Trautmann's Journey

Also by Catrine Clay

Master Race (with Michael Leapman)
Princess to Queen
King, Kaiser, Tsar

Trautmann's Journey

From Hitler Youth to FA Cup Legend

Catrine Clay

Yellow Jersey Press
LONDON

Published by Yellow Jersey Press 2010

2 4 6 8 10 9 7 5 3 1

First published in Great Britain in 2010 by
Yellow Jersey Press
Random House, 20 Vauxhall Bridge Road,
London SW1V 2SA

Addresses for companies within The Random House Group Limited can be
found at: www.randomhouse.co.uk/offices.htm

The Random House Group Limited Reg. No. 954009

A CIP catalogue record for this book
is available from the British Library

ISBN 9780224082884

The Random House Group Limited makes every effort to ensure that the
papers used in its books are made from trees that have been legally sourced
from well-managed and credibly certified forests. Our paper procurement
policy can be found at: www.rbooks.co.uk/environment

Mixed Sources
Product group from well-managed
forests and other controlled sources
www.fsc.org Cert no. TT-COC-2139
© 1996 Forest Stewardship Council
FSC

Printed and bound in Great Britain by
CPI Mackays, Chatham ME5 8TD

For Tom, who loves history
And Charlie, who loves football

Contents

Illustrations

CREDITS: Private collection unless otherwise stated; 1, Daily Mirror; 2, Bildarchiv Preussischer Kulturbesitz; 7, Bundesarchiv; 9, Hulton Deutsch; 10, Ulstein Bilderdienst; 13, 14, 28, 29, 30, 32 and 36: source unknown;15 and 16, BFI; 25, St Helen's Reporter; 26, Corbis; 27, Kemsley Newspapers; 31, Manchester Evening Chronicle; 33, Manchester Evening News

'He was the best goalkeeper I ever played against. We always said, don't look into the goal when you're trying to score against Bert. Because if you do, he'll see your eyes and read your thoughts.'

Bobby Charlton

'I volunteered at seventeen. I was a paratrooper. I fought in Russia for three years. I was in France after D-Day. I was at Arnhem, I was at the Ardennes. I got captured in March 1945, and came to England as a POW. That's when my real education began, at 22, in England.'

Bert Trautmann

Introduction

In October 2007 I got off the train at Manchester Piccadilly on my way to meet Bert Trautmann. He was waiting for me on the platform, tall, smartly dressed in jacket and tie, still handsome at the age of 84. As we walked down the platform a man came up to us. 'You're Bert Trautmann, aren't you?' 'I am,' answered Bert, with a German Lancashire accent all his own. 'May I shake your hand, sir?' They shook hands and exchanged a few words: the football legend, hero of Manchester City, the goalkeeper who broke his neck in the last sixteen minutes of the Cup Final but still went on playing. Then Bert wished him luck and we were on our way.

We took a taxi to the restaurant where we were going to talk over the idea of this book. 'Bert Trautmann, isn't it?' the driver turned round in his seat to greet him. 'You were my boyhood hero. How you doing?' he asked. 'Not so bad, thank you,' said Bert. Later, settled at our table in the restaurant, the chef came out of the kitchens and asked Bert for an autograph for his young son. It was like that wherever we went; that Cup Final was more than fifty years ago, but in Manchester they still remember Bert Trautmann, their very own Jerry goalkeeper, and want to shake his hand. 'It's always like this,' he says with a smile and a shrug. 'I still get fan mail almost every day. Last week I got a letter from China! Unbelievable!' Bert uses the word 'unbelievable' often, partly because so much of his life has been just that. 'In the old days, after a match, I'd be stood there signing autographs for an hour, sometimes more. At the beginning I was overwhelmed by all the attention, but I never liked to say no, so I'd be there, long after the match was over, still signing those autographs, tired out, but I did it. The other players used to say, "Why do you do it, Bert?" But they didn't understand. After the war, when I was a POW just up the road from here at Ashton-in-Makerfield, I had so much understanding, so much forgiveness, so much friendship, that I wanted to give something back; show there were good Germans, not just bad.'

We talked about his life over the meal: the growing up in Nazi Germany, the Hitler Youth, volunteering for the Luftwaffe at just seventeen, fighting in Russia, and all the rest. But most of all, sport. 'Sport has been my life,' he said. 'It's seen me through everything, good and bad, even in Russia when I was fighting the partisans and we had to strap ourselves up in the trees at night by our leather belts because it was the only safe place to be. Even then, the regiment had a handball team, and we got away from the front line from time to time, playing matches against other teams, keeping us sane. Later, after the war, in England, it was the football, becoming Manchester City's goalkeeper and suddenly all that fame. Unbelievable.'

'It's a history book too,' I explained. 'Starting in Weimar Germany, ending in post-war Britain. You're a kind of Everyman who goes through all these dramatic times and experiences, making us think, what would I have done under those circumstances?' Bert agreed with that. 'In a way, it was my childhood that made me what I am,' he said. 'And the war. I was born with a natural sporting talent – in athletics, handball, football, it's true – but the war made me tougher, harder. After fighting the partisan, nothing could ever frighten me again. Not even a broken neck. You can be a good goalkeeper, but to be a great one you have to have heart. All the great goalkeepers have it: courage and heart.'

After the meal he took out a large black and white press photograph. It was taken on 15 April 1964, at the end of his testimonial match at Maine Road, the day he finally retired from professional football, aged 41, and shows him being interviewed in the stands in front of one of those old-fashioned microphones, with the press photographers and fans crowding round in their raincoats and trilby hats, cloth caps and National Health glasses, and Bert in the middle, looking like the star he was, a bit more composed now than when he first came off the field. 'That's when I really cried,' he said. 'Tears rolling down my cheeks. It had rained all day, and I thought, that's it. No one will come. No people, no money. I never earned more than £35 a week in those days, you know, so I needed the money: wife, two boys, and a house to maintain. But they came, from all over – Bolton, Liverpool, Preston, London and Manchester of course – 47,000 came. Magnificent, wasn't it?'

Kick-off was at 7.30 p.m., by which time the rain had stopped, and when Trautmann led the two teams out of the tunnel the noise from the stands was deafening. 'How many outstanding moments are there in your life? But the best ones are the human ones, and this was one of them. I always say, I'm grateful to the people of England, especially Lancashire people and my fellow professionals in the game, for accepting me after the war and as a German, and making me the person I am today.' Even as he's talking about it, 45 years later, he has tears in his eyes. 'Actually, the game never really ended. The people just jumped onto the pitch and a path had to be made for us to get off. Emotionally, that was the moment. I was in tears. Of course I was. I'm not ashamed of it.'

The *Daily Express* put it this way:

BERT GETS 47,000 TRIBUTE

Fans paid £9,000 in a farewell tribute to Carl Bernhard Trautmann, England's best loved German. 5,000 fans ended the game three minutes early in their eagerness to salute this superb servant of football. Players fought to get off the pitch and it was several minutes before Trautmann, looking pale and drawn with emotion, managed to reach the dressing room with the help of police. The quality of the football – between a combined Manchester City and United team and an International eleven – matched the occasion, with the 49-year-old Stanley Matthews putting on one of his top-line acts for the benefit of young Trautmann, the 41-year-old.

Bert and I spent many days together after that lunch, with me asking the questions and Bert sitting hunched over the tape recorder, remembering. His memory proved remarkable, as good as a young man's, no detail too small for his attention. His years under the Nazis during the 1930s followed by the war and the time as a POW in England are bound to have an epic quality to them, and he was often emotional, remembering things which had lain dormant for many years. Then came the football fame, but fame has its own highs and lows, and Bert's life has had plenty of those. I explained that I would tell it as a story. A story of our times. And like most good stories, this one began a long, long time ago.

1

Childhood in Bremen

As a child growing up in Bremen in Germany in the 1920s and early 30s Bernhard was always known as Berni. 'Berni, fetch the potatoes from the cellar,' or, 'Berni, go to Schmidts and get a loaf of *Sauerbrot*,' and, 'Berni, don't be long!' this last called out of the kitchen window by his mother as he was already running down the road. Later, among his *Kameraden* fighting in Russia, he was Bernd. Later still, in England after the war, he became Bert. But for the time being he was Berni.

Berni was eight when he saw his first political demonstration. It was the first Sunday of May 1931 and he went with his father and mother and his brother Karl Heinz, aged five. The day was hot and the lilac was already blooming in the gardens in front of the blocks of flats where they lived, built by the council in uniformly grey concrete, solid and functional, four families to a block. Each block had a cellar below and a large attic above, where Berni's mother Frau Trautmann took her turn doing the laundry once a week, hanging the washing on long ropes with pulleys across the attic during the snowbound days of winter and out in the gardens at the back of the flats in the summer, the white sheets flapping in the sun along with Herr Trautmann's work overalls and Berni's school clothes. There were stone steps leading down to the cellar, but the stairs from the ground floor up to the attic were made of solid wood and always smelt of beeswax because they were scrubbed and polished every day, each housewife taking her turn. The blocks of flats ran the length of Wischusenstrasse, only giving way to large private houses with gables and turrets once you got to the far end by the Heerstrasse, which was the main thoroughfare, and there were lime trees all along and one large old oak, so although it was social housing built for workers in the Bremen docks it was a pleasant place to grow up. The Trautmanns' flat was number 32.

Demonstrations were a constant feature of the Weimar Republic, set up in 1919 to replace the autocratic monarchy of Kaiser Wilhelm II after Germany's disastrous defeat in the First World War. Over two million Germans died in the conflict, and twice as many came home so maimed and mutilated they could never lead a normal life again. The new government of liberal democrats promised to reform the reactionary institutions of the kaisers and improve the lot of the working man, most of whom had only recently returned home from the front. Berni's father was one of these – one of the lucky ones who suffered only minor wounds, though Lord knows what it did to a man to spend the best part of two years in the trenches. He never talked about it. He was just twenty when he came home, and soon after he married Frieda Elster.

Berni and his father walked ahead. They didn't speak, but greeted neighbours coming back from the demonstration or from an afternoon walk in Burger Park. Everyone was wearing their Sunday best, the men in suits, freshly laundered shirts and polished shoes and spats, the women in home-made summer frocks and light jackets, with hats and gloves. Times were hard and many of the men were unemployed, but on Sundays you wouldn't know it. '*Gruess Gott!* What's it like up there?' Herr Trautmann asked his neighbour Herr Wittenburg, speaking in *Plattdeutsch,* the local dialect. 'So far so good,' replied Herr Wittenburg, passing on. It had become something of a Sunday sport in relatively peaceful Bremen to go and watch the demonstrations, as long as you stayed well back in the crowd.

Elsewhere the demonstrations were not so peaceful. Sunday after Sunday the storm troopers of the NSDAP, the rising Nazi Party, pitted themselves against the communist KPD and the USPD, the militant wing of the socialists, in all-out street fighting. Germany, only recently united as a nation under the Prussian kaisers, wasn't used to democracy. There were too many political parties in the Weimar Republic and no sooner was one formed than a splinter group emerged, halving its vote. The Social Democrats, who initially had a majority in the Reichstag, soon lost their hold: for the left they were too cautious with reform, for the right they were too liberal, and far too weak with the Allies at Versailles. And they were led by Stresemann, who was a Jew. By 1931 the political centre had collapsed completely, leaving the stage free for the extremists.

The worst demonstrations were in Berlin, but all the major towns and cities had them, even Bremen with its moderate socialist local government. Against its stated principles, the Weimar Republic resorted to physical force to control the masses, who were close to revolution. Workers' uprisings and strikes were violently put down by the police and military, keenly assisted by the *Freikorps,* bands of right-wing vigilantes mostly made up of disaffected junior officers unable to adjust to life in post-war Germany. The police were meant to arrest troublemakers on both sides, but somehow left-wing demonstrators always came off worse. By the time Hitler formed his first cabinet in January 1933 there had been eleven chancellors.

Berni, at eight, was a striking child with blond hair, blue eyes and a keen, alert expression. He could run fast, jump high, catch any ball, and throw it far. Physically he looked like his father, a handsome well-built man who worked in the docks, first as an electrician and then as a loader for Kali Chemicals, distributing the cargo on merchant ships, but in character Berni resembled his mother, who was more intelligent and spoke a better German. She had attended a *Gymnasium* 'grammar school', while her husband had left elementary school at fourteen with only a basic education, to start his apprenticeship as an electrician. Frau Trautmann was generally considered to have married beneath her, but anyone could see why she had. As time went on the differences between them caused some trouble, and Berni always resented the way his father dominated his mother even though she was the clever one, the better one, and it especially annoyed him that she took it all without a word. It was no secret that Berni was his mother's favourite, her joy and her hope.

Up at the crossroads a large crowd had gathered. There seemed to be many more demonstrators than usual, and the brawling had already started. Berni, keen to get a better view, tried to make his way to the front through the legs of the crowd, but his father grabbed him by the collar and pulled him back. Instead he scrambled halfway up a cast-iron lamp post to where some acanthus-leaf decoration gave him a foothold. His mother told him to come down, scolding him for messing up his Sunday best, but his father let him be, so he stayed and watched the scene unfold.

He'd never seen anything like it. There were dozens of men in various stages of undress, grabbing and swearing and beating hell out of one another. Some of them had proper weapons, others used their banners – trade union, KPD or NSDAP – to batter the enemy, one man was even using a rolling pin; many were kicked to the ground unconscious, and there was blood everywhere. Rather belatedly, an open police lorry came speeding round the corner, horn blowing, with two rows of policemen wearing shiny black tricorne helmets seated on wooden benches, already wielding their truncheons. Taking the corner too fast, the lorry tipped over sideways, throwing the policemen out onto the road helter-skelter. It was a splendid moment and the crowd roared with laughter, clapping and cheering, but not for long. Some of the police were injured, but those who weren't leaped to their feet and started laying into the people with their truncheons; then the mounted police arrived, charging down the middle of the street on their horses, straight into the crowd. At the same time the *Freikorps* and the SA arrived in more open lorries and jumped into the fray, attacking the crowd with rifles and sabres. The mood changed abruptly to one of fear and people quickly dispersed, running in all directions. Herr Trautmann grabbed Berni by the ankle and pulled him down from the lamp post. 'Run, Frieda!' he shouted to his wife, who was already caught up in the stampede, carrying Karl Heinz in her arms.

They raced across the Heerstrasse and down Wischusenstrasse, Berni leading the way and not stopping till they were a good halfway down, out of breath. Berni could still hear the distant shouts, but here the birds were singing and you could smell the lilac and the privet, and Sunday fell back into place again, everything strangely as it had been. Still, Herr Trautmann kept looking over his shoulder to make sure no one was following. Other families were doing the same. No one talked. Everyone went quickly into their flats and locked the doors. Later they heard that three had been killed and over a hundred seriously wounded. One of the wounded was Herr Trautmann's brother-in-law *Onkel* Bencken, a surly man who held loudly to his socialist beliefs, against all family advice.

As soon as they were inside Frau Trautmann gave Berni a good slap. 'Look at your clothes!' she shouted at him, completely distraught. They were standing in the small vestibule, which had wood panelling halfway up the wall and iron hooks for coats and hats with an umbrella stand in the corner. Berni sat on the wooden bench taking off his shoes; the house slippers were ranged in a neat row beneath the bench. 'Look at you!' Frau Trautmann shouted and slapped him again. Karl Heinz began to cry.

Herr Trautmann took no notice; he put on his slippers and went through to the kitchen, sat down at the table and picked up the local newspaper. He never bothered to engage in family matters, that was his wife's job; his job was to earn the money. Originally the family had lived in Walle, a better part of town, but as inflation turned into hyperinflation following the First World War, his wage packet was effectively reduced by more than half and they could no longer afford it. In the year Berni was born, 1923, the German mark wasn't worth the paper it was printed on: in June it was 1,800 to one US dollar, by July it was 160,000, by August it was a million, and the price of basic foodstuffs could double in a day. Foreign investors took their money out of Germany as fast as they could, leaving the economy in even greater chaos. The Trautmann family was forced to move to the east side of Bremen, into the social housing where they still lived. From here Herr Trautmann bicycled to the docks every day, grateful to have a job. By 1931 there were nearly six million unemployed and on his way he passed many old war comrades, jobless and homeless, queuing at the soup kitchens set up at most of the main crossroads. Herr Trautmann himself was never unemployed, but he always worked a double shift, just to make ends meet.

In the early days of the Weimar Republic there had been many attempts at workers' councils in socialist Bremen, especially in the docks, where the trade unions were active, calling strikes and demanding wage arbitration at the drop of a hat, but every initiative failed. It was always the same story: good intentions soon mired in political infighting, each party breaking up into feuding factions, losing sight of the common aim. Originally Trautmann had been a middle-of-the-road socialist, supporting Stresemann and the ruling SPD, but lately he'd pretty much given up on politics. Like most people, he blamed the crushing terms of the Versailles Treaty. How could Germany, already in a parlous state, possibly pay 269 billion gold marks over a period of 42 years in war reparations? Later the sum was reduced to 132 billion, with the rest paid in kind: coal, pig iron, crude steel and so on. But it was still impossible. The only people to profit, he agreed with his drinking companions, were the Jews, who owned all the big department stores and charged exorbitant interest rates from the poor fellows who got themselves into debt. Trautmann was an amiable man who liked to be liked: he was popular with his drinking fellows, who met at their *Stammtisch*, their regular table, in the local *Gasthof* every Sunday morning. He wasn't a weak man, but he tried to avoid trouble, preferring to keep his head down, tell another joke and order another round of beer.

The day after the demonstration life was back to normal. Herr Trautmann left the flat at 5.30 a.m., bicycling down to the docks in time for the start of his first shift at six. Frau Trautmann had been up since five, preparing breakfast: bread and jam and coffee, with hot milk for Berni. There was no bathroom, so everyone took their turn at the kitchen sink, stripped to the waist, washing themselves with a flannel and carbolic soap before putting on their work clothes, fresh every day. Frau Trautmann always wore a large apron, Herr Trautmann had his overalls, and Berni had his school clothes: short-sleeved shirt and short trousers with leather braces, a sleeveless jumper in summer and a thick hand-knitted long-sleeved one in winter. Berni never saw his father in the mornings because he only got up once Herr Trautmann had left for work. Karl Heinz, being just five, stayed in his bed till Berni left for school at seven thirty.

His school, the Humanschule was only 500 metres down Wischusenstrasse and Berni could run there in two minutes. In 1931 he was the new boy, having only recently moved from Walle, and he soon found out how rough it was by comparison. Every class has its bullies and Berni's had Rainer. Rainer was a big tough-guy, top dog in the class hierarchy with no intention of ceding it to anyone. Berni knew how to keep his head down so at first there was no trouble, but as his natural talents began to reveal them-selves and his position in the class rose, he found himself nose to nose with Rainer. There wasn't much Berni could do about it. His class teacher, Herr Koenig, liked him because he was bright, always one of the top three in a class of forty, and the boys liked him because he was already the best sportsman in the class, and always up to some prank, stealing apples from the farmer who had his orchard next to the school, or telling jokes about the teachers, or passing notes to Richard Hohnemeyer or Herbert Behrens, the friend who shared his wooden desk. In a word, Berni was popular, and Rainer didn't like it, didn't like it at all.

One morning not long after the political demonstration Rainer was waiting for Berni at the school entrance. 'Meet me after school and we'll see who's the chief,' said Rainer, showing Berni a clenched fist. School ended at one o'clock in those days, leaving the afternoons free for homework and sport. 'Can't,' replied Berni. 'Have to take Vati his dinner down the docks.' 'Be there,' threatened Rainer. 'Can't,' said Berni and went inside.

The business about his father was true. Now that Herr Trautmann worked a double shift at Kali Chemicals he couldn't come home for his midday meal, so Berni took it to him prepared by his mother, a half-hour there and back. He didn't mind, speeding up Wischusenstrasse and across the Heerstrasse, then down the cobbled streets which led to the docks, billy cans swinging from the handlebars – soup and potatoes, potatoes and soup, and sometimes a bit of *Mettwurst* sausage. If he timed it right the level crossing of the dock railway would be up and then he could speed across the tracks and past the sentries at the entrance gate, right down the Kali quay, past the red-brick office buildings and on to the canteen, where his father would be sitting at a bare wooden table with all the other men on their half-hour break, waiting for their meal before the next shift began.

Bremen had been a city since medieval times, a thriving port trading with the world and always retaining a certain political independence, even within the German Empire. It is situated in the far north-west of Germany, on the River Weser, sixty kilometres inland from the North Sea, and whether it was its geographical position, the trading links with the rest of the world, or the political independence it enjoyed under the kaisers, Bremen held on to the socialist ideals of the Weimar Republic long after most other German cities had given up hope, and the trade unions in the docks remained a strong force – at least till the Nazis came to power, at which point they were disbanded overnight and brutally smashed.

Sometimes Berni bicycled along the other quays in the Bremen docks, past ships from Africa, the Near and Far East and the Americas, ships so huge you could see only their black hulls rising high above, studded with rivets and hung with the heavy chains and ropes which anchored them to massive iron bollards the length of the quays. The passenger ships docked at Bremerhaven, great luxury liners taking the glamorous rich across the ocean to New York and beyond. Berni might cycle past one great iron hull and smell coffee from Africa; from another it was spices from India, from another the sweet smell of tobacco or the acrid smell of rubber. What with the scraping and banging of ships docking, stevedores and lightermen shouting, lorries coming and going, and sailors and dock workers falling out of the bars fighting and swearing, the place was all life.

Kali Chemicals had its own quay and warehouses at the far end of the docks. Herr Trautmann had recently been promoted to master loader, a position of some responsibility because if the cargo wasn't loaded evenly the ship would not hold an even keel at sea. The raw material Kali dealt in was a salt-like mineral transported to the Bremen docks by train from mines the far side of Hamburg, which was used in fertiliser and, later on, as war approached, ammunition. Kali had its own plant behind the quay, where the fertiliser was put on conveyor belts, either in sacks or loose, and loaded straight onto the ships anchored both sides of the quay. It was filthy stuff to work with, and by the end of each day Herr Trautmann was covered from head to toe in a thick layer of dust, which turned his hair and eyebrows white and was so corrosive that the leather on his boots never lasted more than six months, just eaten away. The first thing Herr Trautmann did at the end of each day was to scrub himself clean and unclog his ears and nostrils in the communal showers at the plant. Then he got on his pushbike and made his way home.

Berni didn't fully appreciate the difficulties of his father's working life, perhaps he was too young, but he enjoyed the pride of his father being master loader, boarding ships as soon as they docked armed with his ledger and pencil, making for the first officer's cabin, where they checked their lists and planned the loading over a glass of schnapps. Sometimes Berni was allowed to board a ship with his father; many of the officers knew him already and waved to him from the decks high above as he stood waiting for his father on the quay below. He knew how to handle himself on these occasions, only speaking when he was spoken to and smiling engagingly so that, if he was lucky, one of the officers spun him a pfennig, which he caught mid-air with pleasing ease, a bow and '*Danke Schön!*'

So Berni had told Rainer the truth about his father and the need to take him his dinner after school, but it made no difference: for three days running Rainer was there waiting for him at the school entrance, challenging him, and each time Bernie repeated the same story till, on the fourth day, he got fed up with it. It was typical of Berni to suddenly lose his patience, and his temper with it. Anyone who knew Berni could have told Rainer that once he lost his temper there was no stopping him. So, 'All right,' he said suddenly that day. 'Tomorrow morning, before school.' Stupid Rainer couldn't wait to get his hands on Berni, who was small by comparison, and give the little upstart a good thrashing.

As it happened, Berni had volunteered for English lessons every morning before school began. That was typical of Berni too: he was keen to learn, at least at this early stage of his life, before the Hitler Youth took everything over. The school had asked his parents' permission, and his father at least was surprised that Berni should want to do the extra work, but Berni had made up his mind he wanted to learn this foreign language. Was it a presentiment, was it curiosity, was it his natural intelligence seeking a new challenge? One way or the other, he did it, even though it meant starting school an hour early. His friend Herbert Behrens joined him, along with six other bright ones from his class. The teacher was a Mrs Payman, married to a local businessman who was English.

The next morning Berni turned up half an hour before English class, ready for the fight, but as he walked into the classroom, bang! Rainer, waiting behind the door, punched him in the face, hard. It was a bad mistake: Berni's temper went off like a rocket and soon Rainer had a cut on his chin, a black eye and a bloody nose. The other pupils were shouting and cheering the fight on when Mrs Payman arrived, just in time: big boy Rainer was on the floor, almost out cold. There were two blackboards in the classroom, a large one attached to the wall and a smaller one propped up against it. They put Rainer on the loose blackboard, like a stretcher, and carried him off to the school nurse. Mrs Payman was bound to report the incident, so later that morning Berni found himself standing to attention in front of the large wooden desk in the school director's room. Herr Schweers was the old-fashioned, autocratic type of school director, military in bearing and manner, with an inflexible belief in harsh discipline. He refused to tolerate such behaviour in his school, especially as it wasn't the first time Berni had hit someone in a fit of temper. Herr Direktor Schweers called in Herr and Frau Trautmann to tell them of his decision: Berni was to be expelled and sent to a school of correction.

Herr and Frau Trautmann were shocked beyond belief. They knew that under his normal easy-going nature Berni had a temper: he wasn't past thumping Karl Heinz when he annoyed him, and he shouted at his mother from time to time. But basically Berni was a biddable boy, running shopping errands and helping with the housework, polishing the stairs or putting the washing through the mangle on days when his mother wasn't feeling well. At school he rarely joined in playground fights, preferring to spend his energy on sport. So Herr and Frau Trautmann tried to defend their son to Herr Direktor Schweers, but it got them nowhere until Herbert Behrens, a quiet, shy type of boy, took his courage in his hands and told the full story: that it wasn't Berni who had started the fight, but Rainer, and that in fact Berni had tried three times to avoid it, but that Rainer had gone on challenging him till Berni finally agreed. Herbert saved Berni's skin, thereby cementing a friendship between two boys of very different character who nevertheless shared the same basic beliefs about fair play. But later that day, as Berni walked unsuspecting into the kitchen, his mother was waiting for him and gave him a good hiding with her wooden spoon. His father on the other hand, when he came home from work, and in confidence, congratulated him, saying, 'Well done, *mein Junge*. Don't ever let anyone bully you.' Years later Berni could look back on his life and his father's words, and think, Yes, that's right. And I never did.

When Berni was eight he became eligible to join Tura, the local amateur football club. Football clubs in Germany were brilliantly organised in those days, offering all sorts of sporting activities along with the main event, including athletics, *Völkerball* and handball, as well as chess tournaments, card games, swimming competitions and anything else an active boy might want to do in his spare time. Membership was only a few pfennigs, and as a result big clubs might have as many as 30,000 members. Tura fielded numerous football teams from juniors to the seniors, and they trained every Sunday morning, often coached by famous players. At the pinnacle stood the Second and First Elevens, who travelled the length and breadth of northern Germany playing friendlies against other clubs. Members of the junior teams were sometimes allowed to travel with them in the coaches, to watch and learn, drink in the heady atmosphere and long to be one of the stars themselves. Tura was a club for life, and for Berni, already showing outstanding natural talent, it was life itself.

So although there was little money to spare at home this didn't stop Berni having a happy childhood, and he had his parents to thank for it, because they gave him everything a boy might need: love, discipline and plenty of freedom. Perhaps his mother loved him a bit too much, and she certainly had the greatest influence on him, but in later years he came to recognise that his father had also played his part. When Berni was still young his father often took him to football matches, and afterwards, sitting on the tram on the way home, they would discuss every detail of the match: which players had done well and which hadn't, which team displayed the better tactics, which goalie had made the best saves, anything they could think of, like two old professionals. If the First World War hadn't intervened Herr Trautmann would certainly have gone on playing the game himself, but by the end of those two years in the trenches he'd lost the heart for it.

On summer Sundays the Trautmann family went boating in the Burger Park or for a trip on the River Lesum, on a steamboat, when Frau Trautmann packed a picnic, which the four of them ate on the banks of the river, watching the boats and ships go by before getting back on the steamboat home. But best of all was the fact that every summer, from the age of seven, Berni was sent for two weeks' holiday to *Onkel* Hans, Herr Trautmann's brother, at his house in the countryside outside Hamelin, and right from the start he went alone. Perhaps it was lack of money, but each year his parents took Berni to Bremen station, the *Hauptbahnhof*, put him on the train and waved him off. He was never frightened, only excited. At Hamelin he played in the fields all day long till the light faded with his cousin Hansi, who later became a fighter pilot and was shot down over the Channel, and then, once the two weeks were up, he got on the train again, all alone, and travelled back to Bremen. Freedom is what Berni relished, and freedom is what he got.

Momentous political events were meanwhile shaking Germany, but why should Berni bother? He'd never heard of Stresemann and had no idea that when the great man died the last hope of a stable society vanished, preparing the way for the Nazis. The street fights and violent demonstrations which bedevilled the Weimar Republic had often been orchestrated by the Nazis, whose tactics were always the politics of terror. Now their endless propaganda about the injustices of the Versailles Treaty, the perfidy of the Jews and the inability of the Weimar government to solve inflation and unemployment won over enough of the population to narrowly win the election in 1933, setting Germany on a course which led to the final disaster. When Hitler and the Nazis came to power on 30 January 1933, overnight everything changed in Germany. They called it the *Machtergreifung,* the Seizing of Power, and it was marked by rank upon rank of SA and SS storm troopers goose-stepping past the Chancellery in Berlin for hours on end, saluting Hitler, who stood at an open window, saluting back with that outstretched arm. In those early days few ordinary Germans realised the full meaning of the change which had overtaken them; only the party members knew, those who had been working for years towards this very moment. But the change was like night for day.

In the Trautmann household the shift in political power was quickly reflected in their everyday lives. Herr Trautmann still did his double shift at Kali Chemicals, but now working practices became much more organised, with wages based strictly on productivity. There was better welfare and improved medical care, but every worker was expected to make donations to the Nazi Party, up to a quarter of his salary. There were no more strikes, and no more communist or socialist agitators. The masses of unemployed were put to work, building motorways, factories and new railway networks, all with an eye to the war to come, though the man in the street didn't know it. He might have realised had he read Hitler's own political testament, *Mein Kampf*, written as early as 1924, where he stated again and again that the only solution to Germany's problems was war and conquest to extend the nation's *Lebensraum*, its space to live. 'We turn our eyes to the lands of the East,' he wrote. 'When we speak of new territory in Europe today we must principally think of Russia . . . this colossal Empire in the East is ripe for dissolution.' Rearmament became the overriding priority. 'All other desires without exception must come second to rearmament,' he announced a good nine years before the Nazis came to power. But although many had *Mein Kampf* on their shelves, especially after 1933, it was so rambling, so incomprehensible, that few actually read it.

In the Bremen docks, red and black swastika flags hung from every official building, giving the place a festive air. Each time someone entered an office or a warehouse they gave the Nazi salute. If the 'Heil Hitler!' wasn't executed with proper zeal, soon enough the offender was called in for questioning to the local Gestapo headquarters in the Lehrstrasse, swiftly followed by the loss of their job, or worse. Kali Chemicals was meanwhile awarded a gold flag for its quick and thorough adoption of all the Nazi reforms, including the directive that all workers should join a club and engage in an acceptable hobby. Herr Trautmann, always a good musician, was in the Kali band, playing the flute as they marched about the docks, military fashion, marking some great event in the Nazi calendar. Thinking about the changes, he tried to weigh up the good and the bad: he liked the fact that there were fewer unemployed; he preferred law and order to political chaos; he believed much of the Nazi propaganda about the Jews, the communists and the injustices of the Versailles Treaty. Above all, he was frightened of losing his job. Finally, if not enthusiastically, he joined the party.

Frau Trautmann also found that life under the Nazis had good as well as bad sides. The economy was picking up with prices in the shops less volatile; there were no more dangerous demonstrations; she felt safer in the streets; and there was a general feeling of cautious optimism with a new pride in the German nation. Medals were now struck to honour the German mother who bore three or more children for the Führer and the Reich, which seemed only right and fair, even though it only applied to mothers of pure Aryan stock. On the other hand, the press and radio were censored, and everything was dominated by Nazi Party propaganda. Worse still, while Frieda Trautmann continued to be friendly with her neighbours and the local shopkeepers, she learnt to watch what she said and to whom. There were spies everywhere and any small criticism of the party might be reported.

Berni still attended the Humanschule at the end of the road and still had his excellent class teacher, Herr Koenig, who wore knickerbockers and tweed jackets, English style, and embodied all the traditional values of Germanic education. Herr Koenig was especially fond of Berni in the way that dedicated teachers are often fond of the brightest in the class, but gradually things began to change. Like many teachers in Germany, Herr Koenig was not a fan of Hitler, and in the early days, before 1933, he was quite open about it. But after 1933 he soon learnt to keep quiet. The education department of Bremen Council now came under the State Ministry of Education, and in April, barely three months after the Nazis came to power, the Law for the Reconstruction of the Civil Service was introduced. From now on, any teacher deemed unreliable could be brought in for questioning by the local Gestapo and be summarily dismissed. Teachers were not yet required to join the party because the Nazi hierarchy knew well enough that opposition would be strong, but a new sort of teacher soon appeared in the schools, an 'adviser', who was a member of the Nazi Party and whose thinly disguised job it was to keep an eye on things. But all headmasters and school directors were obliged to join the party. Herr Direktor Schweers didn't need to be encouraged; it suited his temperament perfectly.

Like Berni's father, Herr Koenig had no wish to lose his job; many teachers did. The first to go were the Jews, then came any headmasters and directors who refused to become members of the Nazi Party, soon followed by any teacher who dared to criticise the party. So from now on Herr Koenig kept his own counsel, which didn't prevent him from being a good teacher, only it became more difficult because now he had to learn to live and operate with the Nazis' best weapon: fear. He also had to take on board the new curriculum, introduced as a priority because it concerned Germany's youth, those destined to march on, as Nazi propaganda had it, proudly bearing the flag of the *Vaterland* into the Thousand Year German Reich. To his distress, academic subjects with no ideological import were now downgraded. Instead, the Nazi curriculum introduced racial biology, new-style geography giving special attention to *Lebensraum* and the study of the Reich's territory as it was before the Versailles Treaty, Germanic history, myths and military history, especially Bismarck, and lessons on the

Jews and the ways in which they defiled and destroyed the Reich. And sport, always sport. *Kraft Durch Freude*. Strength through joy.

'We train our youth to use their bodily strength,' proclaimed Hitler at one of the youth rallies now held every year at Nuremberg. 'For I tell you, the young man who does not find his way to the place where, in the last resort, the destiny of his people will lie, but only studies philosophy and buries his head in books or sits at home by the fire, he is no German youth! I call on you! Join our storm troopers!'

As far as Berni was concerned, this was all a plus. Academic studies suddenly seemed boring and unimportant, and he who had been the brightest in his class now turned all his attention to sport. He was the best footballer, the best athlete and the best *Völkerball* player, beating boys two and three years older than himself. *Völkerball* was the national sport preferred by the Nazis, in which two teams in either half of the pitch had to hit players of the other side with the ball. A player who was hit out could only be redeemed if one of his own team hit a player on the other team. Sometimes there was only one player left standing on one side, fielding the ball from four or five players of the other team. Berni, with his large hands, quick eyes and athletic leaps was often the last player left on his side, but still he won, showing the natural talent which would one day, far in the future and far from home, make him the most famous goalkeeper in the world. But whereas in the past sport had been just one of many activities in the school curriculum, now, with the new Nazi ideology, it became the essence, the very pinnacle of achievement, a matter of national importance. And Berni, the boy who could run faster, jump higher, hit harder and catch any ball, became the undisputed star, not just of his class but of the whole school. And now, in 1933, he was able to join the Hitler Youth.

2

The Hitler Youth

Berni was ten in 1933, the exact age at which you could join the *Pimpfe*, the junior branch of the Hitler Youth, the Nazi Party organisation which quickly took over all other German youth groups. It was like the finger of fate pointing at Berni, with his exceptional sporting talent and his blond good looks, the perfect example of Aryan stock. Suddenly he was praised and flattered by all sorts of people who had never even noticed him before. How was he to know that right from the start, long before 1933, the Nazis had designated the Hitler Youth a war machine, the training ground for the hardest men, the toughest soldiers, who would fight to the last in a war which was already planned and openly described as unavoidable? By the end of the war, the Hitler Youth had furnished the Reich with close on eight million soldiers. Time and again they were the ones who fought to the bitter end, who never surrendered, offering up their lives with fanatical dedication for the Führer and the *Vaterland*. History has since singled out 1923, the year of Berni's birth, as the blackest, because so few born in that year survived the war; trained from the age of ten to fight to the death, they did just that, because they knew nothing else.

But in 1933, long before all the death and destruction, Berni Trautmann couldn't wait to join the Hitler Youth. His mother, better educated than his father, had her misgivings. Her bright boy, her special one, hardly bothered with school books these days. But begged by Berni and bombarded with Nazi propaganda, his parents scraped together the money it took to buy the uniform: short black trousers, khaki shirt, black necktie and leather toggle, plus a badge bearing the Hitler Youth insignia, a flash of lightning on a black background. Berni wore it with intense pride as he stood erect giving the Nazi salute before the swastika banner, hair shorn short back and sides, and spoke the oath: 'In the presence of the blood banner, I swear to devote all my powers and my strength to the saviour of our Reich, Adolf Hitler. I am willing and ready to give up my life for him, so help me God.' No one in the Hitler Youth movement seemed to think it strange for a young boy, keen on sport and other outdoor pursuits, to swear an oath to give up his life for the Führer, should the moment arrive.

In 1932 membership of the Hitler Youth had been 107,950. In 1933, after the Nazis came to power, it rose swiftly to 2,300,000 out of a total of 7,529,000 German youth. By 1936 it had risen to 5,400,000 out of a total of 8,656,000. By 1939, at the outbreak of the Second World War, it had reached 8,700,000 out of a total of 8,870,000. Those young boys you see in newsreels with a trembling Hitler in the spring of 1945, just weeks before the end of the war, boys no more than fourteen years of age saluting their Führer with pride in the face of certain defeat, those are the final intake of the Hitler Youth, the last gasp of the dream of a Thousand Year German Reich.

The great leap in membership in 1936 did not happen by accident. In 1934 the party had already issued a proclamation, posted at every street corner:

The Hitler Youth asks you today: why are you standing on the sidelines? Surely we can assume you hold to our Führer, Adolf Hitler? But this can only be achieved by joining the Hitler Youth. So you are faced with a question of loyalty: are you for the Führer, and therefore also for the Hitler Youth, or are you against? In which case state this on the attached form, to confirm it in writing. This is your last chance. Fulfil your duty as a young German. Heil Hitler!

Hitler Youths stood by the posters handing out the forms. Schools were ordered to put up lists in every classroom noting which boys were members, and which weren't. Those who weren't on a list soon received a letter, enclosing the form. Both the father and the son had to sign.

In 1936 came the first Hitler Youth Order, marking the moment when the Nazi Party decided that enough was enough. From now on measures would be taken to force all German youths between the ages of ten to eighteen to join, because time was running out: war was imminent. If a youth or a parent resisted, they would be fined and given a warning, if they continued to resist, the father might find himself out of a job. After that it was to one of the concentration camps, which were springing up all over Germany, designed to contain anyone who opposed the party: communists, socialists, Jews or fathers who didn't want their sons joining the Hitler Youth. This was the year German troops occupied the Rhineland. It was also the first year the Nuremberg Laws were systematically enforced. The First Reich Law of Citizenship distinguished two kinds of humanity: citizens of pure German blood and others, mostly Jews, who were soon forbidden to intermarry with anyone of pure Aryan blood, and barred from all official positions and professions. Not long after, their homes were requisitioned and handed over to good Nazi families, while the Jewish family was moved into a ghetto. Naturally, no Jew could be a member of the Hitler Youth.

As far as Berni was concerned, the Hitler Youth was simply an exciting addition to his everyday life. Every week he presented himself, smartly uniformed, at his Hitler Youth hut next to the allotments, just down the road from where he lived. Leaving aside the lessons in racial biology and Germanic history, he loved it all: the sports, the parades, the singing, the drill, the marching to martial music and the flag waving. But best of all were the weekends when the group went camping. 'What are we now? *Pimpfe!* What do we want to be? Soldiers!' they chanted as they marched along country roads in the hot sun, feeling grand. Once they'd pitched their tents, they lined up on the parade ground, hoisted the flag to the sound of the bugle, sang a rousing Nazi song, then got on with their sports and training. There was rifle practice, grenade throwing, map reading and orientation, and leadership skills. The grenades were lumps of metal of the right weight and shape, the rifles were air rifles for the *Pimpfe,* but real ones for the older Hitler Youth. Bullying was endemic: the strong were meant to triumph over the weak, it was the law of nature. The sports were mostly team games, rough and tough to make the boys hard: one side the home team, the other side the enemy. War games.

Sport was the key, the thing the Nazis valued above all else. As early as spring 1933 all working-class sports clubs were disbanded; likewise the *Deutscher Reichsausschuss fuer Leibesuebungen,* the umbrella organisation for sport in the Weimar Republic, was replaced by the DRL, the *Deutscher Reichsbund fuer Leibesuebungen.* All sports clubs had to have a chairman who was a member of the Nazi Party, and any club which didn't fall into line could be summarily disbanded and have its assets confiscated.

From now on there would be *Gleichschaltung,* the centralisation of all sports activities under Nazi Party administration, the *Reichsportsführer,* the Reich Sports Führer, von Tschammer und Osten, having sole power of decision. Sport was to be in the service of the state and the *Reichsportsführer*'s main task was educating the youth of the Reich in National Socialist doctrine. The newspapers and cinemas were soon full of it: idealised images of blond young athletes in white vests and flannels, shot-putting, hurdling, running, javelin throwing, swinging on the parallel bars; whole fields of them putting on a display of gymnastics at some Nazi rally, row upon row of perfect Aryan specimens, muscles taut, eyes blank, all facing the Führer standing on a distant podium festooned with laurel leaves and swastikas, flanked by Himmler, Göring, Goebbels and all the rest.

In reality most of the top sportsmen didn't look like the idealised Aryans of the propaganda films. Why, after all, should great talent go hand in hand with great beauty? But the racial ideology of the Nazis was never about reality – only look at the Nazi leaders themselves for proof. So, unsurprisingly perhaps, when the two coincided, great sporting talent with Aryan looks, that individual was praised and admired like a young god. And Berni Trautmann was one of those.

Luckily for Berni this didn't apply at home, only at school and in the *Pimpfe,* or his head might have been turned for good. At home things were still hard, though the worst times, when his mother had to send him to join the soup kitchen queue at the top of Wischusenstrasse, were over. But his father still worked a double shift, and when you went to the butcher's you bought not the sausage itself, but the ends left on the slab once the sausage had been through the slicing machine. 'Please can I have the ends of the sausage that aren't too fatty for our dog, because my father doesn't like fat' went the joke among their neighbours, many of whom were in the same boat as the Trautmanns. Food was often bought on tick, to be paid for at the end of the week; vegetables and fruit were mostly grown in the gardens. During the summer Frau Trautmann spent hours in the kitchen, hair tied back under a headscarf, bottling vegetables and jams, which were sealed in heavy glass jars and stored in the cellar along with the potatoes and the wood. One of Berni's classmates was the baker's son, and after a game of *Völkerball* or football they'd sit in the warmth of the ovens at the back of the shop, stuffing themselves with leftover crusts of bread and the bits trimmed off the ends of cakes to make them a nicer shape.

Times were hardest in winter, when days were short and the nights so freezing there was ice on the inside walls. Frau Trautmann was always asking Berni to go down to the cellar for some potatoes or a bundle of brickettes for the kitchen stove. It was no good asking Karl Heinz; he just said no and went on doing his drawing of an airplane or a car at the kitchen table. No came as naturally to Karl Heinz as yes came to Berni. Probably Karl Heinz knew early on that he wasn't the favourite son, so he grew bloody-minded, or maybe he was just born that way. Whatever the reason, Karl Heinz always said no, so Frau Trautmann didn't even bother to ask him.

'Berni, run to Zwimmer's and fetch me half a kilo of sugar,' said Frau Trautmann one evening in December 1934, a few days before Christmas. It was six o'clock and already dark outside. The shops didn't close till seven, so there was plenty of time, thought Berni, nicely settled at the table reading the sports results in the local paper. The kitchen was the only warm room in the flat and the last thing Berni wanted to do was put on his boots, coat, scarf and balaclava, and go out into the cold.

'Let Karl Heinz go for once.'

'No,' said Karl Heinz, right on cue.

'Berni!'

Frau Trautmann was baking the traditional biscuits shaped like hearts and stars for the Christmas tree. Berni could tell by the way she turned round from the stove and looked at him, hands on hips, that he'd better get going. The stove was an iron one with four rings and a hot-water container in the middle, and his mother's face was red with heat and exertion. Later he would remember that smell of Christmas biscuits baking, when he was far from home, but for now it was just annoying to have to leave the warmth of the kitchen for the freezing cold outside.

He took the money from his mother's floured hands and went into the vestibule to put on his outdoor clothes. As he went downstairs Frau Mrozinzsky put her head round her door; it was amazing how Frau Mrozinzsky always seemed to know when Berni was off on a shopping errand.

'Berni!' she called out. 'Berni. You going to Zwimmer's? Get me kilo of flour, good boy. Tell them I pay at the end of the week.'

Why on earth couldn't one of the four Mrozinzsky children go? thought Berni, but then the Mrozinzskys were Polish, and he knew about the Poles. There'd been a lot of propaganda about them lately, though Berni didn't realise it was propaganda; he took it as plain fact. The Poles were a dirty lot, he learnt, lazy and none too intelligent, an inferior race, and he found the Mrozinzsky family fitted the bill. Herr Mrozinzsky was a labourer, often out of work, and Frau Mrozinzsky wasn't much of a *Hausfrau*; their flat was always in a mess, in fact it actually stank. The four children all slept in the same bed and were always bottom of their class at school, and the parents spoke bad German with heavy Polish accents. The contrast with the Trautmanns couldn't have been greater, nor with the Wittenburgs, who lived on the same landing as the Trautmanns. Herr Wittenburg was a teacher who'd fallen on hard times, like so many. Their flat was nevertheless always neat and clean, the children well turned out. On the other hand, and this was the puzzling thing, the Mrozinzsky family was a cheerful one, and Berni played happily with them all in the street, where there was no distinction made between varieties of human species, only whether you were any good at kicking a tin can.

Outside, the snow lay heavy on the ground. On the way to Zwimmer's Berni bumped into a couple of school friends and they skidded along the street together, throwing snowballs. Halfway along, in the light of Berni's torch, they spotted something black against the snow. It turned out to be a purse with 25 *Reichsmarks* inside, which was a fortune. They gaped at one another, stamping their feet against the cold, thinking what to do. There was no one to see them, so Berni, being the leader, took three *Reichsmarks* out, then stuffed the purse in his coat pocket, and it was off to Zwimmer's, where they bought more sweets than they'd seen in a whole month.

When he got home with the flour for Frau Mrozinzsky and the sugar for his mother, Berni wondered where to hide the purse. He muttered something about homework, and went to the bedroom to put it under his mattress, hoping for the best. No one noticed. His father was home early from work that day, but he didn't say much, just sat at the table eating his supper of soup and cheese and bread, then sat on, reading the local paper. Frau Trautmann went back to her baking, Berni sat on the couch under the window, turning the pages of his mother's *Das Beste* magazine, not reading it, just relishing the thought of the sweets. Karl Heinz was still busy at the table with his paper and coloured pencils.

An hour or so later there was a commotion out in the street, a man shouting and a young girl crying. Berni looked out, already half knowing what it was. In the light of the street lamp he could see three figures, father, mother and daughter, searching in the snow. Herr Trautmann came to the window to see what was going on and then he went out to give a hand, taking Berni with him. It was a family from one of the larger private houses up the road, and the daughter had been dispatched with the money to help out poorer relatives who lived in one of the council flats. It took Berni the best part of two hours to come clean but finally he went to his mother and told her the truth. She looked scared as she sat down at the kitchen table to tell her husband and there was an awful row, but somehow they managed to replace the three *Reichsmarks* and return the purse. Berni got the thrashing of his life.

But it was soon forgotten. Herr Trautmann could lose his temper easily enough, but once it was over no more was said and life went on. In the winter Berni and Herbert Behrens and their *Kameraden* went down to the frozen canals and the fields, which were covered in a layer of ice; in the summer they raced across the same fields to the windmills beyond, seeing who could hang on to the sails longest as they rose higher and higher. And every day, winter or summer, they played *Völkerball* or football or handball in the street, at school and in the Hitler Youth. Often Berni forgot the time, coming home when it was already getting dark and missing supper; then his mother would be waiting for him behind the kitchen door, armed with her wooden spoon, ready to give him a good hiding. No matter how often she told him not to be late, he just forgot or didn't care. Usually she was a sweet-natured mother, too soft even, but once she lost her temper, Berni had to watch out. When he was young he'd duck and hop around the kitchen, trying to evade her, but when he got older he just stood there laughing, fending off the blows with his arm.

In many ways, during the hard years, it was his mother who suffered most. Her only free time was on Sunday afternoons, when the whole family: father, mother, Berni and Karl Heinz, went on one of their outings, or on a family visit to *Opa* and *Oma* or one of the numerous aunts: *Tante* Martha, *Tante* Elli or *Tante* Gerda. Berni hated these visits, having to be on his best behaviour, bored to tears, politely listening to all their silly talk. The only good bit was the cake – there was always cake and coffee on a Sunday afternoon. Years later he realised how much his mother loved those Sunday visits and he wished he'd made more effort, but at the time he just counted the minutes till they could get on that tram and go back home.

The strain of those years meant Frau Trautmann was often ill, usually a piercing headache, and on those days Berni stayed home from school to help her with the housework. He polished the shoes every morning, that was his regular task and one he maintained all his life, but on those ill days he scrubbed the stairs from top to bottom, made the beds or helped with the washing in the attic, heaving the heavy wet sheets from the copper kettle to the zinc bathtub for rinsing, then pushing them through the mangle before hanging them out across the attic or in the gardens at the back of the flats. Berni loved his mother intensely, but from early on he was forced to feel sorry for her and he resented it. He couldn't understand why she accepted her life the way it was, with a husband who was her inferior in every way but nevertheless completely dominated her. Why did she put up with him? Sometimes, lying in the dark at night, Berni could hear his father shouting at his mother, perhaps even taking his hand to her, and his heart would beat fast with anger, but by the morning there she'd be, preparing the breakfast, smiling as though nothing had happened. Once he heard Frau Mrozinzsky talking to another woman in the hall in a certain tone, saying how handsome Herr Trautmann was. Berni couldn't have been more surprised; it had never crossed his mind that his father was handsome.

However bright Berni was, he couldn't appreciate the many ways in which his father's life was affected by the political situation in Nazi Germany. He certainly couldn't understand that since 1933 an extra source of stress had entered their daily lives, state-sponsored fear, deliberately designed to undermine any potential political resistance. It wasn't the fear Herr Trautmann had felt during his two years in the trenches during the First World War, which had knocked the stuffing out of him, nor even the fear of losing his job, which had made it worse, but the fear of inadvertently doing something to offend the local Nazis, who would take instant, savage revenge; the kind of fear which ran below the surface of everyday life, cowing people into submission, making them easy to manipulate. Making them weak, just like Herr Trautmann.

To reinforce his grip on the country, as soon as the Nazis gained power in January 1933, Hitler called an election. No doubt he thought the Nazis would sweep the floor, but they didn't. With all their terror tactics and all their propaganda, they still only gained 43.9 per cent of the vote, so they swiftly set about changing the law to achieve what the pseudo-democratic process had failed to deliver. First, in February, hardly a month after the *Machtergeifung*, came the Reichstag fire. Who knows who set the place on fire – it might have been a communist, it might have been a Nazi posing as one; either way, within days the Reichstag Fire Decree had been passed, suspending in the name of national security all personal rights and freedoms. Political prisoners could now be held indefinitely, and there were thousands of arrests, overnight. Some came back, some didn't. Conveniently, by April, Dachau, the first of many concentration camps, was open, operated by volunteer members of Himmler's SS, who became the infamous Death's Head units. Now anyone who opposed the Nazis soon found themselves incarcerated: communists, socialists, liberals, Jews, teachers, lawyers, dock workers, tram drivers. Interrogations were violent: people beaten to a pulp till they signed a 'confession' and testified to their loyalty to the Führer. They could only leave the concentration camp once they'd signed the confession and a further document stipulating they wouldn't speak of their experiences to anyone, on pain of rearrest and certain death. The marvel of it was that so many people resisted; people like Berni's *Onkel* Bencken, arrested in 1934, incarcerated in Farge Camp on the outskirts of Bremen and not let out till 1943, because, stubborn socialist that he was, he simply refused to sign.

In March too came the Enabling Act, giving Hitler absolute power. The socialists voted against it, but the Centre Party, believing Hitler was just a passing phase, supported the measure. It was called a 'Law for removing the distress of People and Reich', but was in fact a sweeping measure enabling the new government to make laws without the approval of the Reichstag, and transferring from the president to the chancellor, from Hindenburg to Hitler, the right to draft laws. This was quickly followed by *Gleichschaltung*, which replaced parliamentary power with Nazi power, the Reichstag now only existing as a fiction, meeting no more than a dozen times in the next six years up to the outbreak of the Second World War. At the beginning of May 1933, the unions were dissolved, replaced by the Nazi Labour Front; on 20 May all Communist Party assets were confiscated; in November the Nazis held a national referendum. The result was in sharp contrast to the election only nine months earlier: 95 per cent of the population approved the Nazi policies; that's how quickly fear works under a dictatorship.

For Berni it was different: he was happy with the new life offered to the youth of the Reich by the Nazis. Whereas before sporting competitions had been haphazard affairs, now, as the outward expression of the Nazi's racial ideology, they were centrally organised from the Hitler Youth Headquarters, known as the RJF, the *Reichs Jugend Führung*, first at local, then regional, and finally, for ultimate glory, at national level. Baldur von Schirach, the Reich's youth Führer, was a fanatical Nazi. He'd started the first Nazi youth group as early as 1924, when he was still a student at Munich University. In 1931 he became the Führer of the Hitler Youth proper. 'We who are of German blood and race accuse!' proclaimed the First Hitler Youth Manifesto of the same year, written by von Schirach:

> Against all justice and rule of law, we, Germany's youth, have been attacked with Terror and Rejection for our following of Adolf Hitler. But we will always stay true to the Flag! We will not be stopped from claiming our rightful inheritance! We demand: down with lies about the war! Freedom to the awakening *Volk*! In the name of the Swastika, fashioned from the Blood of our ancient Race, we will fight and triumph for Land, Bread and Work for our Nation! Youth, join us! Adolf Hitler leads the Way!

From now on every member of the Hitler Youth had to become a member of the Nazi Party at the age of eighteen, when he was expected to move smoothly on into the SA – the party's storm troopers – or the SS. The Weimar government outlawed the movement for a few months in 1932, but as soon as the ban was lifted von Schirach organised the first massive Hitler Youth rally, in Potsdam that October, when 80,000 youths marched past Hitler and the Nazi Party hierarchy, giving the Hitler salute. It took six hours.

The structure of the Hitler Youth was set in stone, as rigidly hierarchical, military and totalitarian as the Nazi Party itself. At the lowest level was the *Bann*, the local area administration. Every *Pimpfe* or Hitler Youth belonged to a unit within his *Bann*, along with other boys from his class and age group, and each unit was led by a *Bann* leader. Above the *Bann* came the district, led by a *Stabsführer*; above the district came the region, and above the regions came the RJF itself, divided into numerous departments, each with its own hierarchy, the main ones being the Education Department, the Social Department, the Press and Propaganda Department, the Administration Department and the Personnel Department. This last had immense powers, bestowing or revoking positions and promotions, always advised by local Nazi Party organisations. Hitler Youth leaders were often seconded as adjutants to the gauleiter of their region. All members of the Hitler Youth were expected to turn out, immaculately uniformed, to march, sing and perform gymnastic displays at the endless party rallies. Older members of the Hitler Youth took part in the violence at political demonstrations and street 'actions'. By 1933, 22 Hitler Youths had already lost their lives for the glory of the cause.

In 1934, when he was eleven, Berni was one of only two boys in the whole of the Bremen region to be awarded a certificate of outstanding athletic achievement. It was signed by President Hindenberg himself. The effect was gratifying, especially at school, where he was treated as a hero and allowed to get away with pretty much anything. Typical was the day not long after he'd received his medal when Berni was sent to the art room, where all the sports equipment was stored, to fetch the football for the match that afternoon. There were a couple of other boys in there and Berni couldn't resist kicking the ball around, showing off what he could do. In a fit of exuberance he tried to score a goal with a header past one of the boys and against the wall. He failed to see that there was a large glass panel leaning there, used for painting during art classes. The football hit it full square and the glass shattered all over the classroom floor. Berni soon found himself in front of Herr Direktor Schweers, waiting for a beating. It didn't come, just a mild rebuke and a secret collusive smile, which said, 'We know it was just high spirits, the kind we expect from a rising sporting star of the Reich.' It left Berni with a strange mixture of feelings: jubilation that he'd got away with it, but also confusion, knowing instinctively that something wasn't right.

Not so with Herr Koenig. Although Berni's class master had learnt the lesson of all schoolteachers in Nazi Germany and no longer openly expressed his views about the Nazi Party, he still managed to convey what was right and what was wrong, not in words so much as by example. Herr Koenig was fair: he praised where praise was due, he punished where punishment was due, and being a natural pedagogue he did his best to maintain proper academic standards, against all the directives churned out by the Reich Ministry of Education, as enshrined in the new curriculum. When he noticed that Berni, once his brightest pupil, was not bothering to listen, but looking out of the window waiting for the moment they could get out of the classroom and into the sun, Herr Koenig would ask Berni what he'd just said, and if he couldn't answer, he'd stride down the rows to the desk Berni still shared with Herbert Behrens, haul him out by his ear and give him a good whack. It hurt, but it also made sense.

But the Hitler Youth actively encouraged Berni's arrogance,

reminding boys that they were the important ones, the strong ones, the modern ones who looked to the future and the Thousand Year German Reich, unlike their parents, who were old-fashioned, boring and weak. It confirmed and increased Berni's perception of his father as a weak man. This was a man, thought Berni, who took almost no part in family life, just came home from work, sat at the table, ate his dinner, read the papers or listened to the wireless, then went to bed. And where was he every Sunday morning? In the *Gasthof* at his *Stammtisch*, his regular table, with all his drinking cronies. The result: by 12.30 Berni's mother would be getting restless, Sunday being the only day in the week when they had meat and the food being almost ready. 'Go and fetch your father from the *Gasthof*,' she'd tell Berni, never even considering Karl Heinz. '*Vati!* Dinner's ready!' Berni would call from the door, and then his father would wave him over to join them, promising him a *Most*, Berni's favourite cider, clapping him cheerfully on the back and calling him '*mein Junge*'. It might be quarter past one before they got home, with his father in a high good mood which didn't amuse his mother one bit.

'Why do you do it?' Berni asked his father once when he was a bit older, a bit more arrogant.

'Do what?'

'Pay for someone else's round. That Seiler's a regular sponger. Every time it's his round, he disappears to the toilet.'

Herr Trautmann just laughed. 'It doesn't matter, Berni. It's not important.'

No, thought Berni, that's wrong; it is important. It's important not to be taken advantage of, not to let anyone push you around. It's important to be strong, strong as iron. His father was weak, he saw it clearly now: he was weak because he liked to be liked. Berni didn't see it as basic kindness, didn't understand that his father paid for rounds happily because, doing a double shift, he earned more money than most of his drinking companions – always assuming they had a job at all – and that they'd been old *Kameraden* in the First World War together, sharing the agony of that wretched time, which had wrecked all their lives. When Berni looked at his father he only saw a timid man who, once home, shouted at his wife. And she took it; that was the worst of it.

Berni had no way of knowing that from the start it had been the policy of the Hitler Youth to wean boys from their parental homes, encouraging an arrogance towards their elders in order to gain total influence over them and channel their loyalty solely towards Adolf Hitler, their Führer. Some resisted, but Berni wasn't one of them. Yes, his father was a weak man, a timid man, always frightened of losing his job; but there was another thing, much worse, and best not talked about: his father was only lukewarm in his praise of the Führer. As far as the Hitler Youth was concerned this was tantamount to treason. Berni didn't go as far as some of his Hitler Youth peers, who shopped their parents to the authorities even though they knew it meant they'd be arrested, but he lost his respect for his father, and he never regained it.

His mother could see it all happening but do nothing about it. She saw less and less of Berni, who spent many weekends away at rallies or on camping trips, or attending one of the endless local, regional or national sports competitions which the Hitler Youth organised as a further means of increasing their influence. Year after year Berni won the same three events: the long jump, the 60 metres running race and grenade throwing, eventually becoming the champion of the whole of northern Germany, flattered and praised by everyone as the very best example of Aryan youth. At home he hardly listened to his parents any more; he couldn't see that it was breaking his mother's heart, losing him in this way.

'This youth, it will learn nothing other than German thinking, German behaviour,' pronounced Adolf Hitler at one of his famous table talks at Reichenau in 1937. 'When these youths come into the *Pimpfe* aged ten, and feel, for the first time, some fresh ideas and fresh air, then we can, four years later, take them into the Hitler Youth, and keep them there for another four years. And then we'll really have them, and won't ever give them back, but take them straight into the Nazi Party . . . thence to the army, into the SA or the SS . . . And they'll never be free again for the rest of their lives.'

3
Off to Silesia

It was August 1936, the Berlin Olympics. Berni was sitting in the kitchen hogging the *Volks* wireless, a basic set designed for those who couldn't afford more fancy ones.

Stubbendorf had just won the gold for Germany on Numi in the individual equestrian event, beating the American Earl Foster Thomson on Jenny Camp, and life was good. Berni reached out to tousle his cousin Helga's hair, who was three and a half and sitting at the kitchen table eating her bread and jam before bedtime at six. Herr and Frau Trautmann had adopted her two years earlier, officially, through the council. She was the child of Frau Trautmann's sister; no one was too sure who the father was. Now there was an extra small bed in the boys' bedroom, leaving no room to move, but Berni didn't mind; he loved Helga with her soft blond curls and her sunny smile. He thought she was beautiful and took her for walks, showing her off to his friends.

'Come on! Come on!' Berni was shouting over the commentator's crackly voice, which was rising in the fever of the last lap of the 1,500 metres as Jack Lovelock of New Zealand put on a massive spurt, overtaking Schaumburg, one of the Reich's few hopes in the track events; the negroes in the American team were winning all the rest. Berni leapt up in hope, then sank down, head in hands. What on earth had happened to Schaumburg? Why hadn't he put his all into it? How could he let the New Zealander win?

His mother looked up from her cooking, laughing.

'It's not funny.' As a sportsman Berni knew it was important to be a good loser or at least to appear to be, but this was bad. Thank God for Schwarzmann and Konrad Frey in the gymnastic events; they were expected to smash all opposition on the parallel bars, the pommel horse, the rings, the vault, everything. They already had two golds and three silvers between them, and each time they stood on the dais to receive their medals, arms stiff in the Hitler salute with '*Deutschland Deutschland Uber Alles*' blaring out over the loudspeakers, it sent shivers down Berni's spine.

It was amazing, thought Berni, the way these American negroes were winning all the track events. His father had been down at the docks on 24 July when the SS *Manhattan* came into Bremerhaven bearing the American Olympic team. There were 381 of them, including eighteen negroes, all dressed in white flannels, blue blazers and straw hats. They were travelling from Bremen to Berlin by train and their route from the port to the train waiting at the *Hauptbahnhof* was festooned with hundreds, maybe thousands, of swastika banners, a marvellous sight, enough to make you proud to be German. The team had only a week to get over their nine-day sea voyage before the games started and most of the track events were in the first week, but that didn't stop the negroes: between the eighteen they took fourteen medals, including eight golds. Jesse Owens alone broke four world records including the 100-metre sprint in 10.3 seconds, with Metcalfe, another negro, beating Osendarp of Holland for second place. He also got the gold in the 200 metres, beating another world record in 20.7 seconds, and another gold and world record for the long jump, when he leapt an incredible 26 feet 5 inches; on top of which another negro, John Woodruff, won the 800 metres, and the team won the 400-metres relay with another world record of 39.8 seconds. Berni was torn in two: the sportsman in him was filled with admiration, the Hitler Youth in him was shocked. Why were the negroes so good at running and the long jump, the very events that he, Berni Trautmann, excelled in? It was confusing, making a mockery of the lessons in racial superiority they got from their Hitler Youth leader.

The broadcast was interrupted by one of Hitler's speeches. These speeches were always the same, long and boring. Berni stood up and turned off the wireless; he knew he shouldn't, but unless he was at school, when they all had to file into the hall to listen with the teachers seated on the platform with Herr Direktor Schweers in full Nazi uniform, Berni rarely paid any attention.

When his father came home from work they sat at the kitchen table poring over the results in Herr Trautmann's copy of the local *Bremer Nachrichten* newspaper.

'These negroes,' said Herr Trautmann. 'We just can't beat them.'

'Wait till I get there.' Berni meant it; he really thought he could do it.

A couple of weeks later Herr Trautmann took Berni to the Alhambra cinema in the centre of Bremen to see the newsreels of the games. It was fantastic, the Olympic stadium alone was a masterpiece, holding 100,000 spectators all chanting 'Heil! Heil!' and giving the Hitler salute as the Führer declared the games open from a podium high above. Three thousand, four hundred and twenty-two athletes had carried the flaming Olympic torch from Athens to Berlin, one kilometre each, the very first time this had ever been done, and it was done by the Reich. The musical fanfares which heralded the awards were composed by Richard

Strauss, and each time there was a German sporting triumph the spectators chanted 'Heil! Heil!' It was exaltation for Berni, watching wide-eyed from the front row of the cinema. At the end of the show everyone stood up to *'Deutschland Deutschland Uber Alles'*, giving the Hitler salute to the blank screen before filing back out into the real world again.

Later, when Leni Riefenstahl's film of the Games, *Olympiad*, was in the cinemas, father and son again gazed up at the screen, awed by the black and white images of Aryan athletic achievement and the sheer beauty of the Master Race. Siegfried Eifrig was filmed carrying the Olympic torch from the beginning of Unter den Linden by the Brandenburg Gate, into the stadium and up a vast flight of steps to light the brazier high above. Was there ever a man more perfect than Siegfried Eifrig, in his pristine white vest and shorts, with his blond hair cut long on top, short at the sides? Prince Siegfried, running with natural ease and grace, keeping up a steady pace, never hesitating, never stumbling, eyes front, focused on the mighty task ahead. Berni didn't know that Eifrig had indeed been chosen for his looks but not his athletic achievements, which weren't good enough for him to take part in the games themselves.

The whole world was watching Nazi Germany in August 1936; it was a propaganda coup of the first order for the new Reich. A few countries hesitated briefly about the rights and wrongs of appearing to legitimise a regime already well known for its policy of terror against all political opponents, especially the Jews. There was a great deal of debate in America, but in the end they fell back on the usual argument: it was a good chance to teach those Nazis a lesson, beat them at their own game. How amusing, thought the Nazis, when you considered the way the Americans treated their negroes, the ones who won most of their medals. The Nazis were more consistent: no Jews were allowed to participate in the games.

The man who masterminded the Berlin Olympics triumph was Joseph Goebbels, the Reich minister of public enlightenment and propaganda. Twenty transmitting vans with 300 microphones were put at the disposal of scores of foreign commentators, who broadcast the games across the globe in 28 different languages. For the locals there was something even better: live television broadcasts transmitted to public booths all over Berlin and Potsdam. The world should know that Nazi Germany was in the forefront of technology, not just sport. Newsreels such as Berni and his father watched in the Alhambra in Bremen were watched by millions. Leni Riefenstahl's *Olympiad* enjoyed as much success as her *Triumph of the Will* of two years earlier, both commissioned by Goebbels to illustrate the superiority of the Aryan race.

Triumph of the Will, one of the greatest works of propaganda ever filmed, used dozens of cameras for top shots, tracking shots, dramatic close-ups and theatrically lit wide shots of rank upon rank of storm troopers and Himmler's SS goose-stepping past Hitler in their black uniforms and iron helmets looking like supermen, hardly human at all, for hour after hour, to immortalise the 1934 Nazi Party rally in Nuremberg. The film declared its purpose from the start with a slow pan down from the imperial eagle to the strains of Wagner, ending on the words '*Triumph des Willens*' written in old Germanic script, followed by a series of captions:

> 20 Years after the Outbreak of the World War
> 16 Years after the Start of German Suffering
> 19 Months after Germany's Rebirth
> Adolf Hitler Flew Once Again to Nuremberg
> For a Military Display

These were followed by mesmerising shots of billowing white clouds and Hitler's plane flying high above Nuremberg to a lyrical orchestral rendering of the '*Horst Wessel Lied*', surely one of the finest marching songs ever composed. And far, far below, in the medieval streets of Nuremberg, marched troops in an endless column, making for the vast stadium where Nazi Party members were foregathering to hear their Führer's prophetic words.

For Berni the best bit of *Triumph des Willens* was the sequence about the Hitler Youth, 60,000 of them marching into the stadium, giving the Hitler salute, chanting 'Heil! Heil!' as Hitler passed. Riefenstahl shot one artful close-up after another of these boys, some no more than ten years old, all blond, all Aryan, all like Berni. Some carried banners, others carried standards, everything festooned with swastikas; but the really lucky ones, thought Berni, were the ones in the bands, beating the drums, blowing the trumpets, playing the marches and the fanfares.

Then Baldur von Schirach mounted the podium to introduce Hitler for his speech to the Hitler Youth, the ones he called the 'flesh of our flesh', the 'blood of our blood'. 'Twelve months ago the struggle for power granted us success,' Hitler declaimed, striking a pose, waiting for the 'Heils!' to stop. 'And since then our Movement, whose young vanguard you are and whose standard bearers you will be, has repossessed one region after another in the Reich, and thus returned it to the German *Volk*.' The stadium erupted into a hysteria of 'Heils!', everyone on their feet, arms out stiff in the Hitler salute. 'Everything has to be fought for and conquered,' he told them. 'You have to learn to be hard men, to accept sacrifice without ever succumbing.' His voice rising, he reached the climax: 'In you the Reich will live on, and when we are long gone, you will still be clutching the flag, which we first grasped from nowhere, in your iron fists.' Hard men, sacrifice, the flag, iron fists, these were the words inculcated into every Hitler Youth, and by which they would die in their millions. Then 60,000 young voices rang out: 'Our flag is showing us the way,' the Hitler Youth anthem.

Goebbels always knew Germany would walk away with the greatest number of medals at the Berlin Olympics in 1936, 89 to America's 56, not least because handball, a variation of Berni's *Völkerball,* made its first appearance at the games and was only played by six countries. Then there was gymnastics, where the Germans excelled and which was subdivided into several events, and the equestrian events, which thanks to their long military tradition the Germans dominated, easily beating the British. But as far as Goebbels was concerned, sport was merely a means to a greater end. 'German sport has only one task,' he proclaimed, ' to strengthen the character of the German people, imbuing it with the fighting spirit and steadfast camaraderie necessary in the struggle for the Reich's very existence.' Hans von Tschammer und Osten, the Reich's sports Führer, agreed. 'Sport is a way to weed out the weak, the Jewish and any other undesirables,' he said. 'With Jewish blood dripping from the knife' went one of the Hitler Youth marching songs, cheerfully joining in the spirit of the thing.

From now on it would be made clear, day after day, week after week, in the newspapers, the cinemas and the radio broadcasts, that it was the parasitic Jews who were to blame for all the Reich's ills. They were the ones, as leading politicians and diplomats, who had accepted the grinding and humiliating terms of the Versailles Treaty; they were the ones who had caused the world economic crisis which brought the Reich to its knees; they were the ones who lent money at exorbitant rates to the poor fellows left washed up by the war; they were the store owners, the publishers, the lawyers, the doctors and the university professors, the ones with all the money and all the best jobs – but not for much longer. By the time of the Olympic Games in August 1936 Jewish shops and businesses were routinely daubed with the Star of David and signs warning, 'Jews! Germans, keep away!' The signs disappeared for the two weeks of the games, but reappeared as soon as they were over and the appeasing foreigners had left.

The positive achievements of the Reich were likewise proclaimed at every opportunity, foremost being the fact that in 1933 there had been some six million unemployed, whereas by 1936 it was a bare two million. For the Nazis there was an especially pleasing aspect to this: not only were the statistics dramatically down and the envy of every other country, but the Reich now possessed a massive new workforce for its main industrial priority: rearmament. By 1935 the Nazis had already renounced the Versailles Treaty and passed the Law for the Reconstruction of the National Defence Forces, immediately forming a new German army to replace the *Reichswehr*, a creature of Versailles, which had hardly amounted to an army at all, merely 100,000 men. In addition there was the *Kriegsmarine*, literally the War Navy, and the *Luftwaffe*, led by *Feldmarschall* Hermann Goring. By 1936 the Germans had marched into the Rhineland, repossessing it from the French.

Leaving aside the thousands recruited for the three branches of the *Wehrmacht*, the unemployed were drafted in to build new military airports, army bases and naval ports, to work double shifts in the new armament factories, and build the motorways. This last meant a ten-hour day, with no more than ten days holiday a year, earning sixteen *Reichmarks* a week, out of which they paid fifteen pfennigs a day for a straw mattress to sleep on in their wooden barracks, and 35 pfennigs for an almost inedible meal. After party donations had been deducted, they were lucky to take home twelve *Reichmarks* a week, less than half the average wage. Not surprisingly, most soon wished to leave, but they were there by order and there was no getting away. The rearmament of the Reich was meant to be secret, but everyone knew. The Allies let it pass, neither their first nor their last act of appeasement.

By now Berni was thirteen. At what age does someone become aware and responsible? Ever since 1933 there had been so-called 'action days' in his area of Bremen, as in every other town in Germany. The Gestapo and the SS would descend on Wischusenstrasse, leaping out of their lorries, firing shots in the air and shouting '*Rein!* Get inside! Close your shutters!' People ran this way and that, gathering up children, racing for the safety of their homes and locking their doors. For as long as the curfew lasted, no one showed their face at any window and Berni's school was closed. There were always older Hitler Youth among the SS, and as people cowered inside, neighbours were hauled out of their homes and thrown into waiting trucks or, if they resisted, were shot on the spot. There were plenty of communists and socialists working in the Bremen docks so, in the early days at least, there were quite a few action days. When the order came, shouted from the street, '*Fertig! Raus!*' people only gradually emerged, cowed and terrified, hardly daring to speak to one another, because no one knew which of them had denounced those who had been taken away.

Many times Berni came out of the flat to find the street covered in blood. It was part of everyday life now, along with the rallies and the marching and the rousing martial music. What could he do? What, for that matter, could he do about the Jewish children, who disappeared from his school following the Nuremberg Laws of 1935, which barred all Jews from state schools, including 'a person of mixed blood of the first degree', meaning someone who had one Jewish parent, and *Mischlinge*, those with three Jewish grandparents? The answer in Berni's case, as with most other people in the Reich, was nothing; just get on with his life, which for Berni meant sport.

Hardly a week went by without a sports competition of some sort: athletics, *Völkerball*, handball or football. Whether they were local, regional or national, all competitions were organised by the Reich Ministry for Sport, overseen locally by the Nazi Party via the Hitler Youth organisation. Only football remained relatively free of state intervention. Ever since he was five Berni had belonged to the junior branch of the local football club, the Blau Weisses, before joining Tura when he was eight. He played centre half, his natural talent helped by an aggressive temperament and a powerful will to win. Had his parents been the only influence on Berni's life in those days, these traits might have been well channelled; as it is, they were exactly the traits most admired by the Hitler Youth. Berni starred in match after match, and won one athletic competition after another.

When he wasn't playing football he was a keen spectator. On Sundays, after training in the mornings, he'd gulp down his Sunday meal then race off with his fellow footballers to watch the Werder Bremen match in the stadium in the centre of town. They each had ten pfennigs for the tram and ten more for the entrance gate. Sometimes they took the tram, more often they legged it, forty minutes there and forty minutes back, running all the way. Once they got to the stadium there was always a debate about whether to pay at the gate or try and get in under the fence; they knew all the gaps but it wasn't easy – the security guards were a mean lot. But mostly they managed it, spending the money on ice creams instead, a luxury they could never normally afford. Berni also had his *Onkel* Karli, who ran a *Gasthof* near the stadium, an indulgent type who laughed when he saw the bedraggled gang hanging around in the street outside after the match. '*Komm rein!*' He'd wave them in and give them something to drink and maybe a pretzel with it.

Berni felt his life was getting better and better. When he was fourteen, in 1937, he left school and the same year joined the Hitler Youth proper. Following the Hitler Youth Order of 1936 this was no longer a matter of choice. 'The future of our German Volk depends on our Youth,' stated the order.

Therefore:
1. The whole of German Youth will be gathered into the Hitler Youth.
2. The whole of German Youth will be raised, apart from the parental home and school, by the Hitler Youth, physically, mentally and in behaviour, in the spirit of National Socialism to serve the *Volk*.

New members were initiated on 20 April, Hitler's birthday.

What happened next sealed Berni's fate: he was chosen as one of only 60 boys from the Bremen area to spend a year away from home on the land, as part of a national scheme run by the Hitler Youth called the *Landjahr*, the Land Year. It was his exceptional sporting talent that did it, helped, no doubt, by his Aryan good looks. The boys were bound for a castle in Silesia, on the Czech–German border, to work on a farm. It was part of the wider Nazi Party *Lebensraum* plan, to extend German living space and gain the hearts and minds of local ethnic Germans in preparation for the imminent invasion and occupation of those territories which had been wrested from Germany by the Versailles Treaty. Hitler had written about this in *Mein Kampf* in 1923; now he was ready to put it into practice. The Reich needed *Lebensraum* 'for food and economy', he announced in a meeting at the Reich Chancellery on 5 November 1937. *Feldmarschall* von Blomberg wasn't convinced, nor was von Neurath of the Foreign Office, nor von Fritsch, commander of the army. They were all removed from office within months, along with sixteen older generals who didn't have the qualities required. 'They should want war, war, war,' said Hitler.

When Berni got the good news he raced into the flat waving the *Landjahr* form, which had to be signed by both parents as well as himself. His father wasn't home yet; his mother read through the form carefully, then sat down at the kitchen table, trying to hold back the tears.

'What's the matter?'

She just shook her head.

'Aren't you pleased? Only sixty of us have been chosen. It's an honour, *Mutti*.'

'You're only fourteen.'

'Nearly fifteen.'

'Will you come home for the holidays?'

'No,' he said, fed up.

They waited for his father, Frau Trautmann cooking but always looking out of the kitchen window, watching out for his bicycle to come down Wischusenstrasse, Berni sitting at the kitchen table with Helga, watching her draw. Then Herr Trautmann came home; they could hear him coming up the stairs, then taking off his leather jerkin in the vestibule and sitting down on the bench to put on his slippers. He looked tired when he came into the kitchen.

'What is it?' He looked from Berni to his wife and back again.

Herr Trautmann read through the form, slowly and in silence, then he asked Berni to fetch his pen and the bottle of ink, and he signed it without another word before passing the pen to his wife. 'There's nothing we can do,' he said, standing up and clapping Berni on the back. 'Well done, *mein Junge*,' he added, then went to turn on the wireless for the evening news. Typical of *Vati*, thought Berni – not that interested. Signing was no more than a formality, Frau Trautmann knew that; it was no more than a formality, and they had no choice, but she sensed that she was losing Berni now, her son, her joy, the light of her life.

Within two weeks he was gone. Herr and Frau Trautmann, Karl Heinz and Helga, all in their Sunday best, went with him by tram to Bremen *Hauptbahnhof*, to see him off.

As Berni waved goodbye out of the train window he could see his mother standing on the platform crying, and his father trying awkwardly to comfort her. He himself felt nothing but triumph.

The castle was called Schweibersdorf, right on the border with Czechoslovakia. At night the boys slept in dormitories and the days were organised along military lines: reveille at 5.30 with flag raising, after which each boy had to take his turn on guard duty, from six till two, and two till ten at night. There were inspections and drills, and each morning after roll-call on a makeshift parade ground the boys marched to work in formation, to the farm in the next village, though soon enough some of the top dogs, Berni among them, managed to lay their hands on a horse and cart. The farm's crop was mostly potatoes and wheat and the boys helped with everything from ploughing with a horse-drawn wooden plough to gathering the potatoes, mucking out the pigsties, milking the cows, plus cleaning and kitchen duties, a foul job they all hated. In addition they had to attend lessons every Saturday morning, given by one of the Hitler Youth leaders, on Nazi ideology, racial biology, and Germanic myths and history, all the usual subjects which no one took much notice of. By now there were over 78,000 Hitler Youth leaders, Führers, trained at the Reich Leadership School at Potsdam or one of the hundreds of smaller training schools which operated right across the Reich. They were mostly recent recruits from the Hitler Youth itself, the type who had flourished in the organisation, the hard men, the bullies, the ones who later manned the SS. Their job during the *Landjahr* was 'to totally educate our Youth over a long period of time, so that schooling, and Hitler Youth Free Time activities, all can be used to influence them'. As well as education, the leaders were in charge of discipline, military training and entertainment. One salon in Schweibersdorf Castle had been converted into a small theatre, where local ethnic Germans were invited of an evening to listen to Nazi Party lectures, or to the Hitler Youth boys, now out of their work clothes and smartly dressed in their uniforms, singing old German folk songs and Nazi marches, generally agreed to be the most rousing in the world.

The farmer was called Henning. In return for the help on the farm, he attended the lectures on Nazi ideology and politics, and was taught to speak better German. But after two months Henning lost almost half his workforce. The best athletes and sportsmen in the group, including Berni, were formed into teams, and spent the next several months touring the eastern regions of Germany bordering Poland, Czechoslovakia and Austria, competing first locally, then regionally, with other teams sponsored by the Hitler Youth movement. Berni's team represented Bremen and Lower Silesia at the same time. It was all athletics, and Berni, the undisputed star of the team, was having the time of his life. They travelled by coach, visiting those regions bordering the countries which they knew from their lectures would soon form part of the Greater German Reich.

They didn't have long to wait. In March 1938 Austria was due to have a plebiscite to decide whether to remain independent or unify with Germany. Hitler wasn't minded to wait for the result, given that it wasn't an entirely foregone conclusion. German troops waited overnight at the border, then marched in triumph into Austria on the morning of 13 March, to wild jubilation from that section of the local populace who already supported the Nazis, cleverly orchestrated by Goebbels. The Nazis called it the *Anschluss*. 'I believe that it was God's will to send a boy forth from this land to the Reich, to let him grow to manhood, to raise him to be Führer of the nation, that he might lead his Homeland into the Reich,' announced Hitler, the Austrian, in a radio broadcast to the now Greater Reich on that day, with everyone in schools, offices, factories, Hitler Youth camps and any other public institution ordered to listen. 'There is a higher providence, and we are nothing but its tools,' the Führer concluded, as though he, a mere mortal, had nothing to do with it. The next day Jews were made to scrub Austrian Chancellor Kurt von Schuschnigg's election slogans for independence off the walls of buildings, in front of crowds which had gathered to taunt them, and for the benefit of the newsreels soon being shown throughout the Reich. Others were made to clean public toilets, including the toilets of the already established local SS headquarters, another symbolic gesture designed to show people who were the masters now. In the next weeks and months hundreds of thousands of communists and socialists, as well as Jews, were arrested and transported to concentration camps. Jewish properties and assets were again confiscated and handed over to deserving members of the Nazi Party.

The wireless set at the castle was old and crackly so it wasn't easy to hear the news broadcasts and the speeches, but the wild cheering and jubilation of what appeared to be the entire Austrian population, along with the military bands and Goebbels' wildly anti-Semitic speeches certainly penetrated the thick walls of

Schweibersdorf Castle, where the Hitler Youth leaders, carrying out party orders, gathered all the boys into the salon to listen and celebrate.

For Berni it was far less interesting than the broadcast they crowded round to hear three months later, in June 1938. It was the rematch between Max Schmeling and Joe Louis, to decide definitively who was the heavyweight boxing champion of the world. Schmeling was a hero in Nazi Germany, feted as an example of Aryan superiority after beating Louis, the negro American, in the Yankee Stadium two years earlier, knocking him out in the twelfth round. There had been a lot of dispute following that result, because Louis was still awarded the world title in a court settlement which the whole of the Reich agreed was fixed. Now was Schmeling's chance to settle it once and for all. Joe Louis spent weeks training at his camp in upstate New York, Schmeling did the same in Germany. On the night of 22 June there was a crowd of over 70,000 in the Yankee Stadium and the fight was broadcast to millions, in German and Spanish as well as in English. At Schweibersdorf Castle the old wireless set was crackling and whistling as usual, the sound waves from America coming and going unpredictably. Berni was thumping the wall, shouting for absolute silence. The fight lasted just two minutes and forty seconds. Louis battered Schmeling with a series of lightning blows, got him on the ropes, and knocked him out. The third time he did it, Schmeling's trainer asked the referee to stop the fight and the Yankee Stadium erupted in triumph. At the castle Berni and his *Kameraden* were sunk in disbelief and despair; it couldn't be true, it was another fix. Louis had played dirty, the Reich later claimed, with an illegal punch to the kidneys. Schmeling knew it wasn't true, but sensibly said nothing, knowing too well what might happen if he did. Not many people knew that

Schmeling was never a member of the Nazi Party. Years later and after the war, he and Joe Louis became life-long friends.

Berni was still based at the castle on 9 November 1938, *Kristallnacht*. It was far from the spontaneous event later claimed by the Nazis. Preparations were made long in advance, just waiting for a suitable opportunity. This arose on 7 November, when Ernst von Rath, a member of staff at the German embassy in Paris, was shot by Herschel Grynszpan, or so the Nazis claimed, though who knows who was really behind it. Grynszpan was a Jew. Immediately instructions went out via telegraph to all Gestapo headquarters across the Greater German Reich, from Reinhard Heydrich at the Reich Central Bureau for Security. 'Only such measures may be employed as will not endanger German lives or property – for example, synagogues may be burned only when there is no risk that fire will spread to neighbouring structures. Jewish stores and dwellings may be destroyed, but not plundered,' the orders ran. 'Only as many Jews – particularly wealthy ones – should be arrested as can be accommodated in available jails. After completion of arrests contact should promptly be established with the appropriate concentration camp to provide for immediate transfer of the Jews.' The special-duty squads which had been waiting for their instructions were made up of SS and storm troopers, plus members of the Hitler Youth. A thousand synagogues were destroyed.

Again everyone was crowded round the wireless at Schweibersdorf, listening. Farmer Henning was nodding in approval, some of the boys were cheering. '*Richtig! Gut!* Serve them right!' Berni wondered what had happened in Bremen. The synagogue was in the Linzerstrasse, in the Jewish quarter. It wasn't very big and he couldn't remember seeing many Jews, the ones with skullcaps and the like, but he remembered a boy called Goldstein in the class above his at school who left to emigrate to America with his family. And why not? America was probably a nice place to live.

That summer, after months of local and regional competitions, Berni's athletic team made it to the national finals of the Youth Olympics in Berlin, held in the Olympic Stadium itself. As they marched into the stadium Berni looked around in awe: he, Berni Trautmann, stood where Jesse Owens had stood, he slept in the quarters where Schwartzmann and Konrad Frey had slept. He came second in the whole of the Reich in three individual competitions: the long jump, the 60 metres and grenade throwing; his team came second overall. It was a fantastic achievement. The Reich's minister for sport, von Tschammer und Osten, handed out the medals. For Berni it was the best moment of the best year of his life. He came home three centimetres taller, tanned, healthy and arrogant. From now on he asked to be called Bernhard.

4

The Apprentice

A totalitarian dictatorship is exactly what it says it is: every aspect of life in that country, however large or small, comes under its power and jurisdiction; anyone who resists is removed, by one means or another. In Nazi Germany it was usually pretty quick, often overnight.

When Berni, now Bernhard, got back from the *Landjahr* in December 1938 he had to find work. The apprenticeship scheme, like everything else, was in the hands of the Nazi Party, in this case under the *Reichsarbeitsamt*, the Reich Labour Bureau. Anyone who wasn't a member of the Hitler Youth needn't bother to apply. Over seven million were members now, either willingly or bowing to the massive pressure of propaganda and political threat. That there were still over 600,000 who resisted is a tribute to the courage of those families who held on to their political beliefs, prepared to suffer the inevitable violence and terror. Many such families moved away from the areas where they were known to live quietly elsewhere. By early 1939 it was the law that every boy of eligible age join the Hitler Youth. That, or their fathers were off to a labour camp.

Bernhard and his father went by tram to the *Reichsarbeitsamt*, which was situated in the centre of Bremen, in Wilhelm Decker Haus on the Nordstrasse. Herr Trautmann was wearing his Sunday suit and homburg hat, Bernhard was wearing his Hitler Youth uniform. He'd only been home for three days. The office at the *Reichsarbeitsamt* was large with a swastika flag on the wall behind the desk, which faced front, square on, a portrait photograph of Hitler in a heavy black frame on the wall to the left, and a map of the Greater German Reich to the right. When father and son entered the office they both gave the Hitler salute. '*Heil Hitler!*' Once, at a Nazi Party rally in Bremen, Herr Trautmann had given a salute which wasn't deemed good enough by a passing member of the SS and got a fist in his face for it, so he'd learnt his lesson.

The official behind the desk indicated without looking up that they sit and wait. He was dressed in party uniform and reading a Gestapo file on the Trautmann family, containing all the necessary information: Herr Trautmann worked at Kali Chemicals, which had been awarded a gold flag for its keen adherence to Nazi Party work directives and for its high rate of production of ammunition, which since 1933 had been the main output, largely replacing the fertiliser of earlier times. Herr Trautmann was a member of the Nazi Party; the boy had been a member of the Hitler Youth as a *Pimpfe* since the age of ten. The report from his Hitler Youth leaders was excellent, describing just the calibre of youth required by the Reich for the coming war, which everyone in the hierarchy knew was imminent. The task, then, was to find an apprenticeship which suited the talents of the boy, and the needs of the Reich, both at once. The main working relationship of the Hitler Youth was with the SS, especially in the *Führerkorps,* the Leader Corps, the *Streifendienst,* the Security Forces, and the *Landdienst,* the Land Service. The best Hitler

Youth leaders automatically joined the officer class of the SS when they left the Hitler Youth, as agreed with Reichsführer Himmler that same year, 1938. Others joined the *Streifendienst*, the section of the SS which included the Death's Head units who manned the concentration camps and wore the skull and crossbones. The rank and file of the Hitler Youth would be placed with the SA or branches of the regular army. The Hitler Youth already had its subsections in preparation for war: the Flier HY, the Marine HY, the Motor HY and the Communications HY, covering field telephone and Morse code. There was also a Music HY, because all armies need rousing songs to keep up morale. This Bernhard Trautmann had only completed elementary school, leaving at fourteen, so he needed something practical.

'First of all let me congratulate you on your excellent athletic achievements at the Reich Youth Games,' said the official, looking up from the file.

Bernhard was gratified to hear his achievements had reached the attention of the authorities; he was certain to get a good apprenticeship.

'What are your interests?'

Bernhard replied they were sports, field and athletics. His father sat mute, hat in lap.

'Are you interested in motor vehicles and mechanics?'

Bernhard agreed that motor vehicles were indeed an interest, and father and son left with the assurance that an apprenticeship would be found.

In September 1938 the Munich Agreement had been signed by Germany, Britain, France and Italy, ceding the Sudetenland of Czechoslovakia to Germany. This was a border territory with a large ethnic German majority which Bernhard knew from his athletics tours during his *Landjahr*. Neville Chamberlain, the

British prime minister, had gone to pay Herr Hitler a visit in August to try to persuade him to desist, and twice more after that, returning home on the third occasion waving the famous piece of paper and proclaiming 'peace for our time'. However, Hitler carried right on with his plans, reclaiming the Sudetenland for the Reich. Six months later he marched into the rest of Czechoslovakia, unchallenged.

It was a disaster for Europe, the effective green light for the Second World War. Now that Hitler knew Chamberlain and the appeasers held the upper hand in Britain he turned his attention to Poland, the next country on his list. Winston Churchill, labelled a warmonger for his criticism of the appeasers, recorded a broadcast to America that month: 'Had the German dictator been confronted by a formidable array of peace-defending powers, this would have been an opportunity for all peace-loving and moderate forces in Germany, together with the Chiefs of the German Army, to make a great effort to re-establish something like sane and civilised conditions in their country.' In 1945, after all the carnage and the nineteen million dead, he amplified this point in a letter to *The Times* on 16 November: 'If the Allies had resisted Hitler strongly in his early stages . . . the chance would have been given to the sane elements in German life, which were very powerful, especially in the High Command, to free Germany from the maniacal system into the grip of which she was falling.' He added, 'President Roosevelt once asked me what this war should be called. My answer was: "The Unnecessary War."'

The Unnecessary War. Few people in Germany in 1938 knew how strong the opposition to Hitler and the Nazis was, least of all Herr Trautmann and Bernhard returning home by tram from the *Reichsarbeitsamt*. One of the first acts of any dictatorship is to curtail the freedom of the press; the only papers people like the Trautmann family read and the only broadcasts they heard were those allowed by the Ministry of Publicity and Propaganda, under Dr Goebbels. These proclaimed a Germany united in its love of the Führer who had led them out of economic turmoil, righted the injustices of the Versailles Treaty and made Germany great again. Just look at the hundreds of thousands who turned out wherever the Führer went, shouting, 'One Reich! One People! One Führer!'

The truth was rather different. The vote of confidence election in March 1933, after two months of terror-filled Nazi rule, had still only delivered 43.9 per cent of the vote. After that the Enabling Act was passed, effectively giving Hitler absolute power, making democratic elections meaningless and hounding anyone who tried to resist the regime. Fearing for their lives and never knowing which neighbour or colleague might give them away, the German opposition went into hiding. But it was still there, just where Churchill knew it was, among the generals in the high command, among politicians and diplomats, bankers and industrialists, among teachers and students, journalists, scientists and university professors, and among the ordinary people of Germany, those who were never one of the eight million members of the Nazi Party, who comprised no more than one in ten of the population. The wonder is that there remained any opposition at all.

Some of the bravest were the workers in the ports of Hamburg and Kiel, traditionally strongholds of the communist and socialist parties. In March 1936, at the famous shipyards of Bloehm and Voss, 5,000 workers were ordered to assemble in the main building to listen to a relayed speech by the Führer. They walked out in the middle. At Germania-Werft, 6,000 workers, again ordered to assemble, openly heckled another broadcast by the

Führer, knowing they'd get beaten up and their leaders arrested by the storm troopers waiting for them at the shipyard gates.

'It is absolutely essential for you, as well as everyone in a responsible position, to understand the vital importance of the internal battleground, which in case of war will mean life or death for us,' Himmler told a group of generals at the High Command in the summer of 1937, speaking of the enemy within. 'We must have more concentration camps. At the beginning of the war, mass arrests on an unprecedented scale will be necessary. Many political prisoners will have to be shot out of hand. Utter ruthlessness is essential. Any way in which we neglect the internal battlefield will lead to catastrophe.'

By 1938 disaffection with the Nazi regime was widespread. 'Our general impression is: among the bulk of the people dislike of the regime is steadily growing, and while it will probably not show itself in open opposition, the Nazi Party are conscious that they no longer have the bulk of the people behind them,' reported an English employee of Hambro's Bank in Berlin to the Foreign Office in London. The reports came in from all over Germany, reaching the Foreign Office in London, mostly in secret, sometimes in code, via the German Foreign Office in the Wilhelmstrasse in Berlin, under State Secretary von Weizsaecker. Week after week the pleas came in, literally begging for help, and week after week von Weizsaecker passed the reports on to his partners in London, knowing he risked his life if found out. Years later, von Weizsaecker explained, 'Such regimes as this one can only be abolished with help from abroad.'

Originally it had looked hopeful. Sir Eric Phipps, British ambassador in Berlin from 1933, reported that unless Hitler was checked there would, sooner or later, be war, but that the Nazis' claim of a united Germany was largely propaganda and something could yet be done. His reports were read by Sir Robert Vansittart, permanent secretary at the Foreign Office in London, who passed them on to the government, along with the reports from von Weizsaecker, forcefully adding his own warnings. The German opposition, knowing Vansittart was on their side, pinned all their hopes on him. But by 1937 Neville Chamberlain was prime minister, and Phipps was moved to Paris, replaced in Berlin by Sir Nevile Henderson, a man entirely in agreement with Chamberlain's appeasement policies. 'Sir NH is a national danger in Berlin,' warned Vansittart, but no one listened. Whitehall took the view that they had no wish to provoke Herr Hitler. Once Chamberlain became prime minister he quickly replaced Vansittart with Sir Alexander Cadogan. 'I fear he is writing a paper,' wrote Cadogan about Vansittart in his diary. 'I only hope it won't be another in his usual German-scare style.'

Bernhard was fifteen when he started his apprenticeship in January 1939. The Reich Labour Bureau had arranged for him to have some simple aptitude tests, after which they found him a position with a firm called Hanomag, which produced agricultural plant, lorries and other vehicles and had a maintenance depot in Bremen. The coming war would be fought with motor vehicles, not horses, and diesel was the new fuel which would see them through. Everywhere in the Reich hundreds of thousands of Hitler Youth were learning their various trades, all in preparation for war.

On weekdays Bernhard got up at 5.30, had his breakfast of coffee, bread and jam, then he bicycled to work, or in bad weather took the tram. The tram stop was three minutes' walk up Wischusenstrasse on the Heerstrasse and the journey only took twenty minutes, with Hanomag no more than a five-minute walk the other end, so he was there and ready to start work with his overalls on by 6.30. For the first year Bernhard was the only apprentice with fifteen qualified mechanics. The foreman of the depot was a bad-tempered man called Budde, a keen member of the Nazi Party, who was addressed by everyone as '*Meister*'. Luckily he wasn't in charge of Bernhard's day-to-day training; that was a man called Karl Wegener who had learnt his trade in Lingen, the home of the famous racing driver Brend Rosemeyer and the Auto Union team who had broken so many world records. Wegener was a nice man, clever at his work, and a good supervisor for Bernhard. They got on well from the start.

Working with diesel was a filthy stinking job, especially in winter when the lorry engines had to be stripped and cleaned with a strong petrol solution. At the end of each day Bernhard's hands were ripped open, his nails black with dirt and oil, and by the end of the week his overalls were so thick with grease they could stand up on their own. There were two breaks in the day, fifteen minutes at 9.45 and another from 12.00 to 12.30, when he ate the lunch prepared by his mother the night before. The day ended at 5.00, except on Saturdays, when it was 12.45, after which the whole workshop had to be scrubbed clean – the windowsills, the work benches, the pits and the concrete floor, which was so filthy the only way to get it clean was to use a chemical from Henkel called P3 – but first of all the thick diesel had to be scraped up. The *Meister* seemed to take a special pleasure in standing about on Saturday afternoons, looking down into the pits watching them work, checking till the concrete was pristine again. For this Bernhard was paid two *Reichmarks* a week, and one extra for getting his overalls laundered. If, on a Monday morning, the *Meister* saw that his overalls hadn't been washed at the specialist laundry but just at home to save money, the extra *Reichsmark* was deducted. Luckily there was an occasional boost to his meagre earnings: since the Reich was gearing up for war there was a massive demand for vehicle repairs of every kind, too much for the workshop to complete in a week. Bernhard's supervisor Wegener did overtime on a Sunday, and some private work too, and Bernhard often helped him, sharing in the profits.

Life was different in those years before the war: narrower, less informed, more innocent. In his spare time in the evenings, and Sundays if he wasn't working overtime, Bernhard would play sport or, when he had the money, go to the cinema. On those evenings his mother waited for him to come home and tell her the whole story of the film from start to finish. If it was a nice weepy one she'd go and see it later, by herself or with one of the aunts, to have a good cry. Girls didn't come into it for Bernhard in those days; he didn't seem to notice if they smiled at him in the street. His mother was the woman in his life, and the passion in his life was all sport.

Once he was an apprentice at Hanomag there was hardly any spare time so he limited himself mostly to football, playing on Sunday mornings at the local grounds. First they had to help the linesman mark out the pitch, then they changed into their team colours. Bernhard played centre forward, aggressively barging past anyone who got in his way – he hardly knew where he got it from, this will to win. The talent for the game came from his father, he knew, but the aggression, the attack, the temper when one of his team made a bad pass, this was all his own. Although he'd learnt over the years to be a good loser, he minded the outcome of a match as though his life depended on it. Either way, he was always the star, the one who outran and outplayed all the rest.

After the match everyone had a shower, then made their way home for Sunday dinner. In Bernhard's case he was often met by his mother calling out to him from the kitchen window, 'Go and fetch *Vati* from the *Gasthof*.' Sometimes his father came home so late his mother was almost in tears, and once Bernhard lost his temper, raising his arm to hit him. 'Never take a hand to a parent!' his father warned him, stopping him in his tracks. But wasn't that just it? thought Bernhard. One law for him, another for the rest of us.

'Why did you marry *Vati*?' he asked his mother one evening. They were sitting side by side on the settee, she doing some knitting under the standard lamp, he leafing idly through a sports magazine. There had been one of those arguments in the night with his father shouting at his mother in their bedroom, and Bernhard and Karl Heinz and Helga lying in their beds in their room, listening, each pretending to be asleep.

His mother looked surprised, shocked even, at the question, but she knew he'd heard the argument and she realised she had to say something.

'You're too young to understand,' she offered.

'I'm not. Just tell me, why do you put up with him?'

His father was on a double shift that day, not due home till half past nine. The Bremen dockyards were working round the clock now, building U-boats for the German navy. Outside it was already getting dark, Helga was in bed, Karl Heinz was listening to the wireless. His mother said something about his father's time in the trenches during the First World War and something about the strain of working double shifts and the constant worry about losing his job, though that was better these days, what with all the rearmament. None of it satisfied Bernhard, who resented his father for making him feel sorry for his mother; all his life he felt sorry for her, but could do nothing about it.

'He was very good-looking, you know,' she added as an afterthought, a touch embarrassed.

When his father came home she leapt up and put the food on the table. Herr Trautmann ate his meal almost in silence, except to tell them he'd had a few whiskies with some of the officers off one of the ships, which they could tell for themselves. After the meal he fell asleep in his chair by the stove with the unread *Bremer Nachrichten* on his lap.

That's when Bernhard found out how much his father earned each week. His mother never knew and never asked, which is how it was in those days. Women like his mother were slaves, thought Bernhard, nothing but slaves. Now he made her come out into the vestibule with him, to where his father's leather jerkin hung on a hook. She went, but was scared stiff, knowing instinctively what he was up to. The payslip was in the inside pocket. Bernhard peered at it in the dim overhead light, then handed it to her. She didn't look at it, so he told her: over 40 *Reichmarks* a week, when the average wage was hardly 25. 'But that's because he works a double shift,' she whispered. And then: 'Put it back, for heaven's sake.'

On 1 September 1939 the Germans invaded Poland. That half of the public who supported the Nazis went wild with triumph, Hitler and Goebbels filling the airwaves with triumphant speeches about *Lebensraum* and the conquest of an inferior people by the Master Race. There were rallies and demonstrations and night marches with flaming torches, with everyone in uniform, military bands and hysterical crowds chanting, *Sieg Heil! Sieg Heil!* The other half of the population kept their heads down, most especially the Jews. There were two labour camps on the outskirts of Bremen: Bremen-Farge, where Bernhard's *Onkel* Bencken still resided, and Bremen-Vegesack, with Missler a bit further out. They were full of communists and socialists, and no one with any sense wanted to add to their numbers. 'There is a bad mood among the population,' wrote General Ritter von Leeb, who would later lead Army Group North into Russia, on 3 October 1939. 'No kind of enthusiasm, no flags flying on the houses, everyone looking for peace. The people feel war is unnecessary.'

In the Trautmann family, opinion was divided. Bernhard and Karl Heinz were full of enthusiasm, spouting all the half-digested theories they'd learnt in their Hitler Youth and *Pimpfe* lessons. Frau Trautmann didn't say much; Herr Trautmann knew it meant war with Britain. 'And we'll lose this one too,' he added. Bernhard nearly hit him. That was exactly the kind of defeatist comment which they hated at the Hitler Youth – weak and cowardly, the kind of thing that got you arrested. Helga, aged nine, just sat and listened, wondering what all the fuss was about.

On 3 September Britain and France declared war on Germany. For the silent German opposition, it came too late. A year earlier, when the Reich was gearing up to invade Czechoslovakia, intervention of some sort could have made a difference. If the Allies had said no to Hitler then, they might have stopped him in his tracks, because the opposition was well organised, armed and ready to take action, with a fully functioning, high-level, anti-Nazi government waiting in the wings to take over, avoiding any vacuum of power. If not that, the opposition at least might have delayed or even derailed the war. But then came Chamberlain's trip to Munich, and Lord Halifax, another appeaser, became the new British foreign secretary. Vansittart had meanwhile been promoted sideways to chief diplomatic adviser, which meant precisely nothing. The German opposition, assuming it was a real promotion, went on using him as a conduit, but as time went on they found that nothing they did or requested had any effect.

Bernhard, his head high in the clouds, gave not a thought to what it meant that Britain and France had declared war on

Germany other than to wonder how long it would take for the Reich to beat them – might be a year, might even be no more than six months. The conquest of Poland had taken no time at all, and no wonder: they were an inferior race, dirty, stupid and uncultured, as explained in Dr Goebbels' film *Conquest of Poland*. Still, it was confusing. Surely the Russians were also subhuman, and yet the Führer had entered into a pact with Stalin, and Poland was now divided between them, the Reich possessing the west, the Russians the east.

'You going to Schmidt's for your *Mutti*?' Frau Mrozinzsky waylaid Bernhard in the hall of the flats. She had a scarf tied round her head, knotted at the back, and she wore her usual large apron, none too clean. She was laughing and smiling at him, holding out some money wrapped in a piece of newspaper. 'Fetch me half a loaf, Berni, good boy.' She still called him Berni. He didn't mind; he liked Frau Mrozinzsky.

The way he saw it, the Mrozinzskys had lived in Germany for so long they were hardly Polish any more, but he wondered how she could be so cheerful when her country was being conquered – that wasn't natural. And what about Herr Mrozinzsky? How did he feel, as a man? These days you hardly saw Herr Mrozinzsky because he had a job in an ammunitions factory on the outskirts of Bremen; left home early, came home late, and Frau Mrozinzsky no longer had to buy food on tick, so even the Poles were benefiting from the Führer's Thousand Year German Reich. Hitler was the greatest leader Germany had ever had, greater than Kaiser Wilhelm, greater even than Bismarck. He knew everything that went on in the Reich, large and small; that's what Bernhard was told, again and again, and he was happy to believe it.

What Hitler didn't know, however, was that Winston Churchill, currently First Lord of the Admiralty, had some plans of his own.

On 5 September, two days after Britain and France declared war on Germany, President Roosevelt proclaimed America's neutrality. Six days after that, Churchill and Roosevelt began their secret correspondence, which lasted throughout the war. 'What I want you and the Prime Minister to know,' wrote Roosevelt, 'is that I shall at all times welcome it if you will keep me in touch personally with anything you want me to know about. You can always send sealed letters through your pouch or my pouch.' From then on Churchill knew that, sooner or later, America would come into the war on the Allied side.

5

The Volunteer

Bernhard and Karl Wegener were bowling along a straight country-road outside Bremen in one of Hanomag's trucks; Wegener was driving, Bernhard was sitting beside him, whistling, looking at the farmland left and right: the fields, the haystacks, the cows, the old farmhouses with apple orchards and the yards with hens and ducks, everything hazy in the late-afternoon sun, and he was thinking that life was good. The previous week the armistice had been signed with France, on 22 June 1940, in the very same railway carriage at Compiègne where the Germans had been forced to sign the armistice at the end of the First World War – the Führer had insisted on that detail, to put right the injustice and humiliation once and for all – and everyone in the Reich felt jubilant, even his father, who was worried about the war. It was hardly credible how quickly those milk-livered French had given in: six weeks of fighting and the Battle of France was already over, blink and you missed it, no fight, no pride. Then the victory parade down the Champs-Elysées which he and his mother watched on the newsreels at the cinema, Waffen SS goose-stepping under the Arc de Triomphe, with the silent Parisians standing on the pavements, looking on. Who were the masters now? Britain was next in line. 'So, we're marching! Yes, we're marching! Yes, we're marching against Eng-a-land!' as a new marching song went, specially composed for the coming invasion. Bernhard couldn't wait to be part of it.

'Have you heard the latest one about *Feldmarschall* Göring?' There were endless jokes about Göring and his many uniforms, and his film actress wife, Emmy Sonnemann – harmless jokes, not the kind that got you arrested. 'Well, this man turns up at the Göring house and rings the bell. Emmy Sonnemann comes to the door.' Wegener was telling the joke; Bernhard was already smiling in anticipation. '"Is *Feldmarschall* Göring at home?" asks the man. "I'll give him a call," says Emmy. She calls out, across the big hall with the chandeliers, down the long corridor, up the grand staircase. No answer. "He must be out," she says. "But I'll check his uniforms, just in case." She goes to the wardrobe: rows and rows of uniforms, for every conceivable occasion. "Ah, he's down in the cellar!" she tells the man. "The miner's uniform is missing."'

They had a good laugh at that one. It was a Sunday and they'd done a whole day's overtime, mending the engine of a tractor for one of their regular customers. It was the usual routine: farmer goes to his local *Post* and rings up the depot; Herr Budde, the *Meister*, says he's sorry but they're much too busy what with the war and all the truck and lorry maintenance; farmer begs and pleads; Herr Budde has a quick think, says he might manage to find someone for Sunday. 'Wegener. Trautmann,' he shouts out across the depot. 'Want some overtime?' The answer's always yes. The farmer's so grateful they come home laden with farm produce as well as the cash, half of which goes to Budde, as well as half of the farm produce.

When he got home that evening Bernhard put a cabbage, five eggs wrapped in newspaper and an unplucked brown hen, head and all, on the kitchen table. His mother leapt up from the couch and kissed him, even his father looked up from the wireless and smiled. 'Can I have a whole egg for my supper?' asked Helga. 'Just this once,' promised Frau Trautmann. 'What about me?' That was Karl Heinz. 'You too.' There had been rationing since the previous August, basic foodstuffs, as well as coal, soap, some items of clothing and materials, and shoes. For a while, when the Nazis came to power, life had been easier, food cheaper, wages steadier, but now that they were at war it was hard all over again. But that wasn't the worst of it; worst, by far, was the thought that sooner or later Bernhard would be called up. And then what? Frau Trautmann preferred not to think about it because it was unbearable.

At Hanomag Bernhard had started out as the only apprentice, but now four others had joined him, each with his own supervisor. Bernhard was put in charge of them as the senior apprentice: he had to see to it that they did their general duties round the depot properly and on time. Mostly, that meant cleaning, especially on Saturday afternoons. They were a decent enough group of fellows, all but one of them, called Alphonse. Alphonse was a lazy good-for-nothing who took no pride in his work and did a bunk whenever the fancy took him. Judging by his name, he wasn't a true German; he certainly didn't act like one. This was especially annoying because, on hot summer days, Bernhard wasn't above doing a bunk himself, but only from the technical college which they all attended once a week. He even arranged a few outings down to the river for all of them, when they lazed around, swimming and smoking and generally having a fine time. But, trust Alphonse, it wasn't enough for him. He had to do his own bunks as well, and how often did he manage to get away with not doing his share of the filthy, back-breaking Saturday-afternoon cleaning? Bernhard let him get away with it a few times, then came the day when he'd had enough.

After work that afternoon he lay in wait for him outside the depot, along with two other apprentices who were there strictly as spectators, Alphonse being bigger than them, and bigger than Bernhard too. Budde was off somewhere, so it was the ideal opportunity. Soon enough Alphonse swaggered out, smoking a cigarette; the very sight of him got Bernhard's temper up. He leapt at him, grabbing his shirt and laying into him like a madman, dragging him this way and that across the forecourt. It took Alphonse a few seconds to realise what was happening, then he fought back, using his full weight; but once Bernhard lost his temper, that was it. He knocked Alphonse to the ground and punched him again and again, shouting and swearing all the time. 'Watch out! Budde's coming!' One of the apprentices had spotted the *Meister* coming down the road on his moped. Bernhard thumped Alphonse once more, just for the hell of it, then leapt to his feet, grabbed his pushbike and made a quick getaway.

He hadn't reckoned on Budde giving chase, but he did. All round the backstreets and right through the nearby allotments, past astonished gardeners with their rakes and hoes, the *Meister* chased his apprentice, shouting all the time. Bernhard finally lost him on the far side of the allotments and made his way home. Once there he went straight up to the attic to have a bath in the old tub to clean himself up. He was soaking there when he heard a lorry drawing up far below, outside the flats, and the engine sounded suspiciously like one of Hanomag's. Next thing he knew, his father was shouting for him up the stairs. When he got down to the flat, there was Budde waiting for him in the kitchen, along with Herr Trautmann; Frau Trautmann was nowhere to be seen. Budde was still furious. What did Bernhard think he was doing, beating up another apprentice? He was meant to be looking after the apprentices, not laying in to them. Was that the way for a true German to behave?

That did it. Bernhard stopped apologising and told him what was what, shouting back that Alphonse was a lazy good-for-nothing, never did his share of the work, always got his supervisor to find him something to do on Saturday afternoons instead of helping with the cleaning, and so on and so forth. Budde wasn't impressed and turned to Herr Trautmann, telling him to take firmer control of his son; he might like to know it wasn't the first time Bernhard's temper had caused trouble at the depot. To Bernhard's surprise his father refused to apologise and stood by him, saying he would have done exactly the same in the circumstances. With that, Budde left. He'd had his say, and he didn't want to lose Bernhard, who was his best worker by far. 'Let's have supper now, Frieda!' Herr Trautmann called out to his wife, who'd been hiding in the bedroom, along with Karl Heinz and Helga. Then he clapped an arm round his son, calling him *'mein Junge'*.

'Wherever rats appear they bring ruin by destroying mankind's foods and foodstuffs. In this way they spread disease, plague, leprosy, typhoid, fever, cholera, dysentery, and so on. They are cunning, cowardly and cruel, and are found mostly in large packs, just like the Jews among human beings.' Bernhard was sitting in the cinema a couple of weeks later, watching *Der Ewige Jude – The Eternal Jew*. He thought it would be one of those short propaganda films you had to endure for a while before the main feature, but this one went on and on. Apparently the Jews had spread like rats through Europe, and then the entire world; now they were responsible for most of international crime and 98 per cent of prostitution. At the same time they bagged all the best jobs and earned all the money. Really, thought Bernhard, they deserved what was coming to them. He knew that one of his father's drinking companions had got into serious debt because of a Jew. The poor fellow had lost his job at the ammunitions factory for some reason, and he had four children to feed. Herr Trautmann was always buying him beers. On the other hand Bernhard had also seen a couple of incidents in shop queues, where Jews were dragged out and beaten up, which wasn't pleasant. But if you made a fat profit out of other people's bad luck, you were bound to be resented, weren't you? Still, he was pleased when the tone of the film started to lift, in expectation of the usual rousing ending. 'Under the leadership of Adolf Hitler, Germany has raised the battle flag against the eternal Jew,' it proclaimed. 'The eternal law of nature, to keep one's race pure, is the legacy which the National Socialist Movement bequeaths to the German people for all time.' Well, that was that then. Now for the main feature.

By the Autumn of 1940 Bernhard was getting restless. Every time he went to his Hitler Youth meetings or to a football match with Tura, one or other of his mates would turn up in uniform, having volunteered. Like him, they couldn't wait to be part of the war, the adventure, the pride of fighting for the Reich. Once you were seventeen you were old enough to volunteer; the war had already been going for over a year, why wait? What's more, if you wanted to choose which part of the *Wehrmacht* you joined, you had to volunteer; if you waited to be called up they just put you some-where, anywhere, where you were most needed. Bernhard wanted to join the Luftwaffe. Without telling his parents he went to the recruitment office in the centre of Bremen to get the forms. It was the week after his seventeenth birthday.

When he got home his mother was already dishing out the soup for supper, everyone seated at the kitchen table.

'You're late back, Bernhard.' His mother's face lit up with the pleasure of seeing him. 'Did you get some overtime?'

'No.' He sat himself at the table. 'I went to the recruitment office.'

His mother stopped mid-action, then put the saucepan back down on the stove, crying 'No, no, no!' and covering her face with her hands. She realised at once what it meant: he'd volunteered; no one was called up till they were eighteen. They said the war would be over in a year, but Berni might be dead by then. 'No, Berni, no!' She just stood there in the middle of the kitchen, crying 'No!' again and again. Helga leapt up and held her hand, stroking it, begging her to stop. Karl Heinz looked at Bernhard with mild curiosity. His father shook his head.

'What did they say?' After two years in the trenches Herr Trautmann knew what war was, and he knew that Bernhard had no idea.

'They gave me these forms to fill in and sign. You and Mutti have to sign them too.' He put the forms on the table, impressive with their bold Germanic print.

Herr Trautmann looked at them and nodded. 'The Luftwaffe?'

'I want to be a pilot.' The very word thrilled Bernhard.

'You haven't got enough qualifications, have you?' Herr Trautmann knew for certain that his son, having left elementary school at fourteen, didn't have the necessary education to be a pilot, but he hadn't the heart to tell him outright.

Later that evening Bernhard stood over his parents as they signed the forms. He was quite belligerent about it and so full of excitement he hardly noticed their reactions. Naturally mothers are upset; naturally fathers give you advice.

'War is not what you think, Bernhard,' said his father before signing. 'You can't imagine what it's like till you're there.' He was trying to find the right words, searching to express the horror. 'Those two years in the trenches were the worst of my life. You can't begin to imagine it. And for what?' He gave his son a quick look to see if he was taking it in, then he tried again. 'The gas attacks. You've no idea. You choke to death; you hope to die. Believe me, Bernhard, you hope to die, just to get out of it.'

'We have to fight for the *Vaterland, Vati.*'

Since he was ten Bernhard had had his head filled with ideas about the glory of fighting for the *Vaterland*; he knew nothing else. Week after week he was taught about the superiority of the Master Race and their right to *Lebensraum*; they sang songs about it, they were told heroic stories, they were trained for war. Now he was too arrogant, too brainwashed, to hear anything else. Wasn't he the best grenade thrower in the team, and the best sprinter, the best at the long jump, the best footballer? He could shoot a rifle too, pretty accurately. And he was hard. That's what the Hitler Youth taught you again and again: in war you had to be hard, do hard things. If you didn't do it to them, they'd do it to you. Your duty was to fight to the very last and, if necessary, die for the Reich. But he didn't mean to die; he meant to live, to survive everything the enemy threw at him. He was the toughest of his friends, the acknowledged champion of them all. His father's comments were well meant, he could see that, but defeatist, as ever. He tried not to feel irritated, waiting impatiently for the forms to be signed.

Originally Herr Trautmann had been all in favour of his son joining the Hitler Youth. With little money, here was a place Berni could go to play sports, march about the town waving flags and feel proud to be German, not something Herr Trautmann ever had the chance to feel. It was an outdoor, healthy life. The Hitler Youth camps took the boys far afield, as far as the Austrian Alps on one occasion, and they were well organised, teaching the boys tough discipline, which his son certainly needed. Berni had thrived on it, growing into a strong lad with plenty of confidence. He had become quite a sporting star, with rows of medals and certificates, and a certain local fame which made both his parents proud. But as time went on Herr Trautmann began to change his mind. For one thing, the Hitler Youth repeatedly told the boys their only loyalty was to the Führer, which undermined parental authority, encouraging an unpleasant arrogance towards their elders. Then came the *Landjahr*, when Berni, aged just fourteen, was away from home for over ten months and returned spouting all sorts of tripe about *Lebensraum* in the east and the glory of dying for the Reich. But what sealed it for Herr Trautmann was his growing realisation that the real purpose of the Hitler Youth was to train the boys for war; but it was too late, because by then it was the law that every boy of eligible age had to join. So it didn't really come as a surprise to Herr Trautmann that Berni had volunteered; he knew there was nothing to be done, just as there was nothing to be done about anything else which was happening in the Reich. And in a way Bernhard was right: at least this way he might make it into the Luftwaffe, not as a pilot, but in some other unit, which was better than landing up in the infantry as cannon fodder, or in the Waffen SS. Herr Trautmann gave the forms a cursory glance and signed, then he passed them over to his wife, who was sitting at the table blank-faced, saying nothing. He dipped the pen in the ink for her. 'Here, Frieda, sign here.' She took the pen and signed where he pointed his finger. It was done.

Herr Trautmann was right about Bernhard's wish to become a pilot. When he took the recruitment papers to the *Rathaus*, the Town Hall, he found he had none of the necessary qualifications and signed up to train as a wireless operator instead, at least still in the Luftwaffe, then waited impatiently to be called up. Meanwhile the war moved into its next phase. One night in December Bernhard was coming home from Hanomag when he heard a droning overhead. At first he couldn't think what it was, then the sky above the Bremen dockyards lit up with flames and explosions. It was the first British raid, a squadron of Wellington bombers targeting the shipyards building U-boats for the German navy. On the night of New Year's Day 1941 they came again, over a hundred of them this time, targeting the Focke-Wulf aircraft factory on the outskirts of Bremen, and again on the following two nights. Bernhard resisted his parents' pleadings to join them down in the cellar and stood out in the street along with his friends, looking up into the night sky, thrilled by the beams of the searchlights piercing the dark, the bright flashes of flak and the sound of the German anti-aircraft guns, sending the enemy packing, defending their city. Now the war had really begun, and he would soon be part of it. The next morning he went out and collected some bits of cobalt-blue shrapnel, twisted and sharp-edged, putting them in an old cigar box in his bedroom, like trophies.

He didn't have long to wait to join the great adventure: by the end of January he was on his way, first stop a Luftwaffe barracks in Schwerin-in-Mecklenburg, eastern Germany, near the Baltic Sea. The weekend before there was a leaving party, held at his *Onkel* Karli's *Gasthof* in the centre of Bremen, the same one where he and his friends used to go when they were boys after the Werder Bremen football match on Sunday afternoons, hoping for something to eat and drink and money for the tram home. Some of the same friends made it to the party, those who hadn't already volunteered, and most of his Hanomag colleagues, as well as numerous members of the family, including his old aunts. Herr and Frau Trautmann laid on the food; the drinks were on the house. Net result: Bernhard, unused to drinking, got drunk as a lord.

The afternoon before he left, his mother helped him pack, each item immaculately laundered and ironed as though for the last time. She did her best not to cry, but she needn't have bothered; Bernhard's head was so filled with excitement he hardly noticed. The following morning the whole family went with him by tram to Bremen *Hauptbahnhof* and stood there on the platform waving as the train steamed slowly out of the station, just as they had done when he left for his *Landjahr*, and as they'd done every summer when he was a boy, off to stay with his *Onkel* Hans at Hamelin. But this time was different, had Bernhard only known it. This time, as he leant out of the window waving back to his father and mother standing motionless on the platform, he was waving to his past, his youthful self, his innocence, his everything.

The train journey to East Prussia was thrilling, looking out of the window eating the bread and *Mettwurst* his mother had prepared for him, thinking how fine the Reich looked in the sharp morning sun with snow still heavy on the ground, the fields, the woodlands, the small towns and villages, all neat and well tended. Then meeting up with a couple of other recruits, telling some jokes, playing some *Skat* cards, agreeing they couldn't wait to show the enemy what's what. And later arriving at Schwerin-in-Mecklenburg, swaggering down the platform with his kitbag slung over his shoulder, going by lorry to the barracks, driving through the town with its narrow cobbled streets, past medieval buildings and old churches with stained-glass windows, and then the first sight of the barracks with recruits marching about in columns, everything spick and span, just as Bernhard had imagined, followed by registration before being issued with their kit and uniforms, blue with yellow flashes on the lapels, one flash for other ranks, two for a lance corporal, three for a full corporal, and

Bert's Testimonial match on 15 April 1964. 'Bobby Charlton and Denis Law lined up with me for the Manchester XI, with Stanley Matthews and Tom Finney for the opposition. We won 5-4, but we never managed to finish properly because the fans just poured on to the pitch. The police had to clear a path for me so I could get up to the main stand for my farewell speech. I was choked, with gratitude really.'

Bert was born in 1923 when Germany was in chaos following World War I. This tenement block is typical with communist and Nazi flags hanging side by side. Revolution was threatening. But it was the Nazis who benefited in the end.

Berni aged four in a street in Bremen. Times were hard, but he was a much-loved child looking to the future with confidence and optimism.

Berni, aged seven, is dressed in his Sunday best and hating it. The future goalkeeper is already present in his stance and expression: physically strong, determined, with plenty of temperament.

The Trautmann family, with Karl Heinz aged five, in their working-class area of Bremen. Berni's father always worked a double shift in the docks, just to make ends meet. But it was his mother Berni loved best, and the feeling was entirely mutual.

Berni in his new Confirmation suit with his first pair of long trousers outside the flats at Wischusenstrasse. Relations gave him gifts of money, which was even better.

The Hitler Youth was a Boy Scout type of organisation involving healthy outdoor pursuits like camping and sport. But from the very start its activities were seen as a training for war by the Nazis, and its insignia, seen here on the banners, was deliberately like the SS. Over seven million Hitler Youth fought in World War II, often preferring death to capture.

Berni with his cousin Helga and a friend at the back of the flats. Berni, a blond and blue-eyed Aryan, already showing exceptional sporting talent, joined the junior branch of the Hitler Youth when he was ten, in 1933, the year the Nazis came to power.

Berni followed every event of the 1936 Berlin Olympics on the wireless. He was torn between admiration for the Americans and puzzlement that they won so many gold medals. Their best athletes were black, which made a mockery of his Hitler Youth lessons in the racial superiority of the Aryan race.

The Berlin Olympics were a massive propaganda coup for the Nazis, with virtually every country agreeing to attend, even though by 1936 the terror tactics of the regime were clear, especially against the Jews. Every time the Fuehrer appeared, the whole stadium rose to give the Hitler salute.

Bernd, aged seventeen, having volunteered for the *Luftwaffe* in 1941.
He hoped to be a pilot, but he'd left school at fourteen and he was
soon told this was impossible. It was his first experience of failure, and
the crestfallen Bernd ended up in a mechanised unit of the *Luftwaffe*,
on the ground. By June 1941 he was in Russia.

By 1942 Bernd was fighting the partisans in central Russia, as a paratrooper, dropped into hot spots. 'You're scared stiff,' he says. 'But it's kill or be killed.'

The Russians attacked in waves, women amongst them, the last wave coming unarmed, picking up the weapons left on the ground by the dead.

After Stalingrad in early 1943 the Germans were on the retreat. Bernd stayed in Russia for three years, then went to France after D-Day, fighting and retreating all the way to the borders of the Reich in early 1945.

Bernd was captured in March 1945 in Germany and transferred to England as a POW to be processed at Kempton Park Race Course, which was hastily converted into a Reception Centre. As a hardened paratrooper, he was automatically classified 'black', meaning Nazi.

As part of their re-education, German POWs were required to watch films and read posters about the extermination of the Jews in the concentration camps.

Lieutenant Colonel Henry Faulk was put in charge of the German POW re-education programme, teaching them about democracy. Here he is giving a lecture in a POW camp, preparing the men for their return to the new, post-war Germany.

the Luftwaffe wings with the small swastika below; how grand it felt, wearing that uniform.

But once training began it was another matter. There were twelve of them in his group, all new recruits and Hitler Youths who thought they knew a thing or two about being tough but soon found out different. *Unteroffizier* Steffan was in charge of the twelve, who would in time form part of a unit of 60, itself part of a company of 120. Steffan was a decent type but he was there to teach them what tough really meant, pushing his recruits through a fourteen-hour day, starting with a cold shower at six every morning, followed by two punishing hours of drill, then on to training in the different aspects of warfare: attack, defence, charging obstacles with bayonets, climbing walls, rolling down ravines, swinging on ropes – all laden with rifles, spades, rucksacks, boots, helmets – running all the time, to incessant shouting and barracking and insults, till you were dead beat and dead demoralised. Then it was back to barracks in the freezing snow and ice, with lights out at 9.30, only to start all over again the next day, and the one after that, till there seemed no end to it.

Even worse was the instruction in Ferma Code, which took place every afternoon in a bleak, cold classroom at the far side of the barracks. There they sat, rows of hopeful Luftwaffe recruits, trying their best to master the complexities of the code system, with a sadistic instructor standing over them, threatening and humiliating them hour after hour, sometimes even waking them from their bunks in the middle of the night to decipher codes for a further hour as a punishment for their dismal efforts that afternoon. It was relentless pressure, and one or two of the recruits broke under the strain of it, suffered breakdowns and had to be sent home. Bernhard managed the first stage, transmitting 30 letters a minute, and then 40; but he never reached the required 60, he who had once been the brightest boy in his class, before the Nazis decreed that old-style academic learning was a waste of time. Within two weeks he was ordered to attend an interview with the camp *Kommandant*, accompanied by his instructor. He couldn't make the grade, they informed him. What did he want to do instead?

He had no idea; all he could think of saying was that he wished to remain in the Luftwaffe. A photograph taken of him at that time shows a pale and demoralised Bernhard, seventeen years old and vulnerable for the first time in his life. *Nachrichten Regiment 35* was being formed that March, under *Oberst* Kurt Loebell, as part of *V Fliegerkorps*. It was an air district communications regiment, operating on the ground, but still part of the Luftwaffe. They suggested he join that.

He left the interview and went to lie on his bunk; he'd never felt so low, so diminished, in his life. Over half the group had failed the test, but it made no difference, it was his first experience of failure and he couldn't bear it. He, the sports hero who had won medals in the Olympic Stadium in Berlin for his athletic achievements, as well as being the undisputed champion of *Völkerball* and handball, and the star football player in his team, had been rejected and dismissed. He longed for home, for his mother's love, for the familiar warmth of the kitchen at Wischusenstrasse. He missed little Helga, he missed his father, he even missed Karl Heinz. He lay on his bunk in a freezing, alien barracks, staring at the ceiling, trying not to cry.

The basic training lasted three months. Normally it would have been more, but recruits were needed fast now; Barbarossa, the invasion of Russia, was imminent, not that Bernhard or any of his *Kameraden* knew it. Hitler had never intended the pact with Russia to be more than a temporary measure, a means of dividing Poland between them and gaining time. By the spring of 1941, every recruit the Reich could lay its hands on was required for the conquest of the Soviet Union. At the end of April Bernhard found himself on a train with the rest of his company, being transported across the wastes of occupied Poland to who knows where. The journey took two days, stopping and starting all the way.

The train had only three passenger carriages; the rest were flatbed railway wagons for the company's vehicles, the usual lorries, half-tracks and jeeps as well as the mobile wireless units, plus covered wagons for the weapons and ammunition, provisions, and the field kitchen. Of the three passenger carriages only one was comfortably upholstered, for the officers and their batmen; the other two, for the ordinary *Kameraden*, were third class, with hard wooden seats, and so crowded there was no room to move or even stretch the legs. The windows were soon so steamed up they had to wipe them with their sleeves to catch a glimpse of the endless flat, white landscape outside. The snow still lay on the ground and every now and again the train passed primitive villages and ill-tended farms with a few heavily wrapped up peasants standing aimlessly about or walking along country roads pulling wooden carts piled high with belongings, everything confirming the Nazi view of Poland as a country of subhumans, dirty and ill-bred. Bernhard found himself thinking nostalgically of the neat farms and villages of his homeland.

As he looked round his carriage he saw few over the age of nineteen. To pass the time they played *Skat*, passed round family photographs, and sang their Hitler Youth songs. One or two of them had mouth organs, and as the light faded and the mood became more reflective they sang the old German songs learnt in childhood, reminiscent of home. At night there was no room to stretch out: some slept head to toe on the floor, others found space in the luggage racks. Mealtimes brought the first grumblings from the *Kameraden*. The train would grind to a halt in some siding, where the field kitchen was set up; the officers were always served first, and got the largest portions, in canisters to keep the food warm, brought to them in their comfortable carriage by their batmen. The *Kameraden* meanwhile had to get out of their carriages and eat their food from mess tins, stamping up and down in the snow, trying to keep warm.

Bernhard had no idea where he was going; everything was rumours. There were starving people standing about the railway stations, that much was clear, people in rags begging for bread, and apparently there were partisans waiting for them further along the tracks. They were told that a new railway took over from the *Reichsbahn* at Lvov, now Lemburg. Someone else said they were bound for Zamość, on the Russian border. In fact there had been a secret Führer Directive on 18 December 1940, once France had fallen. There would be a blitzkrieg to destroy the Soviet army in western Russia and establish a defence line from Archangel to the Volga, to be completed by 15 May 1941. But how was Bernhard to know? After all, not even Stalin knew.

Poland had been occupied by the Germans for over a year by the time Bernhard and the rest of his regiment arrived in Zamość, and terrible things had been done during that time. Poland, designated a slave state by the Nazis, was to furnish the Reich with forced labour and, coincidentally, to house the mass of new concentration camps quickly built to take care of any opponents to the regime, foreign or indigenous – always assuming they were still alive, since most resisting Poles had already been summarily executed. Every town and village had corpses hanging from trees for all to see. The subjugated rest were systematically resettled in the area called the General Government, while the Jews remained in their ghettos for the time being, till further arrangements could be made.

Important were the ethnic Germans of western Poland, who were being resettled in the new *Gau*, or district, of Western Prussia and Danzig, under Gauleiter Albert Foster, or the *Gau* of Wartenau, under Gauleiter Greiser, both now part of the Greater German Reich. Hitler put Reichsführer SS Heinrich Himmler in overall charge, and he, in turn, gave his gauleiters full freedom to operate the system as they wished, as long as the so-called Germanisation of Poland was achieved. He explained that he was in no hurry; he preferred the job well done. 'I wish to have a population which is racially impeccable and am content if a gauleiter can report it in ten years time,' he wrote to Albert Foster. 'You yourself are such an old National Socialist that you know that one drop of false blood which comes into an individual's veins can never be removed.'

The simplest methods were often the best, thought Hans Frank, the governor general of occupied Poland and Himmler's man on the spot. His stated aim was to destroy the nation of Poland, which after all was only a figment of the Versailles Treaty after the First World War. 'We can only talk of these things in the most intimate circles,' Hans Frank told a meeting of police chiefs in Cracow, in May 1940.

> The Führer told me we must liquidate those people whom we have discovered form the leadership in Poland; all those who follow in their footsteps must be arrested and then got rid of after an appropriate period. We do not need to burden the Reich organisation of the German policy with that. We don't need to bother to cart these people off to concentration camps in the Reich because then we would only have trouble and unnecessary correspondence with their relatives. Instead, we will finish the thing off here. We will do it in the simplest way.

By the end of the war six million Poles had been killed, one way or another, starting with the educated classes, the intellectuals and the elite, who were the most dangerous to the Nazis and expected to make the most trouble.

Meanwhile, the Germanisation of the *Gaus* moved on apace. Any Poles living in these designated areas were given no more than a few hours to gather their belongings, abandon their homes, and join the endless columns of displaced persons trekking across the country with their wooden carts piled high, to the General Government, which was soon suffering from massive over-crowding, with nothing like enough food to go round. Families who had once lived in spacious flats now occupied one room. Adults had only menial work, while their children were not to be educated above the most basic level required of a slave labour force. The ethnic Germans who had moved into their hastily vacated homes frequently found meals still uneaten on the tables, so rushed had the exodus been. Some Poles tried to pass as ethnic Germans. A huge administration was set up to assess racial suitability: forms had to be filled in, photos taken front and profile, and a system was devised to categorise the degree of German blood applicants could claim, going back several generations. A new category was agreed for those successful: German 'in the third category', which allowed them better food rations, better education, and, most important of all, to remain in their own homes.

Travelling across Poland in May 1941, Bernhard and his company of the *Nachrichten Regiment 35* remained sealed in their railway wagons, apart from occasional stops in sidings, when they all jumped out to stretch their legs, standing about in the sun smoking cigarettes and getting something to eat. Once they arrived at Zamość they were confined to barracks, awaiting orders. Bernhard's first experience of war was thus a common one: boredom. They hung about the barracks for over three weeks, whiling away the hours as best they could, tense with anticipation yet knowing nothing. Rumours spread like wildfire. More regiments of every type arrived daily, equipment and supplies coming in all the time: panzers, lorries, jeeps, half-tracks, artillery, rations, rifles, boots, helmets, you name it. Bernhard's days were spent unloading the stuff, hour after hour, and doing endless drill. In his spare time he played football against some of the other regiments; it was the best tension buster he knew, along with games of handball and *Völkerball*. Their marching orders finally came through at 10 p.m. on 21 June 1941. By 4 a.m. the next morning they were crossing the border into Russia.

6

Off to Russia

'Dear Mr Stalin,' wrote Hitler on 14 May 1941, just five weeks before Barbarossa, the German invasion of Russia, with his troops and supplies massing on the border, 'I am writing this letter at the moment of having finally concluded that it will be impossible to achieve a lasting peace in Europe, not for us, not for future generations, without the final shattering of England and her destruction as a state.' He went on to describe the problems he faced, most especially with some of his recalcitrant generals, who persisted in thinking of the English as 'fraternal'. He now needed to deceive the English, and divert them.

To this purpose, he explained, he had placed

> a large number of my troops, about 80 divisions, on the borders of the Soviet Union. This possibly gave rise to rumours now circulating of a likely military conflict between us . . . I assure you, on my honour, that this is not the case . . . By approximately June 15–20 I plan to begin a massive transfer of troops to the West from your borders.
> I continue to hope for our meeting in July.
> Sincerely yours,
> Adolf Hitler.

How could Stalin believe it? But he did, against all the evidence gathered by his espionage networks, his diplomats and his army commanders. To these his reply was always the same: he had his own, private, sources of information, and these told him that Hitler was to be trusted, and that the invasion of England was imminent. One of Stalin's problems was his paranoia: by now he had purged his army of over half its senior commanders, and he had also got rid of at least an equal proportion of Soviet political administrators and district commissioners – anyone, in fact, who appeared to pose a threat to his own pre-eminent position. He trusted no one and believed only himself. If Stalin had a margin of doubt, as he must have had following the Nazis' swift advance eastwards earlier that year, he still believed Hitler could be appeased. Or perhaps he was just playing for time.

At 4 a.m. on the night of 21/22 June three million German troops were crouched in ditches, woods, farm buildings and villages all along the border agreed by the 1939 Nazi–Soviet Pact, running some 2,500 kilometres from the Baltic Sea in the north right down to the Black Sea in the south, waiting for the signal to attack. Including divisions stationed in the west, the German army was now five million strong; with 1,700,000 Luftwaffe, 400,000 German navy and 150 Waffen SS units, made up of infantry, motorised and panzer divisions. In Russia it was organised into three massive army groups: Army Group North, commanded by *Feldmarschall* Ritter von Leeb, comprising the 18th and 16th Armies as well as two panzer armies and Panzer Army Reserve *SS Totenkopf*, was poised to attack the Baltic States in the north and make for the area surrounding Minsk; Army Group Centre, commanded by *Feldmarschall* Fedor von Bock, comprising the 9th and 4th Armies and the 3rd Panzer Army, as well as *Panzergruppe* Guderian, named after its famous commander, Colonel General

Guderian, and including *SS Das Reich*, was to attack the vast territory between Minsk and Kiev, encompassing the Minsk–Smolensk road to Moscow, the great Dnieper River, and the utterly impassable 50,000 square kilometres of marshland known as the Pripet Marshes; and Army Group South, commanded by *Feldmarschall* Gerd von Rundstedt, comprising the 6th and 17th and 11th Armies, the 1st Panzer Army and the Panzer Army Reserve, including *SS Adolf Hitler* and *SS Viking*, as well as the Hungarian Army Corps, the Italian Army Corps, the 3rd and 4th Rumanian Armies, and even some Spanish volunteers, was to attack deep into the Ukraine, south of the Pripet Marshes, and beyond to the Crimea.

On paper the Russian forces easily matched the German. They had 110 divisions to the German Army's 106, deployed all along the border in five military districts: Leningrad, Baltic, Western, Kiev and Odessa. There were three types of division: infantry, armoured and cavalry. Cavalry might suggest a leftover of the First World War, but in fact these divisions were some of the Russian army's strongest, because horses were the best form of transport over the vast distances and the terrain, being small Kirkhil horses from Siberia, very fast, and tough enough to be able to tow light artillery through the thick mud caused by the rains and flooding rivers in spring, and withstand the regular thirty-degrees-below-zero conditions of a Russian winter. Once in place, the cavalry regiments, mostly Cossacks and Kalmuks, tied up their horses and joined the infantry on the ground. In addition to this cavalry strength, the armoured divisions of the Russian Army soon possessed more tanks than the Germans, because they were able to produce 25,000 a year, whereas the Germans never managed more than 18,000. But in those first crucial weeks of June and early July the Russians were not just defeated; it was a rout. The surprise

German attack found them completely unprepared. And their main defence obstacle, the Stalin Line, running all the way from the Gulf of Finland in the north to Odessa in the south, and described by German military intelligence as 'a dangerous combination of concrete, field works and natural obstacles, tank traps, mines, marshy belts around forts, artificial lakes enclosing defiles, cornfields cut according to the trajectory of machine-gun fire', turned out to be not so much a solid line as a series of unconnected defences left unfinished once the Nazi–Soviet Pact was signed in 1939.

Worst by far was the extreme brutality of the German attack. Crouched among the ordinary soldiers waiting for the signal to attack, were the SS and *Einsatzgruppen*, the liquidation units. Although these were part of the German army, they were not of it. It was like a body with two heads: the army proper, still led along traditional Prussian lines, practising strict military discipline and organised in a rigid hierarchy, with many of its generals forming part of the secret opposition to Hitler, and the SS troops and *Einsatzgruppen*, who were the creatures of the Nazi Party, and effectively operated quite independently of the rest of the army, receiving their orders directly from Hitler, Himmler or Heydrich. On the eve of 22 June Reinhard Heydrich, chief of the Reich Security Office, issued instructions to the *Einsatzgruppen* sanctioning the immediate liquidation of any Bolsheviks, on a massive scale. 'The following will be executed: all officials of the Comintern; officials of senior and middle rank; provincial and district commissioners; Jews in the service of the party; Jews in newly occupied territories,' detailed section 4 of Heydrich's further instructions on 2 July 1941. The *Einsatzgruppen*, following in the rear of the army, found plenty of locals eager to help with the exterminations. 'No steps will be taken to interfere with any purges that may be initiated by anti-Communist or anti-Jewish elements,' added Heydrich. 'The task of the security police was to set those purges in motion so as to ensure the liquidation goals that had been set might be achieved in the shortest possible time,' reported Walter Stahlecker, commander of *Einsatzgruppe A* in Lithuania, following Army Group North into the Baltic States on 23 June. Everywhere the *Einsatzgruppen* went, there were scenes of such terrifying brutality it called into question the very idea of a civilised humanity.

Witnesses described local volunteers battering their former neighbours to death in front of crowds who laughed and clapped. Apart from known Bolsheviks, the victims were mostly Jewish, Himmler having announced on 30 July that the aim was to have a 'Jew-free' Russia. As to the rest: 'The commissars are the bearers of ideologies directly opposed to National Socialism', Hitler stated on 30 March 1941 to a meeting of army officers by way of explanation. 'Therefore the commissars will be liquidated. German soldiers guilty of breaking international law . . . will be excused.' He reminded them that Stalin had not yet signed the Hague Convention protecting non-combatants in war, which left the Germans free to treat the Russians as they wished. 'The struggle is one of ideologies and racial differences and will have to be conducted with unprecedented, unmerciful and unrelenting harshness,' he added. 'All officers will have to rid themselves of obsolete ideologies. I know that the necessity for such means of making war is beyond the comprehension of your generals, but . . . I insist that my orders be executed without contradiction.' Regular officers and generals of the German army were profoundly shocked, privately calling it mass murder. But, just as under the terror conditions imposed by the Nazi Party before the war when anyone who expressed open opposition to the regime was swiftly arrested and shot, there was nothing they could do. As for Stalin, he had misread Hitler. As far as Hitler was concerned, Russia was made up of 200 million subhumans, to be swiftly subjugated by the Master Race. 'You have only to kick in the door,' he assured *Feldmarschall* von Rundstedt, 'and the whole rotten structure will come crashing down.'

At 4 a.m. on the morning of 22 June Bernhard Trautmann was with his unit in *Nachrichten Regiment 35*, hiding behind some farm buildings on the Polish border just outside the town of Zamosc, waiting, like everyone else, for the signal to attack. Perhaps inevitably, given his apprenticeship with Hanomag, he'd ended up in a motorised unit, in charge of vehicle maintenance. Next to him was Peter Kularz, a friend he'd made during basic training. Peter was two years older than Bernd, as he was now known, and came from Cologne. Being older, he seemed to know more about the ways of the world, and he had the typical wit and humour of the Rhinelander, which could always make Bernd laugh. In civilian life he was a shoemaker, but his real interest, as with Bernd, was sport, and it was with sport that their friendship first began. Peter's particular passion was cycling, and his hero was the world champion cyclist Toni Merkens. The only cycling Bernd had ever done was taking his father's midday meal down to the Bremen docks, or for fun with his mates, cycling out into the countryside on hot summer days with some bread and cheese prepared by his mother in a rucksack on his back. But basically Bernd was interested in any sport, especially champions; anyone who could get to the very top in his sport, whichever one, was of interest to him. It was the natural skill, allied to character, strength of will and ambition, which fascinated him. More than fascinated, it felt familiar to him, like a language he already knew how to speak.

Before taking up their positions the company had been ordered to gather round a padre to join in the German Army Prayer, newly revised for the coming battle, the Nazis having discovered that religion, so despised by them in peacetime, was a good comforter and motivator, without which some of the soldiers could hardly fight at all. 'Let us pray!' it began, conventionally enough.

> Your hand, O God, rules over all empires and nations on this
> earth.
> In your goodness and strength bless our German Nation
> And infuse in our hearts love of our Fatherland.
> May we be a generation of heroes
> Worthy of those who went before us
> May we protect the faith of our fathers as a holy inheritance.
> Bless the German army whose task it is
> To secure peace and protect the home fires
> And give its members the strength
> To make the supreme sacrifice for the Führer, *Volk* and Fatherland.
> Especially bless our Führer and commander-in-chief
> In all the tasks which are laid upon him
> Let us all under his leadership
> See in devotion to *Volk* and Fatherland a holy task
> So that through our faith, obedience and loyalty
> We may find our everlasting home in your kingdom of your light
> and peace.
> Amen!

In spite of the careful rewording adapting the prayer to the new vocabulary of Nazi ideology, Bernd found the whole thing confusing. The Hitler Youth had told him again and again that religion was a lie, even Christmas was meant to be replaced by an ancient Nordic festival, yet now here they were, heads bowed, praying to God in heaven to help and protect them. Still, at this point Bernd would have prayed to any god. He was seventeen, a bit of a mummy's boy with no real experience of life, and now he was expected to die for the Führer and the *Vaterland*. No amount of training had prepared him for this; he was scared stiff.

'Amen, Amen!' rejoined Peter Kularz.

Then came the signal to attack and they were out of the protection of the farm buildings, stumbling across an open field in the first light of dawn. The Luftwaffe planes had gone before them, bombing airfields, villages, towns and munitions factories; next went the panzers, the pride of the German army, spearheading across the terrain with a force and speed which surprised even the most battle-hardened soldiers; far behind came the infantry, slogging along in the heat with 50 pounds of equipment on their backs, including their daily rations and ammunition as well as rifles, daggers and a spade for digging foxholes. In the rear came the *Einsatzgruppen*.

A wooded area lay ahead of Bernd and Peter's unit, on the far side of the field. It was dark in there and they could see no movement. They expected shooting, even hand-to-hand fighting, but none came. Once they'd made their way to the middle of the wood it became clear: there was no one there. All that day they advanced, encountering little resistance: a couple of skirmishes, a few salvos, a handful of wounded *Kameraden*, nothing more. By the end of the first day the armoured divisions had covered 80 kilometres; even the infantry managed 30. The Luftwaffe had destroyed 1,200 Russian planes, on the ground and in the air, a quarter of their front-line strength. By 9 July the Germans had overrun most of the Stalin Line, the area round Minsk had capitulated, and they were no more than 60 kilometres from

Leningrad and 350 kilometres from Moscow. They had taken some 700,000 Russian POWs and destroyed more than 6,000 tanks; they themselves couldn't believe it. But one thing had taken them by surprise: the Russians fought like demons to defend their towns, even in the face of certain death. Perhaps it had never occurred to the Germans that the Russians were prepared to die for their homeland, Mother Russia.

By the beginning of July, Bernd's company, attached to the 1st Panzer Army of Army Group South, had reached an area near Zhitomir in the Ukraine, just south of the dreaded Pripet Marshes. Zhitomir had fallen to the Germans on 12 July. But by now the company was suffering the fate of most others up and down the German front line: the advance had been so lightning-fast that supplies and reinforcements had been left far behind. As the 1st Panzer Army pushed on, making for Kiev, Bernd and a group of mechanics were ordered to set up camp to see to the vehicles. Many were in urgent need of repair and maintenance after the flat-out charge across ground so hard and dry it was literally cracked, absorbing the rain within minutes after sudden summer storms. The Germans were having to convert the Russian railway system to the standard European gauge so that panzers and other equipment could be transferred fast from one field of battle to another, but work was slow and by the end of July less than 6,000 kilometres had been completed across the whole of German-occupied Russia. The highly mechanised German Army had located most of its maintenance depots far behind the 1939 front line, many as far away as Warsaw; spare parts took a long time to arrive. Meanwhile Bernd and his *Kameraden* were left in a clearing in a forest, surrounded by broken-down panzers, lorries, jeeps, and half-tracks. They had tents, some rations, and the weather was glorious. They were in territory now occupied by the Germans, with surprisingly little partisan activity, so they felt relatively safe. They were drunk with the speed of their advance and settled down to enjoy themselves.

And now Bernd made his big mistake: heady with victory and the unexpected freedom, he let the holiday mood overtake him. The nearest maintenance depot was Cracow, certainly two weeks there and back, and some of the group had already left to collect the spare parts and replacement vehicles. The rest of the company was due to set out on their next assault at 4 a.m. the following morning. The evening before, *Unteroffizier* Fritsche, in charge of those staying behind, told Bernd no vehicle was being left for them, and they'd have to fend for themselves. That meant going on foot to barter for food in the local area or forage for it; neither option appealed to Bernd.

He eyed an Opel P4 parked by one of the tents. The car had been brought from France to Russia, and it was so basic it looked more like a box than a car, with three forward gears and one reverse. Couldn't he fix it so it wouldn't start in the morning? Of course he could. He did it that night, once everyone was asleep – just lifted the bonnet, adjusted the ignition and the distributor, and it was done. The next morning he didn't even get up to bid the rest of the unit farewell, but took his ease and emerged at seven, roused finally by the aroma of coffee being brewed. He stood outside his tent in the early-morning sun and looked around, well pleased. Then he noticed the Opel P4 wasn't there.

He called out to *Unteroffizier* Fritsche, 'So they've gone?'

'And they took the Opel P4 as well.'

Bernd tried to look puzzled. 'What do you mean?'

'It wouldn't start, so they decided to tow it.'

'Unbelievable.'

Fritsche shrugged.

They were back to foraging on foot.

Later that day, at about four o'clock, as they were lazing about in the sun bemoaning their bad luck, a young recruit called Dieter from the Friesian Islands in the North Sea reappeared in the encampment. He was a small, thin fellow, and he stood at the edge of the clearing faint with heat and exhaustion. Apparently at some point that morning *Unteroffizier* Gurner, who thought he knew a thing or two about engines, had decided to try and fix the Opel P4, telling Dieter to stay at the wheel while he stood on the mudguard with the bonnet open and fiddled with the ignition, instructing him to do this and that. Gurner must have got something wrong, because suddenly the car caught fire. He shouted to the driver of the towing vehicle to stop, and they threw sand on the engine to put out the fire, but Gurner's arm got badly burnt in the process. Dieter was ordered to make his way back to the camp and fetch help from one of the mechanics. It was 30 kilometres away and it had taken him over five hours to get back, hitching lifts from passing army vehicles and walking. But mostly walking, given that the German army was on the march in the opposite direction.

They gave Dieter something to eat and drink, and once he was sufficiently recovered, he and Bernd set off to collect the car, taking a couple of jerrycans of petrol with them. They hitched rides again with various army vehicles and reached the stranded Opel P4 at nine that evening, when it was still light. Once they'd removed all the sand and cleaned up the engine Bernd quickly fixed the ignition and they filled it with petrol. 'Go on, start it up!' he told Dieter, who was sitting in the driver's seat looking distinctly apprehensive. But the engine fired first go; they were back at camp by midnight.

Bernd thought he'd got away with it. The next few days were even better than going on camp in the heady Hitler Youth days.

Now they had a car to organise food supplies, they soon found a local farmer prepared to sell them a pig. They paid good money for it, as instructed by army regulations, though by no means everyone adhered to those. It was hardly a sacrifice; army pay was in roubles, and what else could they spend it on? They bought milk and sugar and some home-brewed vodka, and they got their clothes laundered by some women in the local village. In the evenings they took turns standing guard, two at a time, at the edge of the clearing, while the rest sat around the campfire, eating, drinking, smoking, talking and playing games of *Skat* and chess. Wherever you went in the German Army, someone always had a mouth organ, so later on, as the light was fading, they sang the old songs, quietly, so as not to alert the partisans. Some wrote letters home, though Bernd was never much of a letter writer; now that things were going well, he hardly gave his mother and father a thought.

The local village was primitive to say the least. There was a single row of cottages, made of mud, timber and stones, with thick whitewashed walls, tiny windows and thatched roofs reaching almost to the ground. A typical house had one room, where the whole family lived and slept, with a mud stove for cooking and for warmth in the winter, fuelled by lumps of turf. The floor was trodden earth and there was no ceiling, only the thatched roof. The furniture consisted of a table, some chairs and a dresser, all hand-made, roughly, of wood. The toilet was a hole out back with two planks laid across; God knows what that was like in the freezing winter. The road was no more than a mud track with a communal well at the end of the village. The Hitler Youth had taught Bernd about the Russian subhuman, but nothing had quite prepared him for this.

The villagers themselves were not unfriendly, just went about their daily business working in the fields with their wooden carts, fetching water from the well, doing the washing at the communal trough, and tending the fruit trees and vegetables in the gardens which surrounded every cottage, mostly without talking to the Germans, almost as though they weren't there at all, though some chatted away in Russian to the soldiers, who nodded politely, not understanding a word.

There was another army unit billeted in the village, on constant alert for partisans, but so far there'd been little trouble. The SS *Einsatzgruppen* had seen to that, and just as well. There were rumours of a vicious group led by a man called Voss, a communist from Germany. Unbelievable really, thought Bernd, that a German could be there, leading a group of partisans against his own countrymen.

The next day they decided to venture into Berdichev, the local town. It came as something of a shock to see men strung up from trees and telegraph poles, but that was war for you, thought Bernd. He knew very well that hard things had to be done in war, though he hadn't yet had to do any himself. Anyway, these were Bolsheviks, enemies of the Reich. Still, it was a shocking sight. There were so many of them, and some were women. Apparently a ghetto had been set up for the Jews, but Bernd never saw it.

Two days later the group who'd gone to fetch the spares and the replacement vehicles arrived back at the encampment. Bernd was sorry to see them, knowing it meant the end of the holiday and his brief respite from war. After fixing the broken-down lorries and half-tracks, which took a good three days, they set off to rejoin their unit. Unfortunately, one evening after a fair amount of the local vodka, Dieter had told *Unteroffizier* Fritsche what had happened to the Opel P4; it hadn't been hard to work out, watching Bernd quickly put the engine right, and Bernd hadn't bothered to deny it, being rather proud of his cleverness. But now, on the very first night back with the unit, *Unteroffizier* Gurner, his burnt arm heavily bandaged and his mind full of suspicion, quizzed Fritsche closely and, before Bernd knew it, the story was out.

Gurner went straight to the company commander, *Hauptmann* Bergenthum. Bergenthum was just 22 and had been a teacher in Duisberg near Düsseldorf in civilian life. Now he was already the commanding officer of a company, that's how good he was: always fair, always correct, the best commanding officer Bernd ever had. When Bergenthum arrived in the company as a *Leutnant*, the first thing he did was put a stop to the shenanigans going on in the supply department – chocolate and booze disappearing in the night and so forth – which meant that poor fellows like Bernd never got their hands on any. Bernd had a lot of respect for Bergenthum, and Bergenthum, another sports enthusiast, liked Bernd. But once he knew about Bernd's offence, he was bound to report it.

Had he known the severity of the punishment which awaited Bernd, he might have acted otherwise. It was back to the beast with two heads: on the one hand there was the German army proper, with its rules and regulations and its Prussian standards of discipline; on the other, the SS troops and *Einsatzgruppen*, who appeared to be answerable to no one. Following the orgy of brutality and criminality which had marked the first few weeks of Barbarossa, the army hierarchy had attempted to regain control, setting up courts martial up and down the line. The courts martial in that part of the Ukraine took place at Zhitomir, and within a week Bernd was waiting in an anteroom of the court, accompanied by *Hauptmann* Bergenthum. The room was full of all sorts, including men from the SS. When his name was called out, Bernd and Bergenthum entered the court, stood to attention and saluted. Before them, seated at a long table on a low podium, was a general and a whole row of officers, all immaculately uniformed, medals gleaming, jackboots highly polished. Bernd was accused of treason and sentenced to nine months' imprisonment.

He left the court reeling. Bergenthum had stood as a character witness for him, assuring them of Bernd's normally good behaviour and explaining that his crime was really no more than a high-spirited schoolboy prank. He reminded them that Bernd was only seventeen and in his first weeks of war. None of it made any difference. Bernd couldn't take it in at all. Apart from anything else, didn't they need soldiers to fight the Bolsheviks? Isn't that what they were there for? It just didn't make sense.

The jail at Zhitomir was vast and dilapidated, three connecting buildings formerly used by the Russian secret police. The *Kommandant* was an officer of the old school who ran the place along the strictest military lines, assuring the prisoners that if they complied, well and good; if not, there would be hell to pay. There was a small yard with high walls, watchtowers and barbed wire, where the prisoners could exercise for fifteen minutes each day; for the rest of the time they were locked in their cells. When Bernd was taken down the filthy stone steps to his cell, a guard on either side, and the heavy wooden door was unlocked, he nearly broke down with the shock of it: the cell was about five metres below ground, with only a small opening at the top to let in some daylight and air; the floor was awash with water, up to and over his ankles, with floating duckboards to walk across, and the iron bedsteads had no mattresses, only springs, so the duckboards were used to lie on at night, covered with a couple of lice-ridden blankets. There was one other soldier in the cell, an SS man accused of shooting a civilian without just cause. He'd already served two months and he had another ten to go. Bernd hardly acknowledged him; he was absolutely shattered, unable to take in what had happened to him. He lay down on his iron bed and, burying his face in his sleeve, began to cry, longing for his mother and for home.

What happened to Bernd was typical enough of those times: the serendipity of war, and stranger than fiction. That first night Bernd was scared stiff and never slept, just counted the hours till dawn. It was dark in the cell even during the day, but at night it was pitch black, and the damp seeped into his bones. On the second day he started suffering from crippling stomach cramps. He'd had them before, for the past two weeks, but never like this. The next day it was worse, and the day after that it was so bad he couldn't even take his fifteen-minute walk round the exercise yard. The SS man hammered on the cell door, shouting for a guard. When the guard finally came he told him, 'This *Kamerad* needs to go to hospital; he's in extreme pain,' and demanded to see the *Kommandant*. Half an hour later the cell door swung open again, and there stood the guard and the *Kommandant*. Bernd was so overawed and frightened he could hardly speak, but he tried to explain the pain, what and where it was, helped by the SS man. Then the *Kommandant* started shouting at him and swearing: if Trautmann thought he could get away with this he had another think coming. He could see the army doctor, but if he was found to be malingering, he'd get three years.

It turned out to be a burst appendix: one more day and Bernd might have died. He was transferred to a field hospital and operated on immediately. He prayed his recuperation would last as long as possible, the very thought of his cell in Zhitomir filling him with terror and dread. Thinking of the SS man, Bernd reckoned he was a good *Kamerad,* whatever he'd done; the *Kommandant* was a real bastard.

The medical staff of the German army were highly qualified, mostly decent middle-class types, well educated, and rarely ardent Nazis; they were there to do the job as best they could, under terrible circumstances. The wounded and dying came in day and night, sometimes hundreds at a time, and there was often little the doctors and nurses could do except ease their last hours. It was the first time Bernd had seen such wounded men, arms and legs shot off, internal organs hanging out, faces half blown off. Up till now he'd just seen Red Cross lorries driving past their marching columns in the opposite direction, and because the lorries were always covered, there was nothing to be seen. This was different and profoundly shocking; suddenly all that Hitler Youth talk of dying for the *Vaterland* sounded hollow.

'Let's try and keep you here a bit longer, shall we?'

Dr Meissen was in his fifties and had spent his whole professional life tending the sick in the local hospital of a small town in Bavaria. With the resilience of youth, Bernd had made a quick recovery and Meissen felt sorry for the lad; he looked scared stiff at the thought of being discharged and returned to Zhitomir Prison, though *Hauptmann* Bergenthum had meanwhile managed to get his sentence reduced to three months. They were also extremely short-staffed, and over the past few days Bernd had made himself very useful helping out when the Red Cross lorries arrived, pushing the wounded on trolleys to the operating theatre, and then out again to a ward, or at least to a bed somewhere. Once or twice, when they were really pressed, he'd even helped in the operating theatre. The most frequent operation was amputation, and Meissen noticed that Bernd was able to go on working even then, not put off by the blood and guts and the sound of men screaming. Anyway, like many of the doctors and nurses, Meissen liked the lad. That was Bernd's luck: people liked him.

By now the prison *Kommandant* knew that Bernd had suffered a burst appendix, and the army being the army, he had to accept the medical reports on Trautmann's progress sent to him weekly by Dr Meissen. It was a good three months before the hospital finally let him go, and not before Bernd had received his release papers from the prison, his sentence being up. At the same time Bernd got his orders to rejoin *Nachrichten Regiment 35*, now based in the area surrounding Dniepropetrovsk in the far south of the Ukraine near the Black Sea along with the rest of Army Group South. It took him three days to get there, hitching lifts, always having his papers ready for inspection at every MP checkpoint, or he'd have been shot on the spot for desertion.

7

Total War

By the time Bernd rejoined his regiment it was October and winter was setting in. It was his eighteenth birthday on the 22nd; he hardly gave it a thought. A letter arrived from home, from his mother, wishing him a happy birthday and telling him about the bombings and the fuel and food shortages. He could just picture her writing it at the table in the kitchen at Wischusenstrasse, carefully dipping her pen in the inkpot, looking up from time to time thinking what to tell him next. She said his father was still working at Kali Chemicals in spite of the heavy bombing of the docks, and that all their production was now concentrated on the manufacture of ammunition. Karl Heinz had left school and was apprenticed to a carpenter; Helga was living back home now that her mother was married, but she still visited regularly. They hadn't had a letter from Berni for weeks, she added at the end. Was he all right? She prayed to God he was safe. Bernd folded the letter in his pocket and made a mental note to write soon. Then he forgot about it.

When Bernd first came back *Hauptmann* Bergenthum got the whole company together and warned them against any bad talk about him. Trautmann's crime, he reminded them, had been more a prank than real sabotage. Standing listening to him, Bernd felt a kind of love for the man, not out of gratitude but respect. If only his father were more like Bergenthum. The *Hauptmann* was a real leader who stood up for what was right and fair; his father, by contrast, was the subservient type, cowed by life, always worried about this thing or that. Bergenthum wasn't addressing Bernd's fellow recruits, who didn't need reminding of his good qualities, but some of the sergeants, who were quite a different matter, seeing Trautmann as the cocky type, the sort who didn't like taking orders, preferring to go his own way. In a way they were right: stroppy is what Bernd was, and had been all his life.

'So, how did you like life in a prison cell?' Peter Kularz thought the whole escapade a good joke. You couldn't blame him; until you'd been in one of those old Soviet prison cells, smelt the fear, you wouldn't know. Bernd laughed it off. Yes, it was quite a joke. Looking round, he could see all the signs of an army on alert for further action: field kitchens packing up, troops arriving, Panzers revving, light artillery hooked up to half-tracks, officers marching about with their goggles and field glasses – action, action, and deafening noise. But it wasn't half as exciting as it had been in that first rush to glory.

There had been a Führer Directive in July postponing the assault on Moscow till Leningrad and Kiev were taken and the area round Smolensk secured. In the event Leningrad was not taken, Russian resistance under General Zhukov proving unexpectedly strong. But Army Group South had taken Kiev in September, after desperate fighting on both sides, with the Russians finally surrendering after five days. Rumour was, 600,000 Russian POWs had been captured. Then *Feldmarschall* von Rundstedt had received another Führer Directive to turn his army group southwards, to pacify the area surrounding Dniepropetrovsk, and now there was yet another directive ordering an advance on Rostov, to capture the oilfields of the Caucasus which lay beyond. Rundstedt wasn't best pleased, was the word going round. But if the Führer ordered it, then surely that was that. The activity and noise was Kleist's 1st Panzer Army gearing up for the advance, which should have included Bernd, but his unit was once more having to stay behind, to wait for spares to repair the vehicles. Bernd didn't mind; he didn't fancy going on another snail's-pace journey, crammed into freight wagons, then another long march, all in the freezing cold.

'Haven't we got any winter clothing yet?'

Peter laughed out loud at that one. 'Winter clothing? You've been with the German army for almost a year, and you really think we'll get winter clothing in time for winter! How naive you are, *mein Lieber*!'

'Luftwaffe, not army.'

'Same difference.'

They went to the barracks and sheltered behind some lorries to have a cigarette. There had been a first flurry of snow on 6 October, quickly followed by heavy rains which turned everything to mud. It was bitterly cold. They flapped their arms about in their greatcoats and stamped their feet, then they started to laugh, punching each other in the ribs, mock boxing. Once they'd warmed up they lit another cigarette.

'Let's get some more cigarettes tonight.'

Bernd was running out of cigarettes again; so was Peter; so were they all. Getting some more meant going into Dniepropetrovsk and beating the hell out of the Italians, who were somehow always flush with cigarettes. They were a useless lot, those Itties, and a useless ally in Bernd's opinion. Some of the Germans did deals with them, but not Bernd and his *Kameraden*; they preferred to get their cigarettes for free, and have some fun at the same time roughing them up.

The next day it was their turn to go out on patrol, a panzer leading the way, infantry following, rifles cocked. As usual there were a couple of skirmishes in the villages, but nothing too serious, nothing Bernd, hardened by his spell in prison, couldn't handle. Dniepropetrovsk lay on the wide Dnieper River, the administrative centre of the province and now one of the six *Generalbezirke* with a Nazi *Generalkommissar* in charge, answering to the *Reichskommissar* in Kiev. The surrounding countryside was fertile, with valleys and forests and water meadows. If it hadn't been for the war and the cold, Bernd thought, it might be a nice place to live. He was shocked. What had happened to him? How could he think it might be a nice place to live? The Ukraine, Russia. the primitive land of the *Untermensch*.

They camped out in the woods that night while the officers requisitioned a cottage close by. The next day there was another skirmish in another village and in the heat of the fighting Bernd and Peter got separated from their unit. They hid in some scrub by a stream for some hours, but they knew they had to move sooner or later. They had no idea where the rest of their unit was. They could see one of the thatched cottages burning and there was no one around. They had a quick discussion and decided the safest course would be to make for the forest.

A hundred metres into the forest they came across a boarded-up log cabin, probably a disused army hut. It wasn't hard to force the door. Once inside they made slits in each of the windows to keep watch, found some logs to sit on, and took out the remains of their rations, famished.

'They say Merkens is somewhere here in Russia. Imagine that. The Reich's sprint cycling champion, freezing his balls off somewhere in Russia, just like us.'

Bernd laughed at Peter's way of bringing Merkens into

everything; it was like a talisman for him, protecting him, taking him back to the safe world of his childhood, when Merkens won the gold at the Summer Olympics. For Peter it was Merkens, for Bernd it was Schwarzmann and Frey.

'Frey got a lot more medals than Merkens.' That always got a rise out of Peter.

'Only if you limit it to the 1936 Olympics.'

'They're the ones that count.'

'Is that so?' Peter laughed and lit a cigarette, one of the ones they'd 'requisitioned' from the Italians the night before.

'Give me one.'

'Make it last. I've only got five left,' said Peter, handing one over.

As night fell they lay on the floor to sleep, rifles to hand and the door of the hut heavily buttressed with logs of wood; further decisions could wait till the morning.

'What's that?' Peter sat upright, head cocked to one side, hand in the air for silence.

'What's what?'

'Shut up and listen!'

At first Bernd couldn't hear anything except the wind in the trees, then he heard it: a salvo of shots, then another.

'*Scheisse!*' Peter went to the door, putting his ear to it. 'What is it!' It only took a second for him to make up his mind. 'Come on. Let's go.' That was typical of Peter, always curious, up for everything. But not Bernd. Bernd had been in a prison cell; he'd had enough excitement to last him a lifetime. He was reasonably warm and he wanted to sleep, and the shots, whatever they were, were a long way off and not coming any closer. But Peter wouldn't be put off. 'Get up, Bernd! Let's investigate.'

It was madness, Bernd knew it, but he went; shades of those times at Hitler Youth camps when they did night orienteering exercises.

They moved the logs from the door and inched out, rifles cocked, then made their way through the forest crouching low, following narrow paths and moving silently from tree to tree. The salvos continued at regular intervals, getting louder and louder. It was dark, but as they neared the shooting they could see great beams of light, like the floodlights at a football match, or searchlights, and Bernd began to feel a kind of dread. He reached out and grabbed Peter's tunic. 'Let's go back,' he whispered.

Peter carried on.

The forest grew lighter and lighter until, quite suddenly, they saw it through the trees, a scene lit up like a stage at the theatre.

It was hard to take it in. There were trenches dug in the ground about three metres deep and fifty metres long, and people were being herded into them and ordered to lie face down, men, women and children. *Einsatzgruppen* officers stood above, legs astride, shouting; a firing squad was lined up at the edge of the trenches, shooting into them. For a while everything went quiet, then another group was ordered forward and the firing squad shot another salvo into a trench. SS guards were standing round the perimeter of the scene, facing outwards, watching the forest. After the second round of shooting, Bernd and Peter were down on their bellies crawling back through the undergrowth as fast as they could to a place far enough away to be safe, where they scrambled to their feet and ran for their lives.

'You could have got us shot!' Bernd was bellowing back in the hut, constantly looking out through one of the slits in the window, just in case.

'Shut up!' Peter shouted back, head in hands. They'd only stopped once on the way, to catch their breath and for Peter to vomit.

'They'd have shot us!'

'I said shut up!'

The next morning they went to the edge of the forest to get their bearings. On the far side of the field they saw a convoy of lorries driving through the village. They ran across waving their arms and shouting and there was hearty laughter as the two lost ones were hauled on board. It felt strange sitting in the back of that lorry with all their *Kameraden,* just like normal. Bernd and Peter told them nothing, and they never spoke about the night shooting ever again.

The rumours spreading through the ranks of the German army in autumn 1941 were substantially correct. By mid-July the Russians, smarting from the rout of Barbarossa, were regrouping. On 3 July Stalin announced his scorched-earth policy in a radio broadcast, calling on all the inhabitants of the German-occupied areas to remove or destroy anything which could be of use to the occupiers: cattle, stores of grain, rail rolling stock, fuel, and anything else the population could lay its hands on. Now that Stalin knew his former ally Hitler had done the dirty on him he began to listen to some of his more trusted generals, especially Zhukov. As for those generals Stalin held responsible for the humiliating defeat, some were sentenced to death, some committed suicide, many more were shot in secret. To match the German Army Groups North, Centre and South, the Russians now formed three new fronts: North-Western, under Voroshilov, Western under Timoshenko, and South-Western under Budenny. Meanwhile in Germany, Hitler, flush with the easy victory of Barbarossa, began to believe his own propaganda and hardly listened to his generals any more. Stalin and Hitler, Hitler and Stalin. They were like a pair of malign twins, having more in common with one another than anyone else in the world.

'He's playing warlord again and bothering us with such absurd ideas that he's risking everything our wonderful operations have so far won. Unlike the French, the Russians won't just run away when they've been tactically defeated; they have to be defeated in a terrain that's half forest marsh,' wrote General Halder, chief of the General Staff, in Berlin. 'Every other day now I have to go over to him [Hitler]. Hours of gibberish, and the outcome is there's only one man who understands how to wage wars.' Naturally Halder didn't say this openly, but wrote it in secret, in his diary, and only spoke about it to the most trusted of his fellow generals, the ones who had been active in opposition to Hitler and the Nazis: von Brauchitsch, the commander-in-chief, was one, von Rundstedt, commander of Army Group South, was another.

Then came Führer Directive 33. Had the Führer gone mad? Instead of marching on Moscow before winter set in, the order was to take Kiev and Smolensk first, to capture the vast territories of the Ukraine with their massive resources of oil and corn, both critical to Germany's war effort. Brauchitsch tried to argue with the Führer, but he lacked the courage for a full confrontation, knowing too well what the outcome would be. On 7 August in Russia, Stalin, suffering from the same delusions as Hitler in Germany, appointed himself supreme commander of the Soviet armed forces.

By November Bernd's regiment was being transferred north-east, to the area around Smolensk, to pacify it while Army Group Centre plus any panzer units Hitler could lay his hands on battled it out in the assault on Moscow, ordered by Führer Directive 35. The journey took three weeks by freight train, from Dniepropetrovsk to Vitebsk. Bernd could hardly believe it: three whole weeks of stopping and starting, with snow piled high, points frozen, and the pioneers going ahead clearing the way, mending the tracks blown up the partisans. Another day, another siding, stamping up and down trying to get the blood flowing into the toes and fingers, and still no winter clothing, just greatcoats and normal army boots and, if you were lucky, a balaclava to cover your head and face. If you managed to find some old newspapers you could stuff them in your boots and down the inside of your coat and trousers; there was nothing else.

Never touch anything metal in the Russian winter, Bernd was told, or your skin would stick to the metal and tear right off. As for frostbite, the German Army lost 100,000 soldiers that winter through frostbite alone. They didn't necessarily die of it, but lost limbs or had their ears, toes and fingers turn black, ballooning like cauliflowers, and had to be hospitalised, and were out of the battle.

'The annihilation of Timoshenko's army group has definitely brought the war to a close,' Goebbels had announced triumphantly to foreign correspondents in Berlin in early October. The word premature hardly covers it; within days heavy snow was falling on the battle front, alternating with heavy rains. By 27 October Goebbels was having to tell reporters, 'Weather conditions have entailed a temporary halt in the advance.' Finally von Rundstedt dared to express his opinion to the Führer: it was not possible to beat the Russian winter; they should winter on the Dnieper River and pursue the assault on Moscow again in the spring. The Führer fell into a rage: who did von Rundstedt think he was? Attack was the thing, not retreat, which is what wintering on the Dnieper amounted to.

The German panzers were no match for the Russian T-34s in this kind of weather. The T-34 might have been a basic design but it was suited to all kinds of terrain, speeding across frozen ground, mounting any incline, crashing through forests and ploughing through snow, floods and swamps alike, while the panzers, with the most modern technology, got bogged down in the mud and stuck in the snow. In addition, the simple Russian tanks could easily be repaired, while the panzers relied on an endless variety of spares which had to be transported from hundreds of kilometres behind the front line on a single railway track which was being constantly blown up by the partisans. Petrol was becoming scarce, supplies and equipment arrived late or not at all. The German plan had been to take over the Russian tank and munitions factories as they advanced eastwards, resuming production on the spot using slave labour. But to their amazement and disgust, the Russians achieved what appeared to be the impossible: by October 1941 they had dismantled 80 per cent of their war industry and transported it further east, mostly to the Urals and Siberia. The man in charge of the move in the southern sector was Commissar Lieutenant General Nikita Khrushchev, the future leader of the Soviet Union.

As for the German infantry, they could find nowhere to shelter. The retreating Russians had blown up any habitable building and the ground was so hard it was impossible to dig foxholes. Luxuries were long gone: soap, razor blades, toothpaste, even cigarettes getting scarce. Dysentery was widespread, which was a severe problem, especially for those trapped in panzers. And still no winter clothing. 'The Russian is completely at home in the wilds. Give him an axe and a knife and in a few hours he will do anything, run up a sledge, a stretcher, a little igloo, make a stove out of a couple of oil cans,' wrote General Heinz Guderian, commander of the famous 2nd Panzer Army, to his wife back home. 'Our men just stand about miserably burning the precious petrol to keep warm . . . Several times we found sentries fallen asleep, literally frozen to death.' On 10 December he recorded a temperature of minus 36 degrees and that 'many men died while performing their natural functions, as a result of a congelation of the anus'. Guderian was another who dared to challenge the Führer's wisdom, but it got him nowhere. In Berlin, Hitler ordered a special medal to be struck for his brave soldiers on the Eastern Front. The brave soldiers were soon calling it the *Gefrierfleisch Orden*, the Order of the Frozen Meat.

On 12 November Halder arrived at Orsha, behind the front line, for a staff conference. He travelled in his special train and the meeting was held in his dining carriage with the train shunted into a siding. There was only one matter on the agenda: Moscow. Many generals questioned the wisdom of continuing the offensive, agreeing with von Rundstedt that the Russian winter could not be beaten. But it was all hypothetical; the Führer wished for the advance on Moscow to be pursued with even greater force and will. It was a fatal mistake. Stalin ordered a counter-attack at the end of November, having recalled Zhukov from Leningrad to Moscow and bringing in ten new Siberian divisions along with 1,000 tanks and 1,000 planes. German casualty returns for the period leading up to Christmas 1941 record 3,000 a day. By January 1942 the Russians had pushed the Germans back almost to where they'd started at the beginning of their assault on Moscow.

Rundstedt resigned on 30 November. Three weeks later Guderian was dismissed, along with 35 corps and divisional commanders. Halder lasted till September 1942, when he was also dismissed. On 19 December Hitler dismissed Brauchitsch as commander-in chief, replacing him with himself.

It was well into November before *Nachrichten Regiment 35* made it to the central sector. When they finally got to the railway station at Orsha, Bernd's unit was detailed to unload the equipment off the train. It took six days because everything was frozen – the differentials, the gearboxes, the engines, everything. They cut up empty oil drums, built fires in them and put them under the lorries just to thaw them out enough to get them moving, otherwise they wouldn't budge, the engines wouldn't turn.

'Have you heard?' Trautmann, Andreas and Kularz were shunting and shoving a vehicle down a ramp and onto the platform, as fed up as could be. Once on the platform they stopped and lit a cigarette, stamping up and down. Bernd had a plan.

'What?' Andreas was another *Kamerad* who was mad about sports and an excellent handball player, though not as good as Trautmann.

'They're asking for volunteers for the *Fallschirmjäger*.' Bernd had always had a hankering after the paratroopers; a bit more like flying, he thought. Everyone knew about Crete and the hammering the *Fallschirmjäger* had taken there, so they needed new recruits fast, and who better than Kularz, Andreas and Trautmann?

'Training in Berlin, someone said. Two months.'

Berlin. Peter could already see the lights, the warmth, the food, the drink, the women.

Before they could volunteer, their unit was transferred to Smolensk, about 100 kilometres east of Orsha but still well behind the front line. Smolensk had been taken by Army Group Centre in July 1941 in the first thrust, and was an important strategic position on the way to Moscow. For this same reason, the Russians had bombarded it for days on end, trying to retake it, but with no success. The result was that Smolensk lay in ruins, and six months on the German *Kommandatur* was still trying to get the roads and the main buildings back into some kind of working order. Bernd's unit was detailed to join the teams doing the job, conscripting local people and prisoners of war to help.

It was Bernd's first face-to-face experience of the way Russian prisoners, unprotected by the Hague Convention, were treated by the Germans, and it was profoundly shocking. Incarcerated in the fort, soon known as the infamous Tower of Smolensk, were thousands of Russian prisoners, literally starving and freezing to death. They were part of a shocking statistic: over the whole war on the Eastern Front the Germans took over five million prisoners of war, of which over three million died in captivity, most during that first winter of 1941/2. It was argued that there weren't enough provisions and supplies to feed the German soldiers, let alone the Russians, but faced with the reality – Bernd had ten Russian POWs in his work unit, all starving – he didn't know what to do. He couldn't share his own rations between them even if he'd wanted to, which he didn't. He ended up shooting crows with his rifle for them. If they were working out of the city they made a fire to roast them; if not, they ate them raw.

By January 1942 Bernd Trautmann was in the recruitment office in Smolensk along with Kularz and Andreas, volunteering for the *Fallschirmjäger*. If they'd known what the training was like they might not have been so keen, but all they could think of was getting out of Russia, getting on that train to Berlin.

The journey back to Germany was hazardous, what with the partisans and the winter, but they made it, along with four other recruits from their regiment. As they finally walked out of Berlin *Hauptbahnhof* to the lorries waiting to take them to the barracks they could hardly believe they were really home. But the Berlin welcome wasn't as joyful as they'd imagined: food and fuel shortages and the first RAF bombing raids had lowered morale and made the people sceptical about the war, so there was no hero's welcome. Pre-war Berlin, like Bremen, had anyway never been a hotbed of Nazi support, the socialists and communists between them getting the majority of votes, at least till the Nazis started terrorising them. In the event the three *Kameraden* didn't see much of the city, the Luftwaffe barracks being in one of the southern suburbs, where there wasn't much going on. The best part of the homecoming was just being out of Russia.

Even after the horrors of Russia, the training came as a shock to the system. The physical and psychological battering was so bad it was too much for some, and four recruits didn't make it. One had a nervous breakdown; three committed suicide, hanging themselves in the toilets during the night. Due to the pressure of war, only six parachute jumps had to be successfully completed to qualify as a *Fallschirmjäger*, but that wasn't the half of it. The basic idea was to break the recruits before building them up again, to make them tough enough, hard enough, to deal with the job they had to do once they were back on the Eastern Front, namely fighting the partisans. The instructors were all *Fallschirmjäger* themselves, many of them veterans of Crete, and there was nothing you could tell them about warfare; they were the hardest men Bernd had ever met.

Day one, the recruits' hair was shorn. They were told it was because the training exercises were done on mud and sand, to approximate conditions on the Eastern Front, and mud stuck to everything like glue, so the hair had to go, but it was as much to break down their individual identities in order to form them into a tight fighting group, a *Kampfgruppe*. 'Cultivate comradeship,' went the *Falschirmjäger*'s credo, given to each of them, written in old German script, 'for together with your *Kameraden* you will triumph or die. Never surrender. Your honour lies in victory or death.' They were the elite, and combat would be their fulfilment, it said. When Bernd, Andreas and Kularz looked at one another, all shorn, they laughed out loud, punching each other in the ribs like good *Kameraden*; but it was shocking really, the change it instantly caused in them, making them almost inhuman.

Bernd thought that as a keen sportsman he'd be fit enough to handle the training, but he wasn't; he was a nobody who didn't know anything, the instructors screamed at him as he battled to complete the assault course before moving on to the practice jumps, and he, the one who could jump highest, run fastest, fight toughest on the football pitch, was half-dead by the end of it.

'Call yourself a *Fallschirmjäger*? You aren't a *Fallschirmjäger* till the blood flows out of your nose!'

Lying on his bunk one night, unable to sleep, Bernd thought about the *Kamerad* who had hanged himself the night before, a lad called Bernd like himself, eighteen years old too, and with parents like his own, he supposed, though he'd never asked. Apparently the fellow had been a bank clerk before the war, a quiet sort of fellow who kept himself to himself, and God only knows how he came to be training as a *Fallschirmjäger* in the first place. But now Bernd wondered whether it was those annual trips to Hamelin as a boy, on his own, from the age of seven, which had made him more independent and less psychologically vulnerable than most. And, he asked himself, which of his parents had wanted this? Which of his parents had done him the favour?

The first practice jumps were from a door like a piece of fuselage, about two metres off the ground, to teach them how to land. Every landing was different and unpredictable, the instructors explained: it might be backwards, sideways or forwards, and they had to learn certain moves and rolls to avoid hurting themselves. The next jumps were from a swing, wearing webbing over the shoulders with a hook attached to the back to lift them off the ground so they swung to and fro like a pendulum. The top of a swing reached about four metres. 'You're 150 metres high! Remember that!' the instructors shouted as they swung from side to side, preparing them mentally for the greater drop. The release came suddenly, without warning, flinging them out another five metres before the landing and the roll. All the rolls were difficult to master, but rolling backwards was the worst.

Some training schools had towers to jump from for the next stage of the training, but Berlin didn't have one, so their next stage was straight to a plane. But first they had to learn how to lay out and fold the parachute, the thing their life depended on.

'The English have service personnel to do this for them, did you know that?'

They were in a large aircraft hanger standing at long highly polished wooden tables. Peter was struggling to get his folds right. Bernd and Andreas, standing either side of him, didn't answer; they were having trouble themselves.

The parachutes were made of silk and were handled on polished surfaces so as not to damage them. There were folding lines to follow for guidance, but the thing was so light and slippery it needed weights to keep it from floating off. The folds were designed to catch the wind when it opened, and you had to create air pockets to help the wind get in there as quickly as possible; if you didn't, the parachute would still open but you would find yourself falling at full speed for the first 30 metres or so. It made you nervous just to think what would happen if you got it wrong, so the atmosphere in the hanger was silent and tense with concentration.

Once they'd mastered the art of folding a parachute the recruits were taken out for their first proper jump, from a Junkers 52, known affectionately as *die alte Oma*, 'old Grandma', or a Heinkel III. The Junkers had only one door, the Heinkel didn't have a door at all, just a hole in the bottom of the fuselage, so you jumped straight down. With *alte Oma* you were told to jump out towards the wings, not the back, or you'd end up hitting the fuselage. 'Jump towards the wings!' the instructors would shout, 'and if you can touch one, we'll let you off the rest of the training!' Of course you never could touch the wings, because the wind took you straight back and then down you went. The instructors always waited for a calm day for that first jump – after all, they didn't want to scare the recruits to death; they needed them alive and fit to fight the partisans. The plane flew low, and, falling at five to eight metres a second, the whole thing was over in no more than 45 seconds. But first you had to jump out of that plane.

Andreas, Kularz and Trautmann all managed it first go and felt like supermen afterwards, joking and larking about once they were safely back on the ground. The instructors just laughed at them: apparently the first jump was always like that, heady stuff, as easy as stepping off a tram. 'Just wait for the next one,' they said.

The recruits were taught how to retrieve their parachutes and roll them up fast, once landed. In real war you might land anywhere, in a tree or an open field, and you had to hide your parachute quickly. Unlike the British and American parachutes, which were attached by a double strap at the back, the German ones, with a single strap, were much harder to steer on the way down and landings were therefore more hazardous. If you landed in a tree you first undid the shoulder webbing, worked your way towards the trunk, then, if you were only three or four metres up, you could jump down; higher was a different matter. After that you had to get the parachute down, and the lines were fifteen metres long, so it wasn't easy. You had to deal with all sorts of weather conditions which affected the way you fell, side winds being particularly tricky, not to mention the enemy who might be waiting for you. Even during training there were sprained ankles and broken limbs and people routinely lost their nerve. You could never tell: sometimes it was the real tough guys, the stars of their Hitler Youth groups in happier times, who lost it first, but once it was gone it was hell to get it back. As the instructors warned, it usually happened on the second or third jump, after the euphoria of the first had evaporated and you realised the full danger; then men would suddenly refuse to jump, barring the doorway with their rifles while the instructors tried to kick them out, or hanging on to the fuselage by their fingertips, literally begging to be hauled back in again. You only got six practice jumps before you were sent to war and it wasn't anything like enough.

'Did you need a kick up the arse?' Trautmann, Kularz and Andreas were marching along a country road after that first jump, going back to barracks. Sometimes the march was ten kilometres in the freezing cold; this time, being the first, it was just four.

'Never!' Bernd wouldn't have admitted it either way, but as it happened it was the truth. 'You?'

'No, just jumped, easy!' Peter and Andreas replied.

The next day they had to start their vehicle training. As *Fallschirmjäger* fighting partisans they had to learn to drive any number of them, including an amphibious VW and a four-wheel-drive Mercedes, plus lorries, reconnaissance vehicles, half-tracks big enough for transporting troops, artillery and anti-aircraft guns, and, most useful of all, motorbikes with sidecars mounted with machine guns. The artillery would be dropped by parachute, which would then have to be located and retrieved in hostile country, and set up. The *Fallschirmjäger* were proud to be known as the 'Führer's Fire Brigade', troubleshooters dropped in wherever they were most needed, 'Agile as a greyhound, tough as Krupp steel,' as the credo went. And all this to be learned in little more than two months.

By March 1942 they were done. They were issued with their uniform, which was a blue tunic with green trousers like the rest of the Luftwaffe but made of better material, with a thick lining, and a different helmet, rim free to be less wind resistant. The three *Kameraden* were now part of the *1st Fallschirmjäger Regiment* of the *7th Flieger Division*, bound for the central sector of the Eastern Front and battle with the partisans.

8

Fighting the Partisans

As Bernd was completing his training in the service of the *Vaterland*, desperate action was being taken by members of the Kreisau Circle, one of the main opposition groups to Hitler in Germany. In spite of their failure to gain the support of the British government during the dark days of 1938 and the first two years of the war, they decided to try once again to make contact and plead with the British to come to their aid. In this they risked their lives, but what else could they do? They wrote another document detailing the strength of the opposition and reminding the British that there was a fully fledged government waiting in the wings ready to take power once Hitler was overthrown. They pointed out the danger to the whole of Europe if the war was prolonged, and promised that the new German government would quickly enter into peace negotiations; but first Hitler and the Nazis had to be overthrown.

It is hard to imagine what Bernd, newly qualified as a *Fallschirmjäger* all set to fight the Russian partisan, would have thought of it. Treason, most likely. Just as it had been impossible for the ordinary civilian in peacetime to know what was going on in the upper reaches of the Nazi state, so now the ordinary soldier went on believing what he was told, though many were increasingly war weary and disillusioned. They had no choice either way; if they tried to desert they were shot on the spot. But Bernd wasn't yet one of those. Bernd was ready to fight to the last.

The Kreisau Circle chose Adam von Trott as their emissary. It was not the first time. As a lawyer and diplomat, von Trott was able to travel to neutral countries, and he had friends in England since his days as a Rhodes scholar at Oxford in 1931 who could vouch for his long record of opposition to the Nazi regime. In 1939, when it was still possible to travel to England, he came three times to lobby Lord Halifax and others to abandon their policy of appeasement towards Hitler. He could have stayed in England, out of danger, but he chose to go back and join the Kreisau Circle in their fight against the Nazis. Now, in early 1942, he travelled to Holland with the secret document hidden in his possessions, knowing he would be executed if caught, and passed the document to a member of the Dutch Resistance, who in turn passed it to contacts in England. Eventually it landed on Sir Stafford Cripps's desk, which was lucky, as he was a sympathiser. He passed it on to Anthony Eden.

'We do not ourselves attach much importance as yet to these people, nor do we propose to respond to any overtures from them. Our view is that until they come out into the open and give some visible sign of their intention to assist in the overthrow of the Nazi regime, they can be of little use to us or to Germany,' Anthony Eden wrote to Stafford Cripps, apparently quite unaware that to 'come out into the open' would mean instant death. Cripps was appalled, especially at the high-handed dismissal of a man like von Trott. 'It is a complete failure to understand either him or what he stands for,' he wrote back to Eden. 'Any such superficial judgement as that indicated in your letter would lead to a grave misunderstanding as regards the outlook of himself and his friends.'

In desperation the German opposition turned to another arm of their network with links to supporters in England: certain members of the Catholic and Protestant Churches. They sent another emissary, Dietrich von Bonhoeffer, a Lutheran pastor and theologian, this time to the Nordic Ecumenical Institute at Sigunta in Sweden. He was issued with a courier's pass by Colonel Oster, a member of a further arm of the opposition, namely a group of generals in the Germany army. At Sigunta, von Bonhoeffer had a secret meeting with Bishop Bell, over from England. He risked everything by giving Bell the names of many of the leaders of the opposition, including Carl Goerdeler, the respected conservative politician and economist who would be chancellor in the new government. Goerdeler was one of the few politicians who had openly stood up to Hitler in the early years, resigning from the government and denouncing the Nuremberg Laws. General Ludwig Beck, who was chief of staff before the war and would become head of state in the new government, was also on the list, as was Dr Schacht, who had been the Nazis' finance minister until he understood the true nature of the regime. There were other generals too, including von Kluge, commander of the 4th Army in Russia, and von Bock, in overall command of Army Group Centre and later Army Group South, and many names from the ruling elite who had always been opposed to Hitler, as well as leading names in industry, business and the radio service.

At the other end of the social scale there were underground resistance groups among the workers, many of whom had been socialists and communists before the Nazis came to power. But Bishop Bell was no more successful than Sir Stafford Cripps: the opposition in Germany would have to go on risking their lives without the help of the British government. And, to an extent, they understood. By now it was virtually too late for intervention.

The British were at war with the Germans, and niceties about not all Germans being Nazis were a luxury.

Bernd and his two *Kameraden* were meanwhile back in Russia with their new unit, risking their lives fighting the partisans. They operated mostly in the area around Bryansk, behind the German lines, and usually in small battle groups called *Kampfgruppen*, which could move swiftly from one trouble spot to another. There were some 250,000 Russian partisans operating behind the German lines, blowing up trains, poisoning the water supplies in German barracks, attacking munitions and supply depots, and torching any building which might be of use to the enemy. Originally the partisans were motley bands of deserters, local resisters and soldiers who'd lost their way and found themselves behind enemy lines, but by 1942 they were highly organised, trained by agitators parachuted in with supplies and new equipment such as wirelesses and explosives. Strict discipline was imposed and Stalin was soon calling these partisans his 'fourth arm'. The reaction from the German High Command was typically brutal: 'For the life of one German soldier, a death sentence of from fifty to one hundred Communists [that is, Russians] must be generally deemed commensurate. The means of execution must increase the deterrent effects still further.' Firing squads should aim at or below the waist, so many were buried alive and in extreme agony from stomach wounds.

Now the war really started for Bernd, and he was scared to death. The bitter winter was the least of it; in the forest, surrounded by partisans, it was either kill or be killed. The Russians were masters of camouflage. They had a network of tunnels to hide in, and they could creep up behind you in the night and knife you before you even knew they were there. Bernd and his *Kameraden* soon found that the safest place to sleep was in the trees, tying themselves to branches with their webbing. The *Fallschirmjäger* were a fully equipped modern mechanised force, with reconnaissance vehicles, jeeps, tanks and machine guns mounted on motorbikes, but when it got down to hand-to-hand fighting they relied on a single-bladed knife which had a split-second push-button release. There were times when Bernd was high as a kite on the danger and the sheer terror of hunting down the enemy. Sometimes when the action went on for days they needed more than their own adrenalin to keep them going and used cocoa or a Benzedrine-type drug. It is astonishing what humans can adjust to, especially young men like Bernd, who were fit, tough and proud. Soon Bernd was as brutalised as the next.

He went for days and sometimes weeks without washing or shaving or changing his clothes. Everyone had lice and everyone got diarrhoea at one time or another. Their rations consisted mostly of processed meat in tins, rusk biscuits and ersatz coffee brewed on an Esbit stove, which could be folded so small it was no larger than a pack of cards. They drank brandy and sometimes vodka, which they 'liberated' from the enemy. When they weren't sleeping up in the trees they rested in blockhouses, single-room log cabins no bigger than ten metres by ten, holding up to fifteen men sleeping in wooden bunks on mattresses of straw. News from elsewhere on the battlefield was unreliable; letters and parcels from home were rare. They might as well have been on the moon.

'What was it really like in Crete?'

Bernd was lying on the top bunk in the blockhouse, Peter Kularz was in the one below. Heinz Schnabel, a veteran of Crete, was in the one opposite.

'We lost a lot of men. Our parachutes were white so we sprayed them with camouflage paint, then we let them dry and folded them into our packs. What we didn't realise was that even though the paint was applied very thinly, it melted in the sun and the 'chutes stuck together, wouldn't open properly. Some poor fellows fell straight to their deaths; most of the others fell badly and broke legs and arms or backs; a few were lucky. I was one of them. But it was terrible, believe me.'

No one could tell Schnabel anything, not the sergeants, not even the officers; he was a typical Crete veteran, hard as they come. Funny thing though, he was related to the famous pianist Artur Schnabel, and was very educated, clever, humorous – dashing wouldn't be overstating it – with a handlebar moustache, broad shoulders and dark skin. No one knew why he wasn't an officer. He must have had some Jewish blood in him, thought Bernd, but he was a great man and Bernd had a lot of respect for him. At thirty-eight he was a lot older than the rest of the unit, and they called him *Der Alte*, the 'old fellow'.

When they weren't in action the unit was billeted in one of the villages, four or five men to a cottage. Sometimes the families were still living there, all in one room, sleeping on mattresses on the earthen ground at night. Bernd often wondered why the Germans didn't get killed then; after all, it would have been easy enough at night, when they were sleeping, and all those families had links with the partisans. But it was rare for a German to be killed like that; perhaps the villagers were too scared. Bernd remembered Zhitomir, where a German soldier had been killed coming out of the cinema one evening. The next day the *Stadt Kommandant* had eight lorryloads of locals rounded up and shot; eight lorryloads for one German. Some of the corpses were strung up later, from the trees and the lamp posts in the town square, for everyone to see. It was enough to scare anyone. It scared Bernd, just seeing it, though he understood why hard things had to be done in war.

'Trautmann! Andreas!'

The unit had just returned from an action and they were dead beat. It was some time in early May 1942 and the Russian spring was giving way to summer, the fields pale green and pink blossom on the almond trees in the village gardens. A dispatch rider, covered in dirt and wearing goggles, had arrived on a motorbike and handed the company CO an order to release the two men, just like that, out of the blue. Trautmann and Andreas were to present themselves at regional headquarters in Smolensk to join a team representing their regiment for a five-day handball tournament. They couldn't believe it. Five days away from the partisan hunt, it was almost too good to be true. Clean uniforms, new sports attire, everything spick and span as though there was no war at all, and off they went in the back of a lorry to catcalls and swearing from the *Kameraden* left behind.

News of Trautmann's sporting prowess and athletics triumphs had obviously reached the front line. Then there was the fact that every time there was a spare hour between actions the unit would get up a football team and Bernd would usually be the one to score the goals. It just came naturally to him; it's who he was. And now sport became his saviour, the thing that kept him sane, taking him away from the front line to play in handball tournaments with the *Fallschirmjäger* team against the infantry, the artillery or the pioneers. In all it happened four or five times during 1942 and 1943, and each time he played it took Bernd back to his youth, the innocence of those pre-war years, the sheer joy of it. Only now he was much tougher, much harder, the war had made him that way; it had raised his game. Usually the *Fallschirmjäger* team won, and when they got back to their unit Trautmann and Andreas were ready for anything.

Spring was followed by a parched summer during which the Germans launched another offensive, but Moscow was still not taken. By the autumn heavy rains had turned everything to mud again, and then came the first snows, so there was no hope of Moscow for another year. In the winter dead soldiers from both sides lay about the Russian steppe frozen into strange shapes, the ground being so hard it was impossible to dig graves and give them a proper burial.

Not long before Christmas 1942 Bernd's unit was detached for a month to guard the railway line stretching back from Wjasma to Smolensk; it was the worst month of his life so far. They patrolled in pairs, up and down a 400-metre stretch of the railway line, guarding 200 metres each and meeting in the middle, rifles cocked, another pair covering the next 400 metres and so on. The pioneers had cut down fifty metres of forest either side of the track to stop the partisans hiding in the trees to detonate their explosives under passing trains, work of real heroism by the pioneers, thought Bernd as he patrolled up and down, scared and frozen to the bone; but the partisans soon adjusted, using remote-control detonators instead. Every train had two flatbed carriages of sand in front to absorb the worst of the blast, but the area cleared by the pioneers unfortunately left the patrolling *Kameraden* completely exposed, like sitting ducks. It was bad enough during the day, but the night was worse: then you found yourself peering into the pitch dark, imagining partisans every-where. Alternatively, if it was a moonlit night, you were a sitting duck again, your silhouette outlined against the sky. Guard duty lasted for two hours, and you were scared to death for every minute of it. Some cracked up under the strain and had to be sent home, raving mad. Bernd turned out to be mentally strong, but it was pure hell and he'd never felt so hopeless and abandoned in his life. Still he never asked himself what they were doing sacrificing their lives in order to occupy a country which wasn't theirs.

Christmas came and went and Bernd felt as bad as he'd ever felt: sick to death of patrolling the railway line, itching all over with lice, and now he had frostbite too, on his ears and fingers and toes. Post from home had pretty much died a death, and the news from Stalingrad was dire. The unit got hold of some bottles of *kümmel* to keep them going, reminding them of Christmas at home, long, long ago. Bernd and Peter Kularz had a bottle to share between them, but since Peter was teetotal it was all for Bernd. Not that he was a drinker, but the *kümmel* was sweet and sticky, and down it went, drowning the misery and fury, and before he knew it he was as drunk as a lord, singing and shouting and swearing at the top of his voice.

'Trautmann!'

Sergeant Kobitska was making his way fast down the block-house to Bernd's bunk. Bernd hated Kobitska, one of those ethnic German Poles who threw his weight around, thinking he was as good as the rest of them. They'd had a few run-ins already, pretty much any time Kobitska tried to tell Bernd what to do.

'Shut up, Bernd!' Schnabel in the bunk opposite was drunk himself, but he knew when to keep his mouth shut.

Not Bernd. He leapt from his bunk as Kobitska came up, and hit him, hard. Then he hit him again, just for the hell of it. Kobitska was mad as hell, but what could he do? Everyone knew it was a court-martial offence to hit a superior, but everyone also knew that the *Fallschirmjäger* were untouchable: the *Kameraden* stuck together through thick and thin, and if Kobitska reported it he wouldn't be alive at the end of the next sortie; someone would have 'accidentally' shot him. Kobitska didn't stand a chance and he knew it, so he grabbed Bernd and dragged him to a hatch in the ground at the side of the bunkhouse which led down to a cellar for storing potatoes, and threw him in. Bernd was so drunk he didn't put up much of a fight, and down he went, right on top of the potatoes. He was down there for two hours, with the *Kameraden* checking on him every half-hour because it was easy to fall asleep and freeze to death.

At the beginning of February 1943 came the German defeat at Stalingrad. Rumours filtered through that General von Paulus, in command of the 6th Army, had defied the Führer's order to fight to the last, and surrendered to the Russians. It was unbelievable, shocking, shaming. Apparently von Paulus had asked Hitler for permission to surrender and the Führer had responded by promoting him to *Generalfeldmarschall*. No *Generalfeldmarschall* had ever surrendered; you either fought to the death or committed suicide. But von Paulus had indeed surrendered, condemning thousands and thousands of Germans, including himself, to becoming prisoners of war in Russia, and God only knew how anyone could survive that. Later there were rumours that as many as 90,000 had been taken prisoner, and that they were half-dead from starvation and disease, but Bernd didn't believe it. Then came news that many had refused to surrender and committed suicide, ordinary decent Germans doing what their commander had refused to do. Others had gone underground, fighting it out in the sewers and cellars of Stalingrad, which was nothing but rubble by now. Later still they heard that von Paulus had been taken to Moscow, where the great man signed an anti-Nazi statement; there were even rumours that he'd been part of the secret opposition to Hitler all along. Some recalled that when he took over command of the 6th Army in Russia, he ordered the lynching of local civilians to stop unless there was positive proof that they were linked to partisans. Von Paulus still believed in the old Prussian military code. No wonder they'd been defeated at Stalingrad.

With grim humour German soldiers up and down the front line were changing the slogan '*Raeder muessen rollen fur den Krieg*' (Wheels must roll for victory) to '*Kopfe muessen rollen nach dem Kreig*' (Heads will roll after the war). In point of fact, the surrender made little difference to the day-to-day existence of Bernd and his *Kameraden*, still fighting the partisans around Bryansk. Except that from now on they knew, deep down, that it was over. No one back home in Germany knew, because Goebbels' propaganda machine could turn even Stalingrad into a kind of victory, but the soldier on the Eastern Front knew that defeat at Stalingrad was the beginning of the end.

In March the unexpected happened, again out of the blue, which is the way things happen during war. Bernd and Peter along with a dozen others were summoned to their regiment's head-quarters, where they were told they were getting three weeks' home leave. It took a while to sink it. Home to Bremen? Home to Wischhusenstrasse? Bernd had almost given up thinking about home; it belonged to another life, young Berni's life, which had almost no connection with life as Bernd now knew it.

The *Kameraden* couldn't wait to get out. They collected their kit and sat in the back of the lorry taking them to the railway station, singing the old marching songs of glory and victory which they hadn't sung for many weeks. But they quickly fell silent as the train steamed out of the station and the outskirts of the town and entered the forest beyond, which was partisan country all the way. They were in covered goods wagons, sitting on the floor, with their rifles, pistols and knives ready and the side hatch open for the machine gun, which they took turns to man, everyone tense, smoking cigarettes, saying little. The journey lasted five days, stopping and starting all the way as usual. The weather was still cold, with heavy rains and sudden bursts of sun, and it was beautiful too, in between the fear, looking out of the side hatch at the passing forest and the open fields. But the fear coloured everything, and the nights were worse because there was no electricity in the wagons and the dark was impenetrable and terrifying. Then they talked quietly about their loved ones and memories of home till they fell into fitful sleep, propped against their kitbags, rolling this way and that with the movement of the train.

By the time they arrived in Bialystok just across the Polish border their spirits were up again. They jumped out of the goods wagons and were marched straight into the delousing sheds, where, stripped naked, they were hosed down with cold water then sprayed with white powder, all over; everyone equal, the generals along with the ordinary soldier, all stark naked, all white. Then they were given fresh underwear and replacement items of uniform followed by a decent meal in a big, echoing hall. There were hundreds of them, from all units: panzer, Luftwaffe, infantry, Waffen SS. The officers ate apart, following Prussian military tradition. The men could see them through the glass doors of their dining room, which had all the appearance of a proper restaurant. Some of the *Kameraden* were incensed. Who do they think they are, these stuck-up officers, served by their batmen wearing white gloves, eating better food than us and drinking expensive wine, at tables with white tablecloths and fine china, as though there was no war at all? Haven't we fought as hard as they have, harder more like? Bernd couldn't care less; he tucked into his *Mettwurst* sausage and potatoes and a large tankard of beer and considered himself lucky to be alive.

After the meal the soldiers sat about in the hall, talking, playing *Skat* and chess or reading old magazines and newspapers, waiting for their transport across Poland and back to Germany, back to the *Vaterland*. Before they left each was issued with a 'Führer parcel'; it weighed ten kilos and contained *Mettwurst*, ham, flour, baking powder, dried eggs, sugar, butter in a tin and real not ersatz coffee, all the things their families back home hadn't seen in months. When Bernd's time came to catch his train, a proper passenger train this time, he dragged his kitbag and the Führer parcel along the platform and into a carriage, and as the massive steam engine pulled out of the station, he fell instantly into a deep sleep.

The journey took two days. Bernd, changing trains at the border and once in Germany, saw for the first time what three years of war had done to the *Vaterland*: the towns and industrial centres were badly bombed, the people looking war weary and hungry, but the countryside was hardly touched, farmers going about their business ploughing and planting with the birds following the plough the same as it ever was and would always be. It was a strange contrast, and long before he arrived back in his own home city Bernd was thinking of Bremen, its port and shipyards, and how much damage the Allied bombing must have done by now.

In fact he arrived at the *Hauptbahnhof* during a bombing raid, sirens blaring and chaos with people running here and there, gathering up their children as they went, and he raced straight down into the public air-raid shelter with them. He found himself sitting on a wooden bench next to a mother with five children about to take a train out of Bremen to the safety of the countryside. She wore her hair in plaits wound round her head in the traditional German style and displayed the Nazi motherhood medal on her lapel, dubbed the Order of the Rabbit by a disillusioned public. The people in the shelter talked to one another about the bombing, the food and fuel shortages, and tried to distract the children as best they could. One or two asked Bernd about conditions on the Eastern Front and he found himself answering carefully, so as not to cause alarm. He soon discovered they knew little of the real situation at the front, still believing victory was in sight. The bombs were mostly aimed at the docks but some fell on the centre of Bremen. You could hear the noise of the explosions and feel the vibration of the impacts, even down in the shelter, built of solid concrete and far below the ground.

When he finally emerged from the shelter Bernd saw devastation everywhere. It took him two days to get home because every time he set off, on foot with his kitbag slung over one shoulder and the Führer parcel on the other, he had to stop to help someone, waving down a lorry to take people to hospital or digging in the rubble of a house along with the neighbours to get someone out. He hardly paused, even at night, fuelled by the kind of energy and anger he had discovered when he was fighting the partisans. It felt normal to him, this battling; he didn't try to get home as quickly as possible even though leave was counted from the moment he presented himself at the *Stadtkommandatur*, which he did on the first day as instructed. In spite of all the chaos, he was regularly stopped by officials asking to see his leave papers. Presumably there were a lot of deserters around thought Bernd; that and the fact that they wanted to check that his passbook was stamped to prove he'd been deloused.

Nobody at Wischusenstrasse knew he was coming; he hadn't bothered to write, not only because all his life he was a bad letter writer, but because he knew how few letters ever got through to their destination, and – who knows – he might never have made it past the partisans. As he walked along the Heerstrasse, past the ironmonger and the horse butcher and the *Zur Krone Gasthof* on the corner, all still in operation in spite of being bombed, a feeling of unreality and sadness overcame him, he hardly knew why; but he shook it off, preparing himself for his family, especially his mother, whom he hadn't seen for over two years. He stopped for a moment at the corner of the Heerstrasse, took a deep breath, then turned into Wischusenstrasse, treading the familiar path to number 32.

As it happened, Helga was at home and looking out of the kitchen window. She was twelve now, and every night, without fail, she prayed to God in heaven to keep Berni safe, she who had loved Berni from the day she came to live with the family when she was two, and who loved him still. When she saw a soldier walking down the road with his kitbag and parcel slung over his shoulder she thought it was a dream. She called out to her aunt, who raced to the window, then flew out of the flat, down the stairs and out of the door, crying to everyone, 'It's Berni! It's Berni! He's home!'

Number 32 was in the third block down, and by now the neighbours were coming out of the flats to greet him as he walked along, and then he saw his mother laughing and crying as she ran towards him. She more or less threw herself into his arms, then she stood back and gazed up into his face, shaking her head in disbelief. Berni was laughing, trying hard not to cry.

'Why didn't you write? Why didn't you tell us you were coming?'

Beside her stood Helga, waiting her turn.

'*Da bist Du*, Helga, grown so tall, with your long plaits!' Bernd swung her round, still laughing.

Karl Heinz held back, standing awkwardly among the crowd of neighbours. Bernd reached out and shook him by the hand. 'So, Karl Heinz!' Karl Heinz said nothing, but he was pleased.

'Where's *Vati*?'

'At work.'

Just as well, thought Bernd; one thing at a time.

None of it felt real – Wischusenstrasse, the old oak tree, the flats all just as before – but he couldn't connect the two, his life on the Russian Front and this. They went into the flats, Helga holding his hand, Karl Heinz carrying the Führer parcel, and there stood Herr and Frau Mrozinzsky, beaming, with their two youngest close by. Then it was up the wooden stairs, his mother leading the way, explaining why everything looked so shabby: that they couldn't get polish any more, not even soap sometimes, and then more greetings on the landing, where the Wittenburgs were waiting, before finally entering number 32. Bernd stood for a moment in the doorway and looked round the familiar kitchen, then he went to his bedroom and then his parents' room, and saw that nothing had changed, though everything looked smaller than he remembered, as everyone always said it would. When he went back into the kitchen he gave his mother the Führer parcel and watched as she unpacked it with gasps of wonderment each time she took out another item. Butter! Ham! Flour! and, *Gott im Himmel*, real coffee!

'Now you can bake one of your cakes,' said Bernd.

By the time Herr Trautmann came home he'd already heard the news of Berni's return a dozen times from neighbours up and down Wischusenstrasse. He greeted his son with his usual '*Mein Junge!*' clapping him on the back, full of bonhomie. Helga had the bowl of warm water and soda salts ready for *Vati*'s feet after a long hard day at work, so he sat in his chair by the window with his trousers rolled up and his feet in the bowl, giving Bernd the Kali news. The works were still functioning round the clock, in spite of the bombing, producing ammunition. The submarine and aircraft factories had both been bombed, but it hadn't stopped production, and there was a large public air-raid shelter in the docks now, so the workers were mostly safe. Berni was shocked at how exhausted his father looked; in the old double-shift days he used to come home tired, but never grey and exhausted like this.

'So what's it like at the front?'

How many times would Berni have to answer that question? An impossible question, which he couldn't answer with any honesty, skirting round the subject with general comments about the bravery of the German soldiers which told them nothing. They were sitting round the kitchen table eating the tinned ham from the Führer parcel, along with a bottle of homemade elderflower wine brought up from the cellar, to celebrate.

'Not too bad,' was Berni's reply. 'Very cold, as you can see.' He pointed to his frostbitten ears, which were still not fully healed. His mother had already put some ointment on them, not that it would make much difference. Then he told them a bit about life in Russia, how primitive it was, hardly mentioning the fighting. 'Lucky you haven't been bombed yet,' he added. It was true that Wischusenstrasse was lucky, seeing as it was so near the docks.

'What about Stalingrad?'

'You have to have some setbacks, *Vati*. Every army has setbacks.'

'Do you eat well?' His mother scanned his face for the truth. He looked fine, she noted, taller and fitter even than when he left; and he was alive, not even wounded, that was the miracle.

He didn't answer, just laughed.

'Are you frightened when you fight the partisans?' Helga was sitting next to him at the table, almost in his lap.

'Sometimes,' he said. 'And now I'm going to bed. I haven't slept for two nights.'

Everyone nodded in agreement, but really they wanted to talk on, late into the night.

9

The Long Retreat

From the moment Bernd got back to Russia in April 1943 it was just one long retreat. There were occasional local offensives when his unit was dropped into some trouble spot and they fought it out, grimly, many preferring death to surrender, but mostly it was just falling back to places they'd taken in the glory days of June and July 1941, defending their position – a bridge, a village, a farm building – for a while before falling further back again. They lost over a million men during that retreat, and God only knows how many men the Russians lost. The Germans used flame-throwers as they went, torching anything which might be of use to the advancing enemy: barracks, factories, supply depots, whole towns and villages, and if a cottage still had people in it, well, war was war and that's how it was.

Bernd's unit was based at Orel by the time he rejoined it. First he did his six annual training jumps, then he was flown straight into the next trouble spot. The planes flew low to minimise the length of time the men could be shot at as they came down, which usually meant being dropped from about 300 metres, falling the first 30 in a couple of seconds, then at eight metres per second once the parachute was open, carrying a pistol, knife and rifle, and one machine gun per group. Those last few seconds of descent, in possible range of the enemy, were like an eternity. There were about twenty men in each *Kampfgruppe*, and Peter and Bernd were always in the same group – the Odenwald, named after the region of forests and hills near Heidelberg. Once you hit the ground it was every man for himself.

When the Russian infantry advanced they came in great waves, women among them. The first wave was followed by another and then another, the last coming unarmed, picking up the weapons dropped by the dead. As for the T34 tanks, when they came rolling at you, line after line strung out across the horizon, you dived into the nearest foxhole, shitting your pants in terror, calling out for your mother and praying to God in heaven. Once the tank rolled over you, you had less than two minutes to get out, throw your grenade and make your escape before the tank rumbled back and ground you into the earth, burying you alive. At Wjasma Bernd's unit jumped in and blew up an airbase; at Willikiluki they relieved a company which was surrounded; at Orsha they held off the enemy for three days, giving the panzers and infantry time to make their getaway. Home leave at Wischusenstrasse was so distant it might never have happened at all.

'One of the T34s has gone.'

Bernd and Peter were crouched behind a burnt-out panzer at a crossing at Orsha, smoking a cigarette during a lull in the fighting. They'd been at exactly the same spot in 1941, and then there'd been two broken-down Russian tanks abandoned there. Now there was just one, because the Russian T34s were so basic you could take the parts from one and fix the other, and that's just what they'd done. The Germans on the other hand had the same old problem of having to send their vehicles back to Poland or even Belgium because their equipment was always being modified with the latest technology, and none of the parts were inter-changeable. And when the lorries and jeeps or motorcycles finally came back, they often wouldn't run properly; time and again they found wire in the oil pipes: sabotage, even some which came back from Germany.

That spring General Kluge, commander of Army Group Centre, attended a Führer Conference, where he tried again and again but in vain to explain the situation to Hitler. By some fluke, a record of the discussion has survived. With another Russian winter coming, Kluge discusses the possible speed of the retreat from Orel to the winter position on the Dnieper, suggesting it will take from August till late September. Hitler wants it sooner and faster.

Kluge: My Führer, I want to call your attention to the fact that four divisions –

Hitler: Are very weak.

Kluge: I have four divisions which are completely exhausted.

Hitler: I'll grant you that. But how many of the enemy's divisions are smashed?

Kluge: Well in spite of that . . .

They look at a map.

Kluge: Bryansk – this part of the line [the Hagen Line, along the Dnieper] is good, but this other piece is not fully constructed yet.

Hitler: That part is not better than this one. If you put these two pieces at Bryansk together, then they make up as much as –

Kluge: But then I have to have time to construct them. I can't do that –

Kluge points out that the rail capacity from Orel is fifty trains a day, but the moment they lose Orel it will be down to eighteen. 'I just want to emphasise that if I give up Orel, I have to retreat in one move, but the important thing is that I have my positions prepared behind me.'

By now many generals in the German army had joined the original conspirators, knowing that the only solution to their impossible situation was to assassinate Hitler. Army Group Centre was the focus of the plans. Hitler had accepted an invitation from Kluge to visit its headquarters in Smolensk, and the generals fighting in Russia had made secret plans with General Oster of the *Abwehr*, military intelligence, and General Olbricht, chief of the German Army Office at Army High Command in Berlin, for an army takeover in Berlin, Munich and Vienna the moment Hitler was assassinated in Russia. The problem which remained to be solved was how to breach Hitler's fanatical SS bodyguard. Kluge was desperately nervous, as well he might be, but agreed to talk to Goerdeler, still leading the secret opposition to Hitler, if he came to meet him at the Russian Front, which Goerdeler duly did.

Admiral Canaris, chief of the *Abwehr* and long-time member of the secret opposition to Hitler, then arranged what was officially entitled a 'conference of intelligence officers' in Smolensk, a week before Hitler was due to visit. The first plan devised was for some of the officers of the 24th Cavalry Regiment, also stationed at Smolensk and already part of the conspiracy, to overpower the SS bodyguard and shoot Hitler, but this was vetoed by an increasingly nervous Kluge. Instead they decided on a bomb attack, to be carried out by a small group of Canaris's officers. For the next two days they practised exploding bombs on a firing range, using three different fuses, one set to detonate after ten minutes, another after half an hour, and the last after two hours.

But when and where to detonate the bomb? Von Tresckow and Schlabrendorff, two of the instigators of the plot and both members of the opposition since the early days of the Nazi regime, suggested that the best plan was an explosion in the air, during Hitler's return journey, which would have the advantage of looking like an accident, and give the conspirators time to put the rest of the coup into action.

Hitler's vist to Smolensk over, the Führer's party got ready to leave. Von Tresckow asked one of Hitler's staff officers to do him a favour: would he be so kind as to take back two bottles of brandy for his friend General Helmuth Stieff? The officer agreed, and Hitler and his extensive entourage and bodyguard made their way to Smolensk airfield, with Kluge and von Tresckow accompanying the Führer in the first car and Schlabrendorff following in the second, carrying the bomb disguised as the two bottles of brandy. At the last minute Schlabrendorff activated the half-hour fuse and handed the bottles over; then the plane taxied off down the runway. The conspirators estimated the bomb would detonate over Minsk. Nothing happened. Had the bomb been discovered? If so, von Tresckow, Canaris, Schlabrendorff and all the rest were done for. Two days later it transpired that the fuse hadn't worked, most probably due to the extremely low temperature in the luggage hold of the plane.

It was neither the first assassination attempt on Hitler's life nor the last. But assassinating a dictator is never easy without outside help, and the half-dozen previous attempts had all failed. The conspirators had to plan in deadly secret, never knowing who to trust and surrounded by spies. And, each time, the conspirators risked not only their own lives but also the lives of their families and dozens of others, because the Nazis never limited their reprisals to the offending individual alone.

To ask the same question as before: what would Bernd have thought if he'd known what was going on that spring of 1943 among his own superiors at Army Group Centre? And the answer is surely still the same: it was high treason. Because, as before, Bernd and the rest of the rank and file didn't know the whole story, couldn't know, and instead fought on even as they knew they'd lost the war on the Eastern Front.

In all this time Bernd, with the luck of the devil, only got wounded once, when a bullet went through his trouser and into his leg. The bullet was easily removed, leaving nothing but a graze – an escape as miraculous, in its way, as Hitler's in his plane. Peter Kularz wasn't so lucky. He was hit in the head by a grenade splinter and had half his face blown off. Bernd heard about it later, when he came back from a patrol and asked where he was; but it was too late: Peter had already been put on a lorry along with the rest of the wounded and the dead. Bernd felt cheated and depressed; he'd lost his best *Kamerad* and couldn't even say goodbye. He vowed to find out, sooner or later, what had happened to him.

In July Bernd was captured by the Russians. It happened between Wjasma and Orel, in a sector where the front line was changing all the time: one minute they were behind the line, the next they were in front of it, fighting skirmishes, defending the sector for a day or two before falling back again, retreating, always retreating.

On the day of Bernd's capture about fifteen of the *Kampfgruppe* were crouched in a ditch, awaiting orders. They were dead beat, all of them, filthy from days of living rough in the same clothes and covered in lice and sores, more like animals than men by now. Bernd took a gulp from his water canister, making it last. The sun beat down hard on them, and the dust from the road, no more than a dirt track, got into everything – eyes, nostrils, armpits, boots. Every time they stopped they fell asleep; they could sleep standing if they had to.

'Give us one.' Bernd stretched out his hand for a cigarette.

'What's happened to yours?'

Heinz Schnabel always had cigarettes; maybe he had a secret source, maybe he was more careful than the rest, maybe he just accepted his role as *der Alte* in the group, the one who looked out for the younger ones. One way or the other he always seemed to have some left in the packet, and if he only had one spare it was always Bernd who got it. So he handed one over, smiling in his reassuring way, and Bernd gave him a joke salute by way of thanks. Then they crouched back down in the ditch, waiting for the enemy.

Bernd was half asleep when he heard it coming, the unmistakeable distant rumble of an army advancing, and instantly his belly tightened in fear. The *Oberjäger* had his field glasses out, counting the tanks, which stretched across the flat land, about fifteen of them, with infantry close behind. Bernd grabbed his helmet and rifle, but there was nothing he could do except curl up in the bottom of the ditch, cover his head with his arms, close his eyes tight like a child and pray to God the T34s rolling towards and then over them didn't crush them alive. This time there was no point trying to fight it out; once the tanks had passed over they scrambled out of the ditch, threw their rifles to the ground, hands high, and gave themselves up – no shooting, no throwing grenades. They were overrun and outnumbered fifty to one.

It was the first time Bernd had ever come face to face with Ivan, as the German soldier called the Russian, when Ivan was the victor. Often enough Bernd had seen Ivan shuffling along in columns, sometimes as far as the eye could see, with not a man among them complaining – that was the extraordinary thing, not a man, and yet most were wounded, some seriously, and all were starving and scared to death. But now it was his turn, and what would Ivan do? That's what scared Bernd. The Germans had done terrible things to the Russians as they marched east, conquering, occupying and exterminating. But now it was Ivan's turn, and God alone knew what he might do.

They were a sorry sight, this bedraggled remnant of the Master Race. The Russians rounded them up, hitting a couple of them round the head with their rifle butts but nothing more, before marching them off eastwards. It rather shook Bernd to find they were being treated with fairness. Up till then he'd kept his head down, avoiding eye contact, but now he looked at his captors and saw that they were just peasants, flat-faced, expressionless, as war weary as he was. They were marched about two miles back to a blockhouse, where they were given water to drink and a lump of bread. There was an officer there, again perfectly reasonable, who asked them a few questions in halting German, to which Bernd gave no answers, after which the officer put them to work with picks and shovels, mending the dirt track along which supplies were brought up to the front line, which had been blasted to smithereens during the recent battle. At night they slept out under the stars with just one Russian guarding them, and early each morning they rose to start digging and filling in, after a breakfast of tea brewed on a samovar and another lump of bread. They did that for three days, after which a German counter-attack redrew the front line, and they found themselves back on their own side and free again.

Kiev fell to the Russians on 3 November 1943. That day Hitler issued Führer Directive 51: 'The danger in the east remains, but a greater danger now appears in the west: an Anglo-Saxon landing. The vast extent of territory in the east makes it possible for us to lose ground, even on a large scale, without a fatal blow being struck to the nervous system of Germany. It is very different in the west.' He was expecting an Allied invasion in the spring, so the Atlantic Wall needed strengthening and the V-1 rocket sites protecting, because it was with these new rockets that the civilian population in England would become demoralised and the enemy finally destroyed.

In other words: forget Russia which is already as good as lost, and concentrate everything on the Western Front. It was probably just as well that no one told Bernd and his *Kameraden*, still fighting to the death, torching and blasting everything as they retreated, day after day, for the next six months.

In the event Hitler got it wrong. D-Day wasn't till June 1944, but more importantly it wasn't in the Pas de Calais, where the Germans were ready and waiting, but in Normandy, where they were not. The Allies' deception code-named Operation Fortitude, with a massive bogus army apparently waiting to invade the Continent from opposite Calais, had worked. An intercept confirmed that the Germans had swallowed the false information passed on to them by their spies in England, not knowing that virtually all the spies had been rounded up and turned, a task made somewhat easier by the fact that many were well-educated Germans who spoke good English, the kind who had never been keen supporters of the Nazis in the first place. As a result, the Germans were taken completely unawares in the early hours of 6 June, when an armada of over 6,000 ships and landing craft appeared on the horizon, making for the beaches of Normandy, backed up by 1,500 fighters, bombers and transport planes of the Allied air forces, Roosevelt having long since fulfilled his promise to Churchill that, sooner or later, he would manage to persuade the American people to join the war.

The Germans were literally caught napping. Rommel, who had arrived in France in December to command Army Group B in Normandy, was back in Germany on home leave for his wife's birthday. Von Rundstedt, commander-in-chief, was back at headquarters, far from the front line and fast asleep, and when he was woken and told there seemed to be something happening in Normandy, he took the view that it was of secondary importance; the meteorologists said the weather was too bad for an invasion, and anyway when it came it would be in the Pas de Calais, not Normandy. Hitler at Berchtesgaden was also asleep, and no one dared to wake him. He'd gone to bed late the night before after watching one of his favourite Hollywood films with Eva Braun, and he didn't appear till 10.00, by which time the Allied troops had landed and were fighting their way off the beaches and into the countryside beyond. Once he was informed, his reaction was odd. 'As long as they were in Britain we couldn't get at them,' he told his despairing generals with the calm of a madman. 'Now we have them where we can destroy them.'

By 22 June the Germans had surrendered at Cherbourg, with Hitler demanding that General Friedrich Dollmann, who was in command, face a court martial. Dollmann preferred suicide, taking poison that night. On 29 June Rommel and Rundstedt went to see Hitler. 'Mein Führer,' said Rommel, 'I think it is high time that I, on behalf of the German people, to whom I am also answerable, tell you the situation in the west. The entire world stands arrayed against Germany.' Here Hitler interrupted him. 'Field Marshal, I think you had better leave the room.' From then on Hitler never trusted Rommel, and Rommel knew that very soon it would be the end for him. But Rommel had told Hitler no more than the truth: the Germans were outnumbered by the Allies three to one, and eight to one in tank strength. By the end of June they had suffered 80,000 casualties, but the Führer's order was to fight on, torching and blowing up everything in their wake, leaving nothing for the enemy. 'Make peace, you idiots,' von Rundstedt told Keitel, Hitler's chief of staff. He was gone within days, replaced by Kluge.

The British, commanded by General Montgomery, had an altogether more cheerful approach to the horrors of war. On 26 June they launched their attack on Caen, calling it Operation Epsom after the famous racecourse and the Derby, which always takes place in June. They put up boards in the midst of battle listing the runners and riders and took bets, then listened to the results on the wireless. When Operation Epsom encountered unexpectedly strong resistance from the Germans and failed, they proceeded to Operation Goodwood, the name of another famous racecourse. This too encountered desperate resistance from the enemy. By the time Caen was taken on 20 July, almost a month after the initial assault and in spite of relentless bombardment from land, sea and air, some 6,000 French civilians had been killed, and Caen was nothing but rubble. The Germans had launched a ferocious counter-attack on 18 July, as defeat stared them in the face. To the British it was incomprehensible; they didn't know about the Hitler Youth and what it did to young boys, turning them into the kind of fanatics who would rather die for their Führer than surrender. How could they? They'd never lived under a dictatorship.

By the time the Battle of Normandy was over the Germans had lost 450,000 men, with more than 40 divisions completely destroyed. In addition, they had lost 2,117 panzers, leaving them with no more than 850 to do battle with 4,500 Allied tanks. The Allies also suffered severe losses – some 200,000 men of which 37,000 were dead – but theirs were losses in sight of victory; the

Germans fought in clear sight of defeat. Kluge wrote to Hitler, warning, 'The moment has drawn near when this front, already so heavily strained, will break.'

In the midst of it all came news of another assassination attempt on Hitler's life, the famous 20 July Plot, executed by one of Hitler's own staff officers, von Stauffenberg, and involving the same conspirators as before at Smolensk. This time the conspirators knew the assassin would have to be someone in daily contact with the Führer, but they used the same device, a bomb, to be placed under the table during one of Hitler's conferences with his staff at the Wolf's Lair, the complex of heavily fortified concrete bunkers which were Hitler's military headquarters at Rastenberg in East Prussia. Von Stauffenberg brought the bomb into the room in his briefcase, then left on some pretext. The bomb went off as planned, killing four but not Hitler. Apparently someone had moved the briefcase to the other side of the table at the last minute. Meanwhile von Stauffenberg was on his way to Berlin to join the other conspirators and help take over the Home Army. When he arrived he discovered that Hitler had been wounded but was still alive. Over the next few days 7,000 people were arrested. The main conspirators were tried by the infamous People's Court, which had been set up by the Nazis soon after they came to power to circumvent normal judicial procedures. These were show trials in the most literal sense, with all the conspirators being summarily sentenced, then executed in the most painful way the Gestapo could devise: slowly hanged with piano wire, after days of torture. Among them were Adam von Trott and von Tresckow, as well as von Stauffenberg. In all nearly 5,000 more were executed: family members, friends and totally innocent acquaintances.

As to the assassination attempt: Hitler may not have been killed, but he suffered from a serious tremor and a lame right arm from then on, and suddenly he looked like an 'old and broken man', as General Bayerlein, commander of the Panzer Lehr Division, recalled, profoundly shocked after a meeting with Hitler not long after. Hitler rambled on for an hour, but 'we dared not fidget or so much as draw a handkerchief. The SS men glowered at our slightest movement.' Hitler, who had never trusted his generals, now trusted them even less and was rampantly paranoid; everyone was against him, and everywhere he saw assassins. Only the ordinary soldier at the front, schooled for years to revere the Führer and obey, could still be trusted. An examination of 45,000 letters written by them at the time reveals that most saw the assassination attempt as an act of foul treachery. As ever, they had no idea what was really going on, nor what was at stake.

The first generals to suffer from Hitler's paranoia were Rommel and Kluge. Hitler had long suspected both of being part of the conspiracy, but he was planning a counter-attack against the swiftly advancing Americans at Saint-Lô in August, so he waited for the result of that battle before deciding what to do. The outcome was not good for the Germans. The Americans won through in spite of the toughest resistance, and went on to take first Orleans, then Chartres, then Dreux. By 19 August a unit of the US 79th Division had crossed the Seine. Paris fell on 25 August. Kluge had been relieved of his post on 15 August, replaced by Model, and told to report to Berlin. At dawn on 19 August he set off, taking a route through the battlefields of the First World War where he had served as a young man. There he stopped to have a picnic lunch, wrote a last letter to his brother and committed suicide with a cyanide capsule. Earlier he had written to Hitler, 'Mein Führer, make up your mind to end this war. The German people have suffered so terribly it is time to put an end to this horror.' If Hitler had had any real concern for the German people he would have made peace a year earlier, as his generals had advised and as the Allied bombs rained down on Hamburg, Bremen, Cologne and Berlin, but in the hour of death Kluge made this one last effort to persuade Hitler. Rommel lasted till 14 October, when two army officers arrived at his home, where he was recuperating from a slight wound, keeping his head down. He was given the choice of appearing before the People's Court or committing suicide; he chose suicide. But he was still so popular with the German people that they were never told the truth and he was given a hero's funeral.

News from the Eastern Front was no better: it was all up with the German army, units and munitions so depleted there was no proper structure left. Hitler's reaction was to order that every regiment be combed for able soldiers to be transferred to the Western Front. Accordingly, by May 1944 Bernd was in France, at Melun near Paris, training recruits, teenage Hitler Youths, to whom he was a veteran paratrooper aged all of 21. The training took place in an old French barracks and lasted no more than four weeks, with the recruits formed into units in the new *6th Fallschirmjäger Division*. Of the 3,000 in Bernd's original regiment there were only 800 left. Trautmann, the war veteran, had by now been awarded two Iron Crosses for bravery in battle and promoted to corporal.

From Melun he next went to Lyons to do his six practice jumps, all in one day, then he was pitched straight into the front line again, at Saint-Valery-sur-Somme, by the Pas de Calais, facing the sea, waiting for the Allied invasion which never came, at least not there. After the rout of D-Day and with the Allies advancing inland, Hitler decided the one thing he would never concede to the enemy were the French ports. Garrisons of German soldiers were left to man them with the usual order to die rather than surrender. Bernd's unit was sent in as troubleshooters to one hot spot after another, and he found himself fighting it out in Boulogne, Cherbourg, Caen, Calais and Dieppe.

As he waited for the invasion in his concrete bunker at Saint-Valery-sur-Somme, peering through the slit and out to sea, had Bernd thought of his father, who'd been fighting not far from there during the First World War? Did he now understand how war could change a man, make him fearful and want nothing more than a peaceful life? Over 60 years later, recalling that time, he shook his head. No, the young Bernd was made of tougher stuff than his father, and the Hitler Youth had toughened him up some more. He'd become the hard man, just as he was trained to be, honed by three years on the Russian Front, earning two more Iron Crosses before the war was done. Nothing much could reach Bernhard Trautmann by then, as he waited for the enemy, knowing full well that there wasn't a chance in hell that Germany could win.

It was in one of those villages of northern France that one of the sergeants was killed. In the midst of a skirmish he was heard talking to a panzer commander. They were sheltering behind a church wall at the time, and some of the *Kameraden* overheard the conversation: the idiot was asking, right in the midst of battle, to be recommended for an Iron Cross; it beggared belief. This was an *Oberjäger* hated by everyone, a useless type who nevertheless threw his weight around, ordering you to parade in your dress uniform straight after you'd come back from the front, wearing the same clothes for days on end, covered in mud and blood. Now you had to go and change into your full uniform and stand there as though you were back at home during peacetime, doing drill, for so-called discipline. But the *Fallschirmjäger* had an unwritten code: they stuck together through thick and thin and no one could tell them anything. Not long after the conversation overheard behind the church, the *Oberjäger* was shot in the head, and not by the enemy.

Everyone knew who did it, but no one said a word, just clapped the *Kamerad* on the back later when no one was looking.

'The war was won before the Rhine was crossed,' Eisenhower, supreme commander of the Allied forces, later stated. But Hitler preferred to sacrifice hundreds of thousands more lives rather than seek peace, which the Allies insisted had to be unconditional. Then, in sight of victory, the Allies made a bad mistake. In August some 300,000 Germans were trapped in the Falaise Pocket and should all have been taken prisoner, but the 12th 'Hitler Jugend' SS Panzer Division managed, almost single-handedly, to keep the neck of the pocket open for more than a week, allowing over 40,000 men and senior officers to get away. Once again the Allies had seriously underestimated the ferocious fighting power of the Germans, especially those, like Bernd, who had been trained for war by the Hitler Youth since the age of ten. Hitler now ordered Model to fall back to the Seine, but General Patton, advancing with tremendous energy and speed, got there first. Nevertheless, in late August, over 280,000 Germans and 25,000 vehicles managed to cross the Seine on floating bridges and small boats, to regroup on the borders of Germany and prepare to launch one last massive counter-attack. Bernd's unit was left behind, dug in no more than 500 metres from the Seine, on the east side, to hold back the Americans as long as possible. It was another daredevil stunt for the *Fallschirmjäger*, and as the Americans crossed the river on their pontoons they were like sitting ducks to the *Kameraden*, armed with machine guns. Bernd could see them clearly, young GIs straight out of college, and he didn't hate them but he didn't care either; he was fighting to stay alive and high as a kite on the adrenalin of war. The GIs were soon backed up by massive air assistance, with almost no Luftwaffe to stop them, so the order came to retreat once again, and Bernd made a run for it, ducking the bullets to reach the lorries, which were revved up and waiting further down the road.

The British had another cheerful name for the next offensive: Operation Market Garden. They had finally captured Brussels on 3 September, Antwerp a day later, and the German garrisons of Le Havre, Boulogne and Calais had surrendered by the end of the month, by which time the whole of Belgium and some of Holland had been recaptured, and the Americans had crossed into Germany at Aachen. Market Garden was launched to capture the Ruhr, the heart of Germany's industrial production. But the more the Allies bombed German cities the more the civilian population rallied to the war effort, just like Londoners during the Blitz, with factories quickly back in operation after the raids and output higher than at any other time. Hatred of the Allies was achieving what Hitler and the Nazis, with all their propaganda and terror tactics, could never do. On 10 September Montgomery met Eisenhower to finalise a plan to launch a massive Allied airborne operation to take the bridges across the Meuse and the Rhine at Eindhoven, Nijmegen and Arnhem; the network of canals and rivers made a conventional ground attack extremely difficult. The Americans would take Eindhoven and Nijmegen, leaving the British 1st Airborne and the Polish 1st Independent Parachute Brigade to take Arnhem. Once the bridges at Arnhem were secured the 2nd British Army would cross the Rhine, advance into Germany and take the Ruhr.

> *Es schienen so golden die Sterne,*
> *Am Fenster ich einsam stand*
> *Und hörte aus weiter Ferne*
> *Ein Posthorn im stillen Land.*

The stars were shining so golden
As I stood at the window, lonely,
And heard from far, far away
A post horn in the stillness of the land.

Heinz Schnabel, *der Alte*, was always spouting poetry. He was good at it, having had a proper education, unlike Bernd. Now they lay side by side, looking up at the stars, somewhere near the Rhine, waiting. They were always waiting – for orders, for the enemy, for the next attack. War was one long wait.

'Who wrote that?'

'Eichendorff.'

'Eichendorff?'

'Yes, Eichendorff.' Heinz was laughing. 'Haven't you ever heard of Eichendorff, you ignoramus? One of our most famous Romantic poets?'

'Yes, I have. I'd just forgotten.'

'Of course, of course.'

'Herr Koenig.'

'What?'

'Nothing.' Bernd lay back and thought about Herr Koenig, his old teacher, in his knickerbockers and his English-style tweed jacket, reading aloud from a book of German poems with his spectacles at the end of his nose, looking up from time to time to see that they were all paying attention. Yes, he remembered that poem all right; they'd had to learn it by heart.

On the morning of 17 September the clear blue sky over Holland filled with thousands of parachutes from 2,000 planes and the gliders of the First Allied Airborne Army. The American part of Market Garden went according to plan, but no one appears to have told the British that the 9th and 10th SS Panzer Divisions were waiting for them in and around Arnhem, backed up by Bernd's unit in the *1st Fallschirmjäger Regiment*. The British 1st Airborne were almost obliterated as they landed. The remainder held the bridge for seven days of bitter fighting, after which they were ordered to retreat. It was a disaster for the British. As for Hitler, it allowed him to indulge his fantasies of ultimate German victory and plan his last-ditch counter-attack in the Ardennes, a dense forest area which lay on the borders of Germany and Belgium.

By the end of September Bernd's unit was on the Dutch–German border and he was employed riding a motorcycle up and down the lines, taking instructions from his company to regimental HQ, to and fro along the straight roads and canals of that flat countryside, waiting for the final Allied assault on Germany.

'You look tired, Corporal.'

Bernd's company CO looked him up and down and told him to go off on leave for a few days back to Tross, the regimental supply depot at Kleve, where units pulled out of the line spent their time off. The men were housed in a small school building dating from medieval times with a pitched roof and pointed Gothic windows. There was a convent next to the school and a narrow lane between the two, which the nuns in normal times crossed and re-crossed a dozen times a day, their black habits and wimples flapping in the wind; but now there were no more children and no more nuns. Bernd went into the school kitchen and got himself some staple German army food, a bowl of pea soup and a thick slice of bread, then out into the yard, where he sat himself down at one of the wooden tables, reaching for a newspaper someone had left behind, talking to no one. After he'd eaten and had a cigarette he realised how dead beat he was. He stretched out on the bench and was quickly fast asleep.

The next day, a Saturday, the sirens went off. Bernd took no notice and nor did anyone else – the sirens were always going off, and Kleve was a small town with nothing much to bomb: a margarine factory and a shoe factory is all there was, and rows and rows of small, neat houses in the north German style. Twenty minutes later Allied bombers were flying over, making for Cologne or Düsseldorf or Berlin. Bernd was hanging around the school yard again, and as he looked up at the bombers, he wondered whether some of them were bound for Bremen and Wischusenstrasse 32. As he watched, half of the planes turned right, following the Rhine; the other half began dropping their bombs on Kleve, perhaps because of the factories, perhaps because they knew German soldiers were there. About 150 of them were billeted in the school at the time, all now racing for the cellars, turning left at the bottom of the steps and running helter-skelter along a narrow subterranean corridor with several small chambers leading off. Bernd, coming down late, dived into a door immediately on the right at the bottom of the steps which turned out to be little more than a broom cupboard. A second later he was joined by another soldier, and together they squeezed into the small space with hardly room to move. The school suffered a direct hit, and Bernd and his *Kamerad* were buried under the rubble for three days before they were dug out. It was pure terror lying there in the pitch dark and the rubble, hardly able to breathe and with only a canister of water to keep them going. Later it transpired that most of the *Kameraden* who had turned left at the bottom of the stairs were dead, and 80 per cent of Kleve had been hit. Bernd was lucky again.

Most of Hitler's generals, including Rundstedt, commander-in-chief, and Model, commander of Army Group B, privately thought the Ardennes offensive was a crazy idea, further proof that the Führer was losing his grip on reality, and tried to dissuade him. But Hitler insisted that the Ardennes, being densely forested, offered ideal camouflage from the air attacks which had so often been their undoing, the Allied air forces far outnumbering a fatally depleted Luftwaffe. Moreover, now, in October, there was already snow on the ground, so the Allies wouldn't be expecting them. The Germans would have surprise on their side, just as the Allies had on D-Day – tit for tat, and death to the enemy.

'All Hitler wants me to do is to cross a river, capture Brussels, and then go on and take Antwerp,' raged Sepp Dietrich, commander of the 6th SS Panzer Army. 'And all this in the worst time of year through the Ardennes when the snow is waist deep and there isn't room to deploy four tanks abreast let alone armoured divisions. When it doesn't get light until eight and it's dark again at four and with re-formed divisions made up chiefly of kids and sick old men.' Dietrich might have added that there was nothing like enough fuel either. But that was part of Hitler's grand plan: once they'd won the battle in the Ardennes they could make for Antwerp and the massive American fuel dumps at Stavelot.

Disagreements at German Army High Command and problems forming and equipping a virtually new army group meant the offensive was delayed till December, when the snow was even deeper and the days even shorter. Nevertheless, the Germans managed to assemble three armies to the east of the Ardennes, and by 15 December Bernd's *Kampfgruppe* had taken up its position deep in the forest along with the rest, waiting in the freezing cold for the order to attack, which came at 3 a.m. the following morning, taking the Allies completely by surprise. Over the next three days the Germans took over 7,000 prisoners and Bernd saw the GI at close quarters for the first time; columns of them trudging through the snow, wounded and defeated. Over the next three weeks, the Americans suffered 81,000 casualties out of 600,000 men, and of these more than 10,000 were killed.

Bradley, commander of the US 12th Army Group, had not given the Ardennes high priority for the very reasons Hitler had listed, and at the start of the battle there were only four American divisions stretched across a front of more than 140 kilometres, with many of the Americans inexperienced innocents in battle. Happily Eisenhower had taken a more cautious view than Bradley, bringing up two extra armoured divisions, just in case and just as well, because it was their presence which managed to stop the 1st SS Panzer Division breaking through to the Meuse valley and capturing the fuel dumps at Stavelot. If it had, the battle of the Ardennes might have had a rather different outcome.

By 19 December the Americans were having a crisis conference at Verdun. Eisenhower handed over the command of the forth-coming battle to General Patton, keeping Bradley officially in overall command but with little real say in the matter. Patton, fat cigar in hand, had plenty to say: 'Hell, let's have the guts to let the sons of bitches go all the way to Paris, then we'll really cut 'em up and chew 'em up.' Eisenhower wanted to know how long it would take for Patton to be ready. Forty-eight hours, said Patton. 'When I said I could attack on the 22nd, it created quite a commotion,' he noted in his diary that night, highly satisfied. 'The Kraut's stuck his head in a meatgrinder, and this time I've got hold of the handle,' he assured his men. And so it turned out. The battle went on into January, but finally Hitler had to admit defeat, as Rundstedt and Model always said he would, and gave orders to start the retreat on 8 January. German casualty figures were almost the same as the Americans, some 81,000, including over 12,000 killed, but they lost 50,000 more, taken prisoner by the Americans, making it almost impossible for the already depleted armies to fight on. 'All in all the Ardennes was a catastrophe really,' wrote Rolf Munninger, recorder for Army Group B. 'What insanity to start an offensive without the necessary resources. I would say it was the *coup de grâce* for our army in the west.'

So it was back to retreat for the Germans – back to the Rhine and yet another last-ditch defence of the *Vaterland*. Bernd's *Kampfgruppe* stayed behind in the Ardennes to the very last, fighting it out, then tried to rescue some of the lorries, panzers, jeeps and half-tracks abandoned in the chaos of battle, leaving nothing to the enemy. The snow was deep, just as Dietrich had forecast, and it was almost as cold as in Russia. After four years of war Bernd's nerves were in shreds, at breaking point – that's how he remembered it 60 years later – but he didn't fully realise it at the time, and he certainly wasn't going to admit it, either to himself nor anyone else. But, looking back, he realised that this was the reason for one of the worst misjudgements he ever made during the war.

Bernd and Heinz Schnabel were on their own somewhere in the forest, hauling a jeep through the snow, both of them at the end of their tether, frozen, starving and scared. Bands of SS were roaming the woods looking for deserters, and if you couldn't produce the correct papers they shot you on the spot. It was hell on earth and Bernd longed to lie down in the snow and sleep, even though it meant certain death. He no longer cared, and it was mainly Heinz who kept him going.

'Give us one.'

They were leaning against the jeep, taking a break from the heaving and shoving and pulling, and Schnabel had lit up a cigarette.

Schnabel shook his head. 'Last one.'

It was like a dagger to Bernd's heart: he felt betrayed, as

profoundly as any betrayal he'd ever suffered. They'd shared everything, he and Heinz, for the last three years – all through Russia, then Cherbourg, Caen, Calais, Arnhem – and now, in this desperate hour, Heinz denied him this – a small thing, and yet at that moment it meant everything. Bernd couldn't bear it. He turned away and walked off into the forest. He never spoke to Heinz again, not that day nor any day after. Heinz did everything to try and make amends, but Bernd, with his usual stubbornness, wouldn't budge. Not long after, they lost sight of one another in the chaos of the final retreat. Later, in saner times, Bernd deeply regretted it; later still, after the war, he searched for Schnabel everywhere, but he never found him.

Terrible things were done on that final retreat back into Germany in early 1945. With nothing but the humiliation of unconditional surrender ahead of them and military discipline more or less gone, many fanatical units carried out the Führer's scorched-earth policy, destroying everything. The blind brutality of it profoundly shocked the Allies as they advanced. Many times they came across German soldiers hanging from the trees, shot and strung up for trying to desert.

One day Bernd reached a village called Kaldenkirchen, close to the Dutch–German border. The place was deserted, the houses long since abandoned by their owners. His *Kampfgruppe*, what was left of it, was charged with checking buildings for unexploded bombs; once cleared they marked the door with a chalk cross to indicate it was safe. Making his way along the deserted main street, Bernd came across a garden centre with a beautiful house attached, an eerie reminder of peaceful times. There was a rough sign outside, ARTILLERY UNIT, so he went inside, along with his sergeant, shouting out to see if anyone was still there. No one answered, the artillery unit having moved on, but they checked the house, starting at the top as usual, rifles cocked, just in case. Eventually they got down to the cellar, where Bernd found shelves and shelves of garden vegetables and fruit, bottled in big glass jars, just as his mother did at home, but all the jars had been smashed to pieces, glass everywhere, the fruit dripping in thick coloured splashes down the stone walls and onto the earthen floor. Bernd nearly wept he was so appalled at the wanton, senseless destruction combined with the sudden memory of home. For good measure the culprits had shat everywhere. Bernd left the cellar fast to breathe the fresh air outside.

'There's someone in the house.' The sergeant had heard a noise in another chamber of the cellar.

They went down again, calling out, and a terrified man emerged, not more than 30 but looking older from sheer exhaustion and fear. His wife and children were hiding in the caves by the Rhine along with his brother, he said, because they didn't want to be evacuated with the rest of the village, but he'd come back to see if the house was all right. He gestured hopelessly at the sight of the smashed jars and the filth.

'It wasn't us,' Bernd said quickly. 'We've only just arrived.'

The man nodded.

'*Gott im Himmel!*' The sergeant couldn't believe any more than Bernd that Germans could behave in this way.

'But you should leave,' Bernd advised. 'The *Amis* are coming.' It didn't cross his mind that the man would be thrilled that the Americans were coming.

It was a time of insanity, that retreat. At one point Bernd and his *Kampfgruppe* came across an army store, who knows where, just somewhere along the way among all the chaos. The store was a large building like a warehouse, full of provisions of every sort, with armed guards at the gates. Bernd and his *Kameraden* were literally starving. 'Open the gates!' they shouted. But the guards wouldn't budge, not for anything, and refused them entry. It was unbelievable: everyone was on the run and soon enough the whole lot would end up in Allied hands, but the guards wouldn't budge. These were provisions for officers – fine hams, real coffee, good butter, bottles of champagne, an Aladdin's cave of provisions – and not for the likes of other ranks. The guards kept their rifles trained on them, and there was little doubt they would have used them, that's how insane things were on that final retreat.

10

Capture

Bernd's last contact with normal humankind had been on his way to the Ardennes. He was driving an ammunition truck at the time, all alone, and it was snowing heavily. At some point Bernd found himself close to Landau in the Rhineland and to the village of Godramstein, where Alfred Andreas, his handball *Kamerad*, came from. Bernd knew the address by heart, almost as though it were his own, so often had Alfred talked about his family, his childhood and his village. His parents were farmers, his sister was a nurse in the German Red Cross. Now, with no one supervising him, Bernd decided on the spur of the moment to make a detour and pay the family a visit.

It was a quiet part of the country and he found the village easily enough, leaving the truck with its load of ammunition by the side of the road as though it was the most normal thing to do and walking the last stretch on foot because of the narrow country road and the snow. Perhaps war had sent him temporarily insane, but that's what he did, and there they all were, even the sister, who was home on leave. Bernd accepted it as the serendipity of war, and told them he just happened to be passing and brought them news of their son. The astounded parents fetched a bottle of schnapps from the cellar, and they spent two happy hours talking like old friends, the parents and sister weeping every time Alfred was mentioned. Bernd told them about Russia, but nothing too bad, and about the training for the *Fallschirmjäger*, which he and Alfred had done together in Berlin, and about Alfred's bravery and his good humour, which kept all the *Kameraden* going, and above all that he was alive and well though, truth be known, Bernd hadn't actually seen him in days. He tried to warn them about the Allies' advance and what it would mean, but they didn't really take it in because the war had hardly touched these small rural villages, and wartime censorship and propaganda still ensured that they thought Germany had a good chance of final victory. They believed in the V-2 rocket miracle weapon, and they still believed in Hitler, perhaps more now than ever before, and Bernd didn't have the heart to disabuse them.

By the time he left the house he was fairly drunk and in a roaring good humour. The truck with the ammunition was still there, covered in snow but safe and sound, and he managed to start up the engine and get back to the main road easily enough. Once there he bowled along, whistling and singing and laughing out loud to himself at the stunt he'd just pulled off in the midst of war. Suddenly he found himself in a ditch, he hardly knew how, with the lorry tipped dangerously to one side and the ammunition precariously balanced. He had no idea what to do and just sat there in a daze. About twenty minutes later, as he was still wondering what to do, an SS panzer unit came by and helped him out; no one else would have done it, what with the live ammunition, but they did, and even laughed at him for getting into an idiot mess in the first place.

After the Ardennes – the Battle of the Bulge, as the Americans called it – the Allies began planning their final assault on

Germany. By March 1945 they had eight armies ranged along the west bank of the Rhine: the Canadians in the north, then the British, the Americans, the French and the Americans again. The main offensive was planned for the north, Montgomery having pounded the Germans for most of February, softening them up. The artillery was backed up by massive air strength and two divisions of the Allied Airborne Army, to be dropped on the east bank of the Rhine. This is where Bernd and his *Kampfgruppe* were transferred some time in February, to Hamminkeln, between Emmerich and Wesel, waiting for the onslaught to begin and knowing that the German forces were fatally depleted, with the Luftwaffe virtually non-existent. There were about fifteen of them crammed into a log bunker built by the *Volkssturm*, the Dad's Army of Germany. These old *Kameraden,* whether through incompetence or sheer lack of time, had built the bunkers with no windows; they just felled the trees along the Rhine, hammered the logs together, and that was that. So there they were, the *Kameraden*, shoulder to shoulder in the bunker, with no room to move, no air to breathe and no way of seeing or even hearing if the enemy was coming. Bernd preferred to stay outside.

On 10 March Hitler relieved Rundstedt of his command for the third and last time, replacing him with Kesselring. After that it was just a waiting game, knowing the final attack was imminent, but not knowing exactly when or where. Reconnaissance units reported massive Allied artillery and air concentrations on the other side of the Rhine, but the only guidance the *Kameraden* in their bunker got came in the form of another Führer order not to abandon their post, to fight to the death and never surrender. On 22 March the artillery attack began with a non-stop 24-hour barrage. It was unbelievable; in all his time of war, four years of it now, Bernd had never experienced anything like it: Armageddon, hell on earth, the end of civilisation. Then, on the night of 23 March and throughout the next day, the skies filled with an armada of planes of every description, thousands of them, and the bombing started. There were so many planes that the sky was dark with them and the noise was deafening. Bernd, facing the Canadians, saw them coming – hundreds of paratroopers like himself, jumping from planes, landing, gathering up their parachutes and running for cover, just as he did, and he felt – how did he feel? It was so confused, that feeling, so divided and dividing, he just shut it out and got on with it. It went very badly for the Canadians, who were mostly young and inexperienced: gliders crashed, paratroopers hung in the trees, and the *Kameraden* picked them off easily but reluctantly because they were paratroopers too.

But the overall outcome was a foregone conclusion. Once the Allied forces had crossed the Rhine the Germans were in chaotic retreat again, fleeing in every direction, committing suicide or giving themselves up, starving and half dead, with their hands in the air and their heads bowed with shame and resentment. Noticeable exceptions were the Hitler Youth *Kampfgruppen*, who refused, against all the odds and all logic, to give up. Everyone else might have fled or surrendered, and they might be completely surrounded by the enemy with a British army officer shouting at them through a loudhailer to pack it in and come out with their hands high, but those Hitler Youths would start shooting all over again, fighting to the death, because defeat was not an option for them. But for most it was finished. By early April 325,000 men had surrendered from General Model's army alone. Still, on 16 April Hitler issued another Fuehrer order, to fight on to Berlin. On 18 April Model spoke to his men for the last time: '*Meine Herren*, it's over. There is nothing more we can do. It is up to you what you do from here.' Three days later he went into a wood and shot himself.

After 24 March 1945 it was every man for himself. In the chaos of battle Bernd lost contact with his *Kampfgruppe* and there was no sign of anyone giving orders or discipline of any kind. He was scared, racing round and round in circles, not knowing what to do. Then it hit him in a flash of inspiration: go home. It's all over here; get back to Bremen. It was 500 kilometres away, but so what? Before being immured in the *Volkssturm* bunker Bernd had taken note of his surroundings, as he always did after years of orientation exercises in the Hitler Youth. He knew the names of the surrounding villages and roughly which direction to take. It was only a question of timing, because he knew he couldn't yet get past the SS and the military police, who were shooting deserters. So he waited for two days and then, in the turmoil of the fighting, made a run for it. He took nothing but his rifle and a standard P38 pistol with him. It was strangely easy, or maybe it was just lucky Bernd again.

He soon ditched the cumbersome rifle, moving swiftly from cover to cover, crouching low, pistol to hand, keeping to the woods and the hedges, always avoiding open fields. As he moved further from the battleground it got quieter, and he saw it was good agricultural land. That first night he risked it and slept in an abandoned barn, the P38 at his side. By the middle of the next day he was half dead with exhaustion and starvation. There was a farm not far ahead and he decided to take another risk: he stumbled into the yard and banged on the door, and when the farmer's wife answered, he asked for some food. She was middle-aged, buxom, wearing an apron, looking just as a farmer's wife should; the farmer stood in the doorway close behind her, both wary. There were chickens in the yard and Bernd could hear the cows stamping about in their stalls because it was still too early in the year for them to be out in the meadows.

Without a word, the farmer led him through the kitchen and down some stone steps into the cellar. There were five wounded German soldiers down there, lying on the floor moaning in pain, staring at Bernd through the darkness. One of them told Bernd they'd been on the road, fleeing in a lorry, three in the cab, two on the front mudguards looking out for enemy planes, when a grenade went off in the back. They all had shrapnel wounds, many of them serious.

'If you take them away, you can have whatever you want to eat,' said the farmer. 'Ham, bread, milk – anything.'

They went back up into the farm kitchen and the wife gave Bernd some ham and bread and poured him some milk from a jug, which he gulped down, muttering thanks. They sat opposite him at the large wooden table watching him eat, saying little, waiting for him to leave, taking the wounded with him. When he'd finished they went out into the yard, where the lorry was parked under an old apple tree. The engine, fuel tank and radiator were all fine; only one front wheel, the windscreen and one of the side doors were damaged.

'I'll need help fitting the spare wheel.'

The farmer nodded.

'And some fuel.'

He nodded again.

'And something for us to eat.'

Again the farmer nodded.

His wife, who'd been standing to one side listening, arms folded, went into the farmhouse to get the food together while the farmer helped Bernd with the spare wheel. Then they took the broken glass out of the windscreen and bound the damaged door up with some string. There were boxes of ammunition in the back of the lorry, machine guns and grenades, and Bernd told the farmer they'd have to unload them and put straw down for the wounded men instead. They did this gingerly, with Bernd giving instructions, and he kept one sub-machine gun, placing it in the cab beside the driver's seat, just in case. It was mid-afternoon by the time they'd finished, but the farmer was in a hurry to see them gone, so they went down to the cellar and together they managed to get the wounded soldiers, moaning and swearing, up the steps and into the back of the lorry, one by one. The wife came out with a basket of food and some home-made elderflower wine, and then Bernd drove the lorry out of the farmyard and back onto the road.

He vaguely remembered passing a hand-painted sign nailed to a tree with an arrow pointing to a field hospital; it meant going back towards the fighting and the SS, but what else could he do? He was cursing as he drove along, wanting to be going east, not west; going home. It was madness, and all the time they were under attack from Allied planes, with explosions left and right, but somehow he found the sign and hurtled down the road, hell-bent on getting the soldiers out of the lorry and being on his way.

The hospital was at the end of the village, in an old castle. They were about 600 metres from it when a bomb exploded close by with such force that the lorry careered off the road. It was total chaos, people running around all over the place, and there he was shouting his head off trying to get someone to help him pick up the wounded *Kameraden*, who were scattered about on the ground, screaming; but everyone was ignoring him. Finally he lost his head completely and forced a passing officer to help at pistol point. Holding the P38 to his head, Bernd screamed at the *Hauptmann*, 'If you don't order some men to help me with these wounded . . .' The *Hauptmann* could have had Bernd shot for gross insubordination, but he gave the order and they got the men into the courtyard of the castle, which was pure bedlam, and laid them among all the other dying and wounded, and that's where Bernd left them, duty done.

He went back to the lorry and a passing reconnaissance unit helped him get it up on the road; then he found an old rag in the cab, cleaned out the radiator and got it working again. By the time he was finished it was dark. He looked around, trying to decide which direction to go, back the way he had come or a different way? He decided to go back along the road he knew, and he set off without anyone noticing him in the chaos.

He drove flat out. There were farms on either side of the road, and a full moon, and it was eerily light. It must have been about midnight when he realised he couldn't hear anything. He stopped the lorry and listened: everything was quiet, no firing, no bombs. He felt elated as though a huge weight had been lifted off his shoulders, but at the same time he had the feeling something wasn't right. He stood in the middle of the road and looked around, then he walked into one of the farmyards and banged on the door. There was no reply, nothing and nobody. It was ghostly out there and he was quite alone. He sat for a while by the side of the road, eating some food from the basket prepared by the farmer's wife, then he got back into the lorry and drove on for another couple of hundred metres to the next farm. He jumped out of the cab to open the yard gate and heard the click of a gun being cocked. It was the *Amis*, and they were everywhere, hidden behind the hedges. Now he realised they'd been there all the time, just watching him. They must have parachuted in, and here they were, a whole unit of them, just watching the Kraut soldier wandering along the road, in and out of the farmyards. He had his P38 in his hand; his arm came up automatically, out of sheer habit, and he pulled the trigger. After that they grabbed him and hit him a few times, but nothing serious, then they took him into the farmhouse, where the American officers and their staff had established themselves. Bernd could hardly believe it when one of the soldiers started speaking to him in fluent German. He was a Jew of course, one of the hundreds of thousands who'd fled Nazi Germany and landed up in America, and it did nothing to raise Bernd's spirits.

Bernd gave his name, rank and number and nothing else, but it was irrelevant; they already knew it all, where he'd come from, what his unit's position had been on 24 March, the lot. After that they led him away, a sergeant and two men with rifles, and they were talking to one another all the time, joking almost as though he wasn't there at all. Bernd spoke only the little English he'd learnt from Mrs Payman at the Humanschule all those years ago, and he couldn't understand the American accent at all, and anyway he had better things to worry about than stupid *Ami* jokes, but still it irritated him, the way they ignored him. They took him to the back of the farm and out into a field to a large oak tree. He had his hands above his head and the sergeant started shouting at him, jeering, poking the rifle in his back every time his hands came down, because he couldn't keep his hands up all the time, they were shaking so much. They told him to face the oak tree and then they started playing with the safety catches of their pistols. That's it, thought Bernd; this is the end.

Then one of the GIs turned him round and shouted at him, waving his arm, apparently telling him to scarper. Bernd got the message all right, but he wouldn't go, reckoning they wanted him to run so they could shoot him in the back, as though he'd been trying to escape. But eventually, after more shouting and shoving, he went; and they just let him go. He never did understand why, except that it was war and things like that happened in war.

First he walked slowly, deliberately not turning round because he didn't want to give the *Amis* the satisfaction of knowing he was scared to death. Then, when nothing happened and he was far enough away to give himself a chance, he broke into a trot. Finally he ran, the fastest sprint of his life. The landscape was full of hedgerows, and he leapt over one after another like a hurdler, and if not over them then through them, racing on until he leapt over another one and landed straight in the middle of a British signals unit, who either saw him coming or got the shock of their lives. They took him to their senior officer, who interrogated him in a mixture of English and pidgin German, and again it was just a formality because they already knew whatever they needed to know. Then he was told to sit under a tree and shut up. After a bit one of the soldiers came over to him bearing a tin mug. 'Want a cup of tea, Fritz?' he asked. Bernd couldn't believe it.

He remained a prisoner of the signals unit for no more than three days, but it was long enough for doubt to creep in. He was seeing this enemy at close quarters for the first time and it was unsettling. There were about 25 of them and the thing that unsettled him most was how different they were. Everything about them seemed different to Bernd: the way they walked, the way they addressed their officers, the way they talked to one another – all of it was strange to him. In the midst of war there was a cheerfulness about them, a kind of banter going on, quite different to the way the *Kameraden* talked to one another. Not that he could understand what they were saying, but he got the drift, and he could see who was the joker among them, who the quiet one, and who the popular one taking his place naturally at the centre of any group. They were all young, even the officers, and they didn't seem to mind him, calling him Fritz, offering him mugs of tea and occasionally even a cigarette. He made a point of accepting politely but never smiling, never conceding defeat. Of course the Tommies were just hanging about with nothing much to do, knowing the war would soon be over and that they were the certain victors, but still it surprised him, that cheerfulness of theirs, that way of going about with one another as though they were out for a bit of a lark, nothing too serious about it.

After those three days Bernd was transferred to Weeze on the Rhine, to a POW camp which held about 5,000 men. It was very makeshift, just a field really, and at night they slept out in the open with no blankets against the cold, but still, they were alive and safe, and all but the most fanatical were secretly relieved, including Bernd. Most didn't talk much – perhaps they were too exhausted, too lost in their own thoughts, too demoralised by defeat – only the real Nazis went about damning the enemy, praising Hitler and swearing revenge. Bernd, as a tough and hardened *Fallschirmjäger* and a former Hitler Youth, was somewhere between the two camps and thought it best to keep his head down.

One evening he was sitting by one of the fires which the British military authorities had allowed the POWs to make at night against the cold, staring into the flames, deep down in the dumps, when one of the men stood up and began to sing. Apparently he'd been a member of the Nuremberg opera company before the war, and now he sang '*Heimat Deine Sterne*', a sentimental song popular in the 1930s full of longing for home. Many of the men, hearing the voice rise up like that in the night air, began to cry with homesickness and despair, Bernd among them. Long after the singer had finished, he stayed by the fire, talking to no one, hearing his mother humming that same song as she prepared the evening meal at Wischusenstrasse. He could smell the soup and he could see little Helga, head bent, doing one of her drawings at the kitchen table. The following day they were transferred to Ostend, where they were held in an old brick factory till they were shipped off to England.

*

In Berlin meanwhile Hitler and Goebbels took their last revenge on members of the opposition who had fought the Nazis for so many years and now had victory finally in sight, albeit too late to save Germany or themselves. Over 4,000 had been executed immediately after 20 July 1944, including one of the leaders of the plot, General Ludwig Beck, chief of the General Staff. But some lingered on in prisons and concentration camps, and they were quickly executed in the spring of 1945, with the Allies at the gate, before it was too late. Among them were lawyers, politicians, generals, priests, trade union leaders, Social Democrats, local government officials and many unknown except to their families and friends who had had the courage to risk their lives for their country in a way completely foreign to the Nazis and their glorification of death. Flossenberg concentration camp and Ploetzensee prison were the two main places of execution.

Dietrich Bonhoeffer, the theologian and pastor who had met Bishop Bell in Sweden, arrested for treason in 1943, was executed on 9 April; his brother Klaus, a lawyer, two weeks later. Admiral Canaris, chief of the *Abwehr*, was also executed on 9 April, along with Major General Hans Oster, all at Flossenberg. Arthur Nebe, chief of the National Police, had already been executed on 2 March, as had Dr Johannes Popitz, Prussian minister of finance, and Professor Alfred Delp. The diplomat Count Albrecht von Bernstorff was executed on 22 April, in a last flurry of activity, with the leading Social Democrat Ludwig Schwab and Major Busso Thoma a day later. Goerdeler, long-time leader of the opposition, was on the run after 20 July 1944. Heinrich Himmler offered a reward of one million marks to anyone who turned him in. He was captured after three weeks and sentenced to death by the infamous People's Court, but not before weeks of torture. He was finally executed on 2 February 1945. His brother, Fritz, was executed later the same month.

By April 1945 Hitler had moved into the *Führerbunker*, a massive concrete complex of over thirty rooms and long dimly lit corridors deep below the Chancellery buildings in Berlin. On 22 April, with the Russians already on the outskirts of the city, he held his last military conference, which consisted of a three-hour rant, denouncing the Germans for their 'treason, corruption, lies and failures'. Joseph Goebbels, true to the last, moved into the bunker with his wife and six small children, where they remained to the end. Martin Bormann also stayed, with two of Hitler's most devoted secretaries, a handful of military aides, a small group of Hitler's personal SS bodyguard and Eva Braun. The rest fled the bunker, making their way out of burning Berlin as best they could. From the relative safety of Obersalzburg Hermann Göring wrote Hitler a telegram: '*Mein Führer!* In view of your decision to remain in the fortress of Berlin, do you agree that I take over at once the total leadership of the Reich.' Hitler fell into one of his rages and ordered Göring's immediate arrest for high treason.

By 27 April the Russians were so close that the Chancellery was hit many times. Hitler, head in the clouds, sent Keitel furious telegrams ordering the relief of Berlin. The next day the BBC broadcast that Heinrich Himmler had offered to surrender the German armies in the west and enter into peace negotiations, an offer which had not been accepted. Hitler, 'raging like a madman', ordered Himmler's arrest, but even he knew this was a vain gesture so, by way of consolation, he ordered Himmler's representative in the bunker, SS Lieutenant General Fegelein, who had tried to escape and who was also Eva Braun's brother-in-law, to be shot. The following evening, having sorted through his papers and had them burned, he dictated his last will and political testament. In the testament he blamed the Jews for everything, much as he had done in *Mein Kampf* in 1924, at the very beginning of the Nazis'

Götterdämmerung, before six million were exterminated. He had warned all along, he ranted, that millions of Aryan children would die of hunger and millions of grown men would suffer death, and hundreds of thousands of women and children would be burned and bombed to death, if the real criminals, the Jews, weren't stopped. In the second part of his political testament he dealt with the succession, starting with those to be expelled from the party, first Göring and Himmler, and then naming Admiral Doenitz as his successor. It was pure fantasy and made no sense, just as many of his speeches had made no real sense, but now that the declaiming voice and melodramatic hand gestures practised for hours before mirrors were gone, there was nothing left but the mad rant. 'Above all,' he ended, 'I enjoin the government and the people to uphold the racial laws to the limit and to resist mercilessly the poisoner of all nations, international Jewry.'

That night, just before midnight, he married Eva Braun, drinking a last glass of champagne in the doomed circle of their few remaining followers. The next day, with the Russians no more than a kilometre away, Hitler poisoned Blondi, his adored Alsatian bitch, then handed out cyanide capsules to the faithful few left in the bunker.

'Although during the years of struggle I believed that I could not undertake the responsibility of marriage,' Hitler wrote in his private will,

now, before the end of my life, I have decided to take as my wife that girl who, after many years of faithful friendship, entered, of her own free will, the practically besieged town in order to share her destiny with me. At her own desire she goes as my wife with me into death. It will compensate us for what we both lost through my work in the service of my *Volk*.

What I possess belongs – in so far as it has any value – to the Party. Should this no longer exist, to the State; should the State also be destroyed, no further decision of mine is necessary.

My paintings, in the collections which I have bought in the course of the years, have never been collected for private purposes, but only for the extension of a gallery in my home in Linz on Donau.

It is my most sincere wish that this bequest may be duly executed.

I nominate as my Executor my most faithful Party comrade, Martin Bormann.

He is given full legal authority to make all decisions.

He is permitted to take out everything that has a sentimental value or is necessary for the maintenance of a modest simple life, for my brothers and sisters, also above all for the mother of my wife and my faithful co-workers who are well known to him, principally my old Secretaries Frau Winter, etc., who have for many years aided me by their work.

I myself and my wife – in order to escape the disgrace of deposition or capitulation – choose death. It is our wish to be burnt immediately on the spot where I have carried out the greatest part of my daily work in the course of twelve years' service to my people.

Given in Berlin, 29 April 1945, 4.00 a.m. (signed) A. Hitler

Witnesses: Dr Joseph Goebbels, Martin Bormann, Colonel Nicholaus von Below.

The next day, at 2.00 p.m., Hitler ate his last, vegetarian meal. Then he bade a final farewell to his staff before returning to his private apartments with Eva Braun while Goebbels and Bormann waited outside. A few minutes later they heard a shot. At 3.30 they went inside and found Hitler sprawled across the sofa, dead, with Eva Braun beside him, poisoned. They carried the bodies up to the Chancellery gardens, where Hitler's chauffeur had left 200 litres of petrol, and burnt them, as ordered. The next day Goebbels and his wife poisoned all six of their children before going up to the Chancellery gardens, where they were shot in the back of the head by a devoted SS officer. Bormann escaped and disappeared.

Rumours of Hitler's death spread fast. Bernd was still captive in the disused brick factory at Ostend when he first heard. Sleep in the factory was almost impossible – there were no beds, just the old brick ovens and the floor, everything covered in a thick layer of red dust, which got up your nose, in your mouth and into your lungs – and he was lying on one of the ovens, counting the night hours, his mind blank, when he heard, 'Hitler's dead, the Führer's dead.' The whisper raced up and down the corridors from floor to floor, and there was uproar in an instant. '*Scheisse!* Lies! All lies!' Now everyone was awake, alarmed, scared. It couldn't be true, it wasn't possible; life without Hitler was unimaginable; they knew nothing else. Most of them had grown up in the Hitler Youth then gone straight into the long hard years in Russia and France, all for the *Vaterland,* all for the Führer. He couldn't be dead. 'A guard heard it on the BBC,' whispered the voices in the dark, and then another voice was shouting, 'Propaganda! Enemy propaganda! All lies!' But Bernd wasn't the only one who thought it might be true, and, just daring to contemplate the possibility, he felt the fight drain out of him, but also relief.

11

Prisoner of War

The sight of the famous white cliffs of Dover didn't impress Bernd much. They weren't very white and it was raining. He leant over the rails of the prisoner-of-war ship taking him across the Channel into captivity and looked down into the waves and the wash, thinking that this narrow stretch of water had been the only thing, as far as he knew, to stop the German forces invading England back in 1941, the year of unstoppable victory and conquest for the Reich. The smell of the sea made him think of Bremen and boyhood days when he had bicycled down to the docks to bring his father his midday meal. It made him smile just thinking of it.

From Dover the POWs were transferred first by train, then lorry, to Kempton Park racecourse, which had hurriedly been made into a reception centre. There followed hours of queuing in long, sullen lines, hundreds of bedraggled and demoralised POWs wearing odd bits of uniform which they'd somehow managed to salvage on their travels, some with kitbags, some carrying cardboard boxes done up with string and a few even carrying small brown leather suitcases, though God alone knows how they'd kept hold of those through the turmoil of the last few weeks, thought Bernd, shuffling along with all the rest. Everyone was mixed in with everyone else, officers and other ranks, SS men among them, and no one any the wiser, or if they were, no one was saying.

Bernd had never been to a horse race so he didn't know what Kempton Park would normally look like, except from scenes of English high-society life which Nazi propaganda films sometimes featured: men in top hats and tails leaning on canes looking arrogant, and women in long gowns and large hats, sipping champagne while starving urchins gazed hungrily through the railings. Now the middle of the racecourse was full of tents, rows and rows of them, housing what he judged to be about 5,000 German POWs. Bernd joined the queue outside the stands waiting to be let in via the turntables one by one, moving slowly along to be processed by British army personnel seated at long wooden tables, taking down their details. It was all very formal and correct: name, rank and number. Bernd had hidden his papers and dog tag in a sack of grain in a barn during the three days he was a captive of the signals unit, and gave no information other than his name, rank and number, and the fact that he was a *Fallschirmjäger*, and proud of it.

Once inside, the men were ordered into makeshift showers, quick march, all naked, generals and other ranks alike, and afterwards, still naked, they were given a thorough medical check-up and doused with DDT powder and gentian violet against lice and any other nasty parasites they might have brought with them. Then they were issued with their POW uniforms, old British army ones dyed brown with yellow diamond patches sewn on the back of the jacket and each trouser leg. They stayed at Kempton Park for five days while the authorities worked out what to do with so many men. Eventually there were 1,500 POW camps all over Britain, but in those early days only half of these were up and running.

Bernd's feelings during those five days in April 1945 penned in at Kempton Park were a confusion of emotions. Above all, he was relieved to be alive and safe, no longer engaged in the horrors of life at the front and the daily battle for survival, kill or be killed; but he couldn't accept defeat, couldn't admit that the Reich was over and that Germany lay in ruins. As to war guilt, the Allies had been as much to blame as the Germans, insisting on the harsh terms of the Versailles Treaty and doing business with the Jews. The Führer had saved Germany from humiliation, restored her national pride and solved the scourge of unemployment, allowing everyone the chance of a better life in freedom and equality, unlike in class-ridden Britain. Bernd was just 22 but he'd already lived a hundred lives, and now he was filled with resentment and disillusion, like an old man. From the age of seventeen he'd known nothing but war – the exhilaration, the terror, the brutality and the adrenalin. Sitting around at Kempton Park for hours on end with nothing to do but think and despair, he found he couldn't adjust to the sheer boredom of peace.

Kempton Park was only a transit camp, with minimal interrogation, just enough to decide to which camp each POW would be sent. Bernd went to Marbury Hall, Camp 180, in Cheshire, where many of the real Nazis were sent. They went by train to a place called Northwich, and as Bernd looked out of the grimy train window at the rows and rows of tiny terraced houses all backing on to the railway line, with their grey washing hanging out in blackened, cramped backyards and hardly a tree in sight, he laughed at the sight with the *Kameraden* sharing his carriage. 'How did these people ever win the war!' they exclaimed to one another, momentarily cheered by the joke. When they got to Northwich they were transferred by lorry from the railway station to Marbury Hall, giving them their first sight of British civilians, ordinary people walking along the streets, out shopping or chatting on their doorsteps. Some of them shouted abuse at the passing POWs, but others gave them a wave or a cheerful V-sign. That unsettled Bernd, to see how little animosity there was, knowing that most of them must have had sons in the war, young men just like himself.

It turned out that there were two camps at Marbury Hall, East and West: East for the anti-Nazis, West for the Nazis. After registration the POWs were interrogated, then assigned to one or the other. Bernd, as a hardened paratrooper, was automatically assigned to West Camp. The classification dated back to the weeks following D-Day, when thousands of German POWs arrived in Britain and the screeners identified three categories who were almost always fanatical Nazis: SS officers, U-boat engineers and paratrooper NCOs, which was Bernd. Later the classifications were refined into a system of 'A' or white for anti-Nazis, 'B' or grey for those in the middle, and 'C' or black for convinced Nazis, with roughly 80 per cent falling somewhere in the greys, while 10 per cent were white and the other 10 per cent, mostly ex-Hitler Youths, were black. Bernd was black.

Once they were settled in West Camp, the camp commandant, a smartly uniformed army officer, addressed them from a platform in one of the Nissen huts. He used an interpreter who was also in British army uniform, but anyone could hear from his accent that he was a Berliner and a Jew. The CO began by talking about democracy and the fact that few of them would really know what it meant, and then he went on to say he was sorry for them, having only ever experienced a dictatorship, and not ever having had the benefits of a democratic system. They would have to learn about it from scratch, he said, and it would feel alien to them at first, and take time, but they should be patient and not expect too much too quickly. It wasn't what Bernd was expecting, and it came as a bit of a shock. The British officer went on to explain the idea of the two camps, East and West, and then he said something which puzzled Bernd: he said the camps would have German *Lagerführers*, camp leaders, and that would be 'punishment enough'. At first Bernd didn't get it, then he realised the CO meant anti-Nazis – communists, socialists, old trade unionists and the like – would be given positions of responsibility in West Camp. Apparently they were meant to be scared of them. That made Bernd smile; scared of some bloody communist, he didn't think so. Still, the CO seemed a decent sort of man, not excessively militaristic like some German officers, and when some of the *Kameraden* made fun of him and his quaint ideas about democracy once they were back in their own Nissen hut, Bernd didn't join in, just held his peace, keeping his head down and out of trouble.

There is archive film of some of the Nazi-dominated POW camps in 1945 and it is shocking to watch. The Nazi contingent saunters about the barbed-wire perimeter fence, greeting *Kameraden* with the Nazi salute, their whole demeanour saying that nothing had changed or would change, almost as though Hitler were still alive and the Reich still the victor. What it doesn't show is what happened to those *Kameraden* who didn't give the Nazi salute in return or transgressed the Nazi code of honour and loyalty in some other way, speaking ill of Hitler or expressing some small doubt about the methods of the Nazi regime.

These were put on trial in kangaroo courts held in secret in the middle of the night and were often found hanging in the toilets the following morning. If they were lucky they got away with a severe beating so that next time they were greeted by an SS officer they returned the Nazi salute with zeal, just like in the Reich during the twelve years of Nazi rule, when people were called into the local Gestapo office if they were reported for giving a half-hearted Nazi salute. Naturally when the British camp administrators heard of such cases and called men in for questioning, it got them nowhere. No one had seen or heard anything, and the British officers, unused to the methods of a dictatorship, didn't know what to do.

There were about a thousand POWs in West Camp, and the same again in East Camp. East, housing the anti-Nazis, was a bit more relaxed, but West was bad, the atmosphere heavy with resentment, depression and fear. Marbury Hall was only a holding camp for further interrogation and screening, classifying the POWs once more before transferring them to a permanent camp, so there was nothing for the men to do but sit around in their Nissen huts and wait. Each hut held 50 men, with their camp beds in two rows at the far end and five tables and benches plus a pot-bellied stove at the near end, and that was it. When it was time for a meal, two of the men went to the canteen and carried the food back in tin canisters along with a large pot of tea. When the weather was good Bernd hung about outside the hut; when the weather was bad he spent hours lying on his bunk, half asleep, thinking of this and that, wondering if his mother knew he was a POW in England, wondering if Karl Heinz, who must have been called up in the last year of the war, had survived, wondering about Helga, his school friends and neighbours like the Mrozinzskys and the Wittenburgs, whom he now realised must have been secret anti-Nazis all along. He thought about his father too: was he still working at Kali Chemicals; was he even alive after all that bombing of the docks? He kept his thoughts away from his own war as much as possible. Mostly he thought about sport: the football matches he'd gone to with his friends at Werder Bremen, the goals he'd scored in his own matches, his triumphs in the handball team, the athletics medals he'd won in Berlin in 1938 – great moments lived and relived – just to keep himself sane.

Two weeks in he'd had enough. He and a couple of *Kameraden* went to the *Lagerführer* and asked him to request a football from the English on their behalf. They got it the next day and quickly organised two teams. Sometimes they played football, sometimes it was handball, and it felt good, throwing a ball around again, like taking a step back in time to another life, long, long ago. Then someone told them that East Camp had a proper field to play on, with goalposts. That was like a red rag to a bull. Bernd and ten of the best players got together and, again through the *Lagerführer*, requested a football match against them, and again it was granted. About 300 men were allowed to go the 800 metres from West Camp to East to watch the game, marched there under English guard. They soon found out why: once they were through the East Camp gates their path was lined with POWs shouting catcalls and abuse: 'You Nazis! You should be hanged! You pigs! You murderers!' Without the guards, war would have broken out between the two camps. Bernd was shocked. Unbelievable, he thought. These are Germans like us! He tried to take a swing at one of them, but two guards leapt between them. Still, West beat the East traitors, and with ease. It was a rough game with plenty of fouls and abuse on both sides, but as he leapt in the air to head the ball or passed it before the other team had time to think, Bernd felt alive again, himself again, for the first time in months.

The next week it was announced that the POWs were to be shown a film in one of the Nissen huts. They went in batches of 100 men, filing in under the gaze of their guards, many of whom were Poles in British army uniform. Imagine it, Poles, designated a slave race by the Nazis, now lording it over the Master Race! It wasn't pleasant, and the men sat themselves down on benches in front of the temporary screen scowling and swearing under their breath. Then the camp commandant stood up beside the screen and explained what they were about to see: the first film to come out of a concentration camp, Belsen. The black curtains were drawn and the lights turned off. At first the men hardly knew what they were watching. There were great piles of naked corpses, no more than skeletons but with hair, their legs and arms indecently splayed as bulldozers driven by British soldiers dumped them into massive pits. As the POWs gradually took in what this was, a hum of indignation and anger went round the hut, expressions of outrage and disgust that they were being forced to watch this horror. Perhaps in East Camp the reaction was different, but in West it was mostly outrage. 'Silence!' The CO and the Poles ordered complete silence for the rest of the film, after which the men filed out, back into the bright spring sunshine.

Bernd filed out with the rest of them, keeping himself to himself again. Many of the men were protesting that the film was a fake, a cheap piece of propaganda. Bernd was keen to believe them, but the scene in the Ukraine kept coming back to him, when he and Peter Kularz had crawled through the forest in the night to investigate the shooting, and had seen what they had seen. Other scenes returned too, at Zhitomir and Berdichev and Kiev, where he had seen officers of the *Sicherheitsdienst* hauling old men out of queues in the market square and cutting off their hair and beards, publicly humiliating them. Now Bernd had to admit what he had always secretly known: that they were Jews, those old men, and so were the women and children he and Peter had seen standing trembling at the edge of the pits waiting to be shot, just as the piles of naked corpses at Belsen were Jews. The CO and two or three army officers and interpreters were standing outside the Nissen hut as the men filed out, quietly taking notes. It was easy enough to pick out the ardent Nazis, protesting their outrage and objecting that the film was a fake, but perhaps they also noticed the ones who filed past in silence, eyes to the ground, like Bernd.

A few days later Bernd and a *Kamerad* were wandering around West Camp, passing the time, when they stopped to watch a scene unfold which had them bent double with laughter. The day before a notice had gone up on the board in the camp office requesting volunteers who knew how to drive. Apparently, with so many of their own soldiers still abroad in Germany or the Pacific, the British needed drivers for their camp COs and their interpreters and screeners. Bernd didn't bother to put his name down. Call it cussedness, his usual bad temper, his unwillingness to collaborate with the enemy, call it what you will, he just couldn't be bothered. Now here was one of the volunteers in the cab of a lorry which he'd just stalled trying to impress the Scottish sergeant, and the sergeant was shouting and swearing at him that he was a useless driver, a bloody Nazi, when anyone could see that this *Kamerad* hadn't a clue how to drive a cumbersome lorry like the Bedford 1500. The Scottish sergeant was well known to everyone at West Camp for his foul language and temper, and he was really letting the fellow have it, with Bernd and his *Kamerad* standing on the sidelines laughing so much they didn't notice the sergent jump out of the cab and march up to them, shouting, 'You! Clever Dick! Get over there and drive, you bloody Jerry!'

He grabbed Bernd by the collar and gave him a shove towards the lorry, then went and hauled the other *Kamerad* out of the cab shouting at him to 'bloody push off'. Bernd just shrugged his shoulders, grinned and sauntered over to the lorry, all in his own good time. The Scot was a stocky little bloke, red-haired and red-faced, and Bernd, tall, blond and blue-eyed, felt a flash of the old superiority as he jumped up into the cab and turned on the ignition, knowing he could drive that lorry better than anyone, the little Scottish sergeant included. He drove 300 yards and that was that; he got the job. Two days later a call went out for POW Trautmann to present himself at the camp office with his kitbag. That same afternoon he was transferred to POW Camp 50 at Ashton-in-Makerfield, to be the driver for the camp commandant, Sir Arthur Glendenning, and his team of screeners and interpreters. Someone had obviously noticed that POW Trautmann wasn't only a trained car mechanic; he was a Nazi who was beginning to have doubts.

Camp 50 was full of POWs when Bernd arrived but they were all Italians, 1,500 of them, with Bernd the only German. As a driver, he didn't sleep in the POW barracks but in the British quarters near the entrance to the camp. The change in his life was extraordinary: from one moment to the next he'd crossed the lines and joined the enemy. He still ate with the POWs in the Nissen hut which was the camp canteen, Italian food like macaroni cooked by their own men, but his free time was spent away from them, in a kind of no-man's land. For his driving work he answered to Mr Maynard, the civilian manager who organised the POW labour force. Every day lorries left the camp, delivering workers to local farms and bringing them back again in the evenings; for the rest of the day Bernd did vehicle maintenance, drove the CO, or took the screeners to the various satellite camps to do their classification work. He also drove the interpreters round to check whether the farmers were happy with their workforce, and whether the POWs were happy with their farmers. This last came as a surprise to Bernd; he hadn't expected the POWs' wishes to be taken into account. Perhaps it was because the Italians were soon to be repatriated, he thought; but later, when the camp was full of Germans, it was just the same.

Ashton-in-Makerfield had been a quiet sort of place before the war, but now it was the scene of a lively nightlife, especially on Saturdays. The Italians were basically free to come and go as they pleased, so down to the town they'd go, looking for girls and a bit of fun. But there were also still a lot of GIs based up the road at Burtonwood, the biggest American supply depot in Europe, and they were after the same girls, with the result that most Saturday nights there'd be a fight, sometimes just for the hell of it. Each time a fight broke out, a bugle would go off in the POW camp and a hundred Italians would descend on the town to join in, easily outnumbering the GIs. These Italians, they all stick together, thought Bernd, remembering them from Berdichev when he was bartering for cigarettes. Clever too, he decided once he'd been driving the interpreters from farm to farm for a few days. Apparently the Italians often refused to work, or only very slowly, larking about instead. One farmer who had pigs and chickens complained that his Italian POWs went into the chicken run and ran about imitating the hens, clucking and squawking and flapping their arms, causing havoc. The farmer reported them to Mr Maynard several times, but it made no difference. Naturally, as more and more farmers complained, the British government thought they might as well send them home. Clever, thought Bernd.

It hadn't yet crossed Bernd's mind that, to the British government, Italians and Germans were not comparable, the Nazis having caused the war, which they'd planned from the moment they came to power in 1933. In addition, they had exterminated six million Jews, as well as six million Poles, not even mentioning the Russians. No, the British were pleased enough to repatriate the Italians, but they had no intention of doing the same for the Germans. Clement Attlee, prime minister of the post-war Labour government elected in a landslide victory in July 1945, had no qualms about it: the Nazis had inflicted untold bomb damage on the towns and villages of Britain, with a million homes destroyed and factories, roads, railway lines, hospitals and schools all gone, so now the German POWs could stay and repair the damage. In this Attlee went against the terms of the Geneva Convention, which stated that prisoners of war should be repatriated once hostilities ceased. But Attlee pointed out that the convention was merely a guideline with no standing in international law. There was the usual outcry from a few MPs in the House of Commons and a certain amount of discussion in the newspapers, but Attlee held firm: countries ravaged by the Nazis were entitled to war reparations, and POW labour, he maintained, was just one aspect of reparation.

After five weeks the Italians left Ashton-in-Makerfield and the camp was cleaned up and freshly painted before 1,500 German POWs arrived in their stead. Once they were settled, Mr Maynard formed them into working parties and Bernd drove them to their various farms, just as he'd done with the Italians. If the farmer had had six Italians before, he was now allocated six Germans, but soon enough the farmers were contacting Mr Maynard telling him they didn't need six Germans, because two could do the work of six Italians. How stupid the Germans were, thought Bernd. As for the quartermaster, a big man called Captain Woolf who came from the Isle of Man, he said, 'With the Italians I had to watch everything except the soap – I always had plenty of soap! With the Germans I don't have to keep an eye on anything except the soap!' That's the way it was.

By early 1946 there were 400,000 German POWs in Britain, almost half of them transferred from America, where they'd been sent for the duration from D-Day onwards. There was hardly a town or village which didn't have a POW camp nearby, and the British civilians got used to seeing them marching out of the camp, two by two, in their brown uniforms with the yellow diamond patches, to work on building sites, clearing bomb damage or mending roads and railway tracks, or, more often, sitting in the back of a lorry, off to one of the local farms. There were specialist camps for certain categories of POW, but most were just plain work camps, housing those men categorised as grey, the majority of POWs who fell somewhere in between the fanatical Nazis on the one hand and those who had, even before the war, been actively anti-Nazi. There was a specialist camp at Wilton Park in Surrey for the strong anti-Nazis: teachers, lawyers, journalists, trade unionists, politicians, businessmen and ordinary workers, who were seen as possible leaders of the new post-war Germany once they'd completed their courses in history, social policy and democracy. And there were a few camps which held most of the fanatical Nazis, so that no grey camp had too many at any one time. Lastly there was the youth camp at Trumpington near Cambridge, specially set up for those under the age of 24 who had never known anything but life under a dictatorship, members of the Hitler Youth since the age of ten, just like Bernd.

Reports written about this camp for the War Office by screeners and trainers all agreed that these young men hardly had minds of their own, so brainwashed had they been, and they were often profoundly disturbed and depressed, feeling that the whole structure of their lives had disintegrated along with the collapse of the Reich and the death of Hitler, their Führer – something which many still didn't believe, because to them it was literally unimaginable and unbearable. Reports quoted them as saying it was 'the end of the world' and they were 'standing before the void'. All the ideals they'd lived by – patriotism, courage, fidelity, comradeship, honour, self-sacrifice, obedience – seemed gone. So too was their sense of racial superiority, their 'will to power', and their total identification with Hitler: '*Mein Führer*, you command and we will follow.'

Camp 50 was a work camp like most of the others, with the majority of its POWs coming in the grey category. The men weren't allowed out of the camp other than for work and were forbidden to fraternise with the locals, but they were left free to organise the daily life of the camp themselves, with only a minimum of overall control exercised by the British, which meant the CO with a small staff of army officers and one or two civilians like Mr Maynard. The British supplied food, clothing, heating, transport, library, study materials, medical equipment and so on, but the POWs ran everything within the camp themselves, from the kitchens, to the laundry, to the camp shop, to the dental and medical services and the recreational facilities, as well as organising the allocation of duties, the distribution of supplies and the issuing of passes and pay, all from the camp office, which formed part of the central complex, along with the canteen, the chapel and the recreation area. The food was German and good, with each POW getting 2,800 calories a day, more than the local population, until rations were reduced somewhat in 1946 because of the world food shortage. And by 1947 every POW was being paid for his work, fifteen shillings a week, a third in British money, a third in tokens which could be spent in the camp, and the rest on credit, to be paid when they were repatriated. For many POWs this treatment was in itself an illustration of the advantages of a democratic system.

The decision to re-educate German POWs had already been taken by the Allies at the Potsdam Conference in July 1945. The British and the Americans were clear about the need to cleanse the Germans of Nazism and teach them about democracy before they could be repatriated, but they also agreed, following the

Geneva Convention, that there should be no indoctrination or propaganda and that the lessons should be voluntary. Stalin agreed with the former aim, but had no intention of following the latter: all German POWs in Russia, those who survived, were heavily indoctrinated, destined to return to East Germany in order to spread the word of communism. In Britain a new department was formed, initially under the War Office, called the POWD, the Prisoner of War Division. It was run by Henry Faulk, who had been a teacher in a grammar school before the war and an officer in the Intelligence Corps during the war, where his potential was quickly spotted. In July 1945 he was seconded to the Prisoner of War Division and told to get on with it.

Luckily Faulk was a remarkable man, and he knew Germany from pre-war years. His firmly held view was that all Nazis were bad, but not all Germans were Nazis; and that even Nazis, if carefully re-educated, might see the error of their ways. In this he joined a hot debate: in America a report had been written in 1944 by Henry Morgenthau, secretary of the Treasury, which came to be known as the *Morgenthau Plan for a Defeated Nazi Germany*. This argued that the German character had pathological defects and that the existing state would therefore have to be totally eradicated and its political and economic structures dismantled before a new Germany could be rebuilt, based on a pastoral, agrarian and non-military society. Roosevelt was inclined to share Morgenthau's views, and in Britain there were plenty among the ruling elite who agreed, but in the event the Faulk approach prevailed, strongly supported by the Churches and those who before the war had urged the British government to support German opposition to the Nazis.

The POWD was divided into two sections: the Field Section for the screeners and trainers who went into the camps, and the

Supply Section, which provided the teaching materials, the weekly *Die Wochenpost* POW newspaper, films, radio programmes and the literature and pamphlets for the information rooms in the camps. Re-education would be by group discussion and lectures, voluntarily attended. But there were always a few fanatical Nazis in any camp who tried to sabotage the groups, not only by refusing to attend them, but by actively preventing others from attending, through threats and sometimes violence. Screening went on well into 1947, weeding the fanatics out, but it wasn't easy to move them to other camps without causing resentment and reprisals.

However, gradually Henry Faulk and his teams began gaining ground. Instrumental in this was his insight that re-education was not so much political as psychological. In Nazi Germany everyone had been drilled in allegiance to the group, and it was this group identity which had now disintegrated, leaving a frightening void. Those under 24, who had literally known nothing else, were especially affected and intransigent. In addition they had received a very poor education under the Nazis, who had doctored the school curriculum for political purposes, neglecting the traditional academic subjects for 'modern' subjects like the history and biology of the Aryan race, with school textbooks showing grotesque caricatures of Jews, and geography concentrating on the Reich's entitlement to *Lebensraum*. Sport, seen as the purest expression of the superiority of the Master Race, came first, and anything else a poor second. Then, aged seventeen or eighteen, these boys, like Bernd, were plunged into war. 'The mass of our youth has been badly retarded in maturity, capacity and knowledge,' reported one anti-Nazi German officer to a screener. 'On the other hand it is way beyond its years in experience of life.' Subjected to Nazi indoctrination and propaganda from the age of ten, they had, in effect, been brainwashed.

The POWD had one basic aim for its re-education programme: to promote a new group attitude. Apart from the voluntary group discussions and lectures, the POWs had free access to pamphlets, newspapers and radio programmes in the camp information rooms, so they could pursue the subject for themselves if they wished. *Die Wochenpost*, produced weekly by the POWD, played a significant role in this. It had eight pages, the first two covering news from Germany and the rest of the world, deliberately offering the news without comment, at least until March 1946 when a POWD report stated, 'Changing conditions have transformed the policy of the paper from an objective presentation of reports without comment to a direct projection of democratic thought and life. At first despised as propaganda and often destroyed in bulk by the Nazis, it has become an essential feature of the life of the German POW, whose interest is shown in the flow of contributions.' These appeared in the last two pages of *Die Wochenpost*, which were devoted to the POW: letters, sport, news from other camps, features, entertainments and, most importantly, 'Search Corner', because the post-war chaos in Germany meant that many POWs had no idea where their families were, nor even whether they were alive. 'A member of the defeated German army seeks next-of-kin', went the postcards POWs were allowed to send to Germany via the International Red Cross from September 1945.

The middle four pages of *Die Wochenpost* were given over to cultural matters – literature, music, politics – and held little interest for the average POW. This applied equally to *Der Ausblick*, a high-minded cultural magazine read almost exclusively by the officers, who were better educated, and moreover had plenty of time on their hands since they didn't have to work. But 'English For All' was a great success, because most POWs sooner or later decided it was a good idea to learn some English, if only to chat up the local girls once the fraternisation ban was lifted. Documentaries were another success, presenting information in an interesting and unbiased way. Each camp also produced its own magazine. Everything organised by the POWD was based on the same humanitarian principle: 'The object is neither reproach nor conversion but enlightenment, that will help the prisoners to form their own opinions.' In due course many camps set up camp parliaments as a democratic way of deciding disputes.

Henry Faulk was quite realistic about the limits of the POWD. Most of the Germans flatly denied ever having been National Socialists and tended to deny any recollection of specific Nazi events. No one had been a member of the party; no one had attended Nazi rallies and festivals; no one knew what the concentration camps were really for; and no one was present at *Kristallnacht*. Meanwhile, the POWD depended on recruiting good people as screeners and trainers, and it had to be people who spoke German, which usually meant Jewish refugees from Nazi Germany. It takes little imagination to see how explosive such a situation might become if not carefully managed. For the Jewish trainer or screener, now a sergeant or captain in the British army, formerly a teacher, doctor or tradesman in Germany who had lost his job, his home, perhaps even his family to the Nazis, to now be confronted with a room full of Germans who were moreover his own countrymen, was highly disturbing and relied for its success on careful preparation and training. For the German POW it was also difficult: it took a certain courage to attend a group discussion on the merits of democracy against taunts from the Nazis in the camp, only to find the group was being led by a Jew. But somehow they managed it. Nine reports were written on one or other aspect of German POW progress from 1945 to 1948, and they included noticeably few complaints from the Germans about bullying or acts of retaliation by their Jewish trainers and screeners. By September 1946 the first white POWs were being repatriated, at a rate of 15,000 a month, ready to serve the new, democratic Germany.

The goodwill and understanding of individual camp commandants were critical for the success of the POWD. At Camp 50 the CO was Sir Arthur Glendenning, a traditional army officer of the older generation with his upright military bearing, his swagger stick, his moustache, his highly polished shoes – always smart, always fair and very British. Glendenning thought the re-education classes were all very fine in their own way, keeping the men occupied and so on, but he wasn't enthusiastic. For a staunch conservative like Glendenning the POWD seemed a bit too soft, a bit too liberal. 'Posh' is what Bernd called Glendenning, having learnt the word from a local farmer, and it puzzled him that the British CO had a photograph of a German army officer complete with Iron Cross prominently displayed in his office. Why was that, Bernd wondered? Was he saying he had German friends from pre-war days? Was he saying that Germans too could be decent, upstanding men, just like himself? Bernd never found out. After a few months Glendenning retired and another commandant came to take his place, a large bluff man who had been a POW himself in Germany, and was extremely well liked and respected by all the *Kameraden*. He was the swashbuckling type and very friendly, regularly walking around the camp with one of his officers greeting the men in a relaxed manner, using a few words of German, asking them how they were, and had they had any news from home? Bernd noticed that he only inspected the outlying camps once. 'That's OK. I know the Germans!' he said, amazing Bernd with his easy-going trust. But the trust was well placed; there was little trouble in most of the camps, and only 0.5 per cent of German POWs ever tried to escape.

Bernd was kept busy driving the new CO and the screeners and interpreters around, and was pleased to be doing it. But the hardened paratrooper wasn't dead yet. There was one screener he had to drive around, a Jew, and Bernd couldn't stand him. This Jew was high-handed, deliberately lording it over him in many small ways, which Bernd found insulting and intolerable, but he never let the man have the satisfaction of knowing it, just took it in his stride, remaining aloof and quietly superior, driving him from this camp to that. The man was obviously full of resentment, and Bernd often heard him laying into the German POWs he was screening, bullying and taunting them. Bernd never stopped to think that this man might have had good reason to hate the Germans; he just couldn't stand him, and it had nothing to do with the man being a Jew, he said.

One day in March 1946, Bernd had to drive the man to one of the outlying POW camps. It was terrible weather, sleeting and raining with snow on the high ground, and bitterly cold in the unheated car. They left Ashton-in-Makerfield at eight in the morning, just the two of them, and not much was said on the way. It took the man all day and part of the evening to screen six or seven men, which Bernd found ridiculous – as was the whole screening process, in his opinion. How could a nineteen-year-old be classified as a Nazi or an anti-Nazi? These people had no idea of how the party worked. Sitting on a bench outside the information room where the interrogations took place, hanging around for hours on end in the cold, Bernd could hear the screener questioning the men in his usual supercilious, haughty manner. The man had been a university professor, and it was that superior manner which really got to Bernd, triggering feelings of inferiority about his own inadequate schooling – he who had been a hero at his school, the best athlete, the best footballer, the best handball player, and a leader all ways round.

At the end of the day the two men, the German and the Jew, made their way back to camp via Wigan, in the dark and the rain. The pubs closed at quarter to ten in those days, and the screener suddenly ordered Bernd to stop. It was ten minutes before closing time, but this man decided he wanted a drink and POW Trautmann was to wait for him outside in the Hillman Minx, in the freezing cold. After ten minutes he came out, opened the passenger door and thrust a glass of whisky at Bernd saying, 'Drink that, you German pig!'

Bernd leapt across the car and hit him, hard, slammed the door and drove off, leaving the man lying by the side of the road in the rain, in the middle of the night. It never crossed his mind that the screener, though insulting, was offering him a drink. He just lashed out. He hadn't fought three years in Russia for nothing.

Back at camp he went straight to the drivers' quarters and climbed into his bunk, frozen and still furious. Two hours later the lights went on and the sergeant major marched in, fully uniformed. They called him the 'King of Kirkby' because he was seven foot tall, with a huge handlebar moustache, and the CO of one of the POW hostels at Kirkby.

'POW Trautmann! Out of bed! Get dressed!'

Bernd was fast asleep, but he was up, out and dressed double quick.

There were two guards with the King of Kirkby, and they marched off, one guard ahead of POW Trautmann, the other behind, with the King alongside barking orders. Bernd spent the rest of that night in the detention cell. At 7.30 there was the King of Kirkby again, and POW Trautmann was marched over to the CO's office. The CO dismissed the King and the two guards and waited to hear what POW Trautmann had to say for himself. Bernd could speak a little English by then, but not enough to explain himself properly. The CO stopped him halfway; he'd already heard the screener's version of the story, and he'd more or less worked out the rest. He stood up and held out his hand.

'In your boots I'd have done the same,' he said.

According to the War Office, who had already been consulted on the matter, POW Trautmann had to be punished, fourteen days in detention. But the CO, being the swashbuckling kind, had other ideas. He needed his driver; he liked him; and he didn't mean to do without him for fourteen days. The screener had to be at Speke airport by ten that morning. As punishment POW Trautmann was to drive him there, with two guards in the car, and he was to conduct himself correctly, and no mistake. It was a clever idea because Bernd still hated the man, and for some reason he just couldn't let go of it. A year or two later he might have been able to work it out, but in March 1946, only a year after the collapse of the Reich and everything he had once believed in, it was too early: deep down he still thought of the Jews as moneylenders and profiteers. Bernd fitted neatly into that category of under-24s who remained intransigent, hardly affected by the re-education groups, when he attended them, which wasn't often.

The road to Speke was treacherous, covered in sleet and patches of ice, with snow piled high on both sides. Who knows whether Bernd was going slow on purpose, but the screener was getting nervous about the time and kept pushing him to go faster.

'I can't go any faster!'

'I'm ordering you to go faster!'

It was a dual carriageway, and now Bernd swerved abruptly from the slow into the fast lane. He knew what the result would be – it had happened plenty of times in the Russian winter – the sleet went under the bonnet and into the distributor, the engine spluttered and the car gave up the ghost. Bernd just managed to swerve back onto the side of the road, and that was that. He turned to the man and shrugged. There was no way anyone could prove anything, but they were stuck there, the screener fuming and Bernd openly grinning. 'You can kiss my ass!' he said, pleased with the colourful phrase he'd learnt from the Americans. The guards leapt out of the car and flagged down another vehicle to take the screener on to the airport. Bernd never found out whether he made it, but he ended up doing his fourteen days in the *Kibosch*.

12

Football Heaven

Bernd's next encounter with a German Jew was much happier. Hermann Bloch had been the owner of a factory in Berlin which was 'Aryanised' by the Nazis in 1936, after the Nuremberg Laws came into effect and action against the Jews was stepped up. Unlike the hundreds of thousands of Jews who watched helpless as their situation in the Reich deteriorated but couldn't bear the thought of leaving their homeland, Bloch saw how it was and decided to pack up and go. Now he was a sergeant in the British army seconded to the Ministry of Agriculture as an interpreter, reporting back on German POWs working on farms in the area around Ashton-in Makerfield. POW Trautmann was his driver.

The first time they met wasn't auspicious. Sergeant Bloch marched into the camp office in his British army uniform and discussed matters with Mr Maynard before addressing POW Trautmann in what sounded like perfect English. 'My name is Sergeant Bloch,' he announced, short and sharp, pronouncing his name 'Block' as in English. He ordered Trautmann to wait in the car, ready for a day of inspections. Bernd had never been good at taking orders, not as a boy at school, not as a soldier from some old-style army officer who'd just arrived at the front and hadn't a clue, and certainly not from some fellow in a British army uniform who was only a sergeant, which is what Bernd was by the end of the war. He turned on his heel and left the office without a word.

They had eight farms to visit that day, which meant being on the road for a good twelve hours. Bernd concentrated on the driving, not inclined to make polite conversation though his English wasn't bad by then, certainly enough to say 'Nice weather' or 'It looks like rain', the kind of thing he heard from farmers every day, but why bother? Bloch didn't seem to mind. He sat looking out of the window at the passing countryside, smoking a cigarette and humming contentedly. He was a big man with a wide girth and seemed to have an easy temperament. After a while Bernd's curiosity got the better of him.

'I thought you interpreters spoke German.'

'We do,' he said in English, adding, 'I'm as German as you are' in German in a strong Berlin accent, and laughing.

Bernd had to laugh as well, at the way Bloch had caught him out, like a typical Berliner. But after that a silence hung between them, because they both knew why Bloch was in England not Berlin. 'I left in 1936,' Bloch said after a few minutes, again in German. 'I used to have a brush and comb factory, but the Nazis took it off me, so I came over here.' There was no resentment in his voice, and he didn't include Bernd in 'the Nazis'. Bernd didn't know what to say, so he said nothing.

'How about you?'

'I was in Russia for three years. Then France, Arnhem, the Ardennes. Got captured in March, by the Americans, then the Tommies; ended up at Kempton Park.'

'All the hot spots.'

'That's it.'

'You were a *Fallschirmjäger*, weren't you?'

So Bloch knew all about him.

When they got to the first farm Bloch spoke his English to the farmer and his German to the POWs. Was the farmer happy with his workers? Of course he was; they worked hard and gave him no trouble. He had four of them, living out of camp in a hostel. Afterwards they walked out to the potato field to talk to the POWs. Were they happy; were they well fed? How were their sleeping conditions? Really, it beggared belief, thought Bernd, that POWs should be asked whether they were happy or not; they even went to inspect the sleeping quarters.

The usual routine at dinnertime was for Bloch to eat with the farmer and for Bernd to sit in the car outside with his bread and cheese, which the camp kitchen provided for the drivers, wrapped in greaseproof paper in a tin box. But after a few days Bloch said they should try what he called the water trick. Bernd had never heard of the water trick. Bloch explained: when the farmer invited Bloch in for his dinner, Trautmann should come to the kitchen door and ask the farmer's wife for a glass of water. Simple as that; it worked every time. The wife would look at her husband, he would nod, and she'd ask Bloch if it was all right to invite the German POW to sit down with them for something to eat. Bloch would hesitate for a moment, then agree.

Driving back in the evenings with the light fading they would often stop by the side of the road and smoke a cigarette together, talking of this and that.

'What was the worst time for you? Was it Russia?' They usually avoided the war, but not this time apparently.

Bernd couldn't tell him about the worst time, because it was that night in the Ukraine. So he told him about Kleve instead, when he was buried alive for three days under the bombed school, which was bad enough. But later that night, lying in his bunk, the old feeling came back to him, the one he always tried to forget, the same feeling he'd had after watching the concentration camp film: a bad, bad feeling, deep down. Mostly he managed to push it away, but lately it had been resurfacing: those people at the edge of the pits in the night. Eventually he fell asleep and by the morning it was gone again, buried in his subconscious till the next time something happened to resurrect it.

The following day when Bernd got back to camp the wireless was relaying a BBC programme into the camp canteen via the loudspeakers. The wireless was available for general use, but every day there was also a special POW programme, produced at Camp 7 at Ascot by a team of 30 POWs who'd worked in journalism or teaching before the war. They had all been anti-Nazis, secret or otherwise, and now, finally, they could speak out, in freedom with no fear of reprisals, and they were determined to put the record straight, which they did day after day to the chagrin of men like Bernd, who were still confused about who they were and what they believed in. He liked the programme for the camp news and especially for the greetings service to families in Germany, but he hated the talks. Today it was 'Who still wants to die a hero's death?' What a stupid question; obviously the answer was no one. This fellow's argument was that they'd been brainwashed by the Nazis to die a hero's death, which, Bernd had to admit, was true; but who said they still believed it? Quite a few, apparently. Well, not POW Trautmann. He bought a packet of Woodbines from the counter, paying with his camp tokens, then left the canteen, walking off towards the camp gates and the drivers' quarters beyond, out of earshot of the tannoy. Still, it annoyed him more than it should have.

'If it is treason to refuse to let patriotism be an excuse for crime, if it is treason to advocate understanding between peoples and to renounce all nationalist lust for power, if it is treason to recognise the rights of other human beings and nations, if it is treason to refuse the sacrifice of our lives, demanded without sense of justice by a government whose first duty is not the welfare of its citizens, then we will willingly be traitors.' That was the text of one of the previous talks in January 1946, reminding POWs of what was considered treason in Nazi Germany, should they have forgotten. The discussion groups, often led by one of the anti-Nazi POWs who had been transferred from the Wilton Camp after passing courses on the workings of democracy, were along similar lines, subjects like 'Is Russia a democracy?' or 'United States of Europe, yes or no?' which were meant to help the POWs come to terms with the past and prepare for a better future, but were too high-minded for the average POW like Bernd, who only attended the groups if they were discussing some aspect of daily life in the camp which was causing friction. Then he did appreciate the freedom to express his views openly, unlike in Nazi Germany. He still remembered how careful his parents had been when talking to friends and neighbours, because you never knew who was a party spy; he even remembered his father, who had after all joined the party so as not to lose his job at Kali Chemicals, warning him not to tell anyone what was said in the safety of home.

The Britain Bernd was coming to know in 1946 was a very different place from today. The towns and cities were grey with dirt and smog caused by all the factories and coal fires, and there were shortages and queues everywhere. One day there would be a queue outside the shoe shop and all down the High Street, because news had got round that they had in some children's shoes; another day it might be a queue for coats, or sheets, or saucepans. And housewives queued every day for food – a half-hour at the

butcher's, another at the baker's, another at the greengrocer's –
and everything was rationed: tea, sugar, jam, meat, cheese, sweets,
butter, lard and most items of clothing. You could usually get fish,
but it often stank. The black market flourished for those who could
afford it, as did petty crime of all kinds. For the middle classes
income tax was nine shillings in the pound, while millions of the
working classes still lived in two-up two-down back-to-backs, the
kind Bernd had seen on his journey north, with no inside toilet, no
running hot water and no bath other than a tin tub. The August
bank holiday was spent at Margate or Blackpool, and they went by
tram or bus, then queued for hours at one of the railways stations
to go by steam train, soon to be nationalised as British Railways.

Entertainment is what people craved, and there were cinemas
on every High Street, sometimes two. Theatres were booked out
night after night and the dance halls were crammed with people
doing the quickstep or the American jitterbug to the music of the
big bands. On BBC radio there was a new Light Programme
replacing the Forces Network, playing the kind of popular music
which some of the more educated middle classes called common.
Workers' Playtime was meant to cheer up factory workers,
encouraging them to increase output of the nation's much-
needed exports; *Woman's Hour* and *Housewives' Choice* were
there to lighten the burden of wives and mothers who up until
recently had been out working, replacing the men away at war,
and were now meant to stay at home and look after the family.

Four million servicemen had returned from the war, exhausted
and disorientated, and now they needed jobs. They also needed
homes. There were bomb sites and slums, but no new houses to
replace the old. Instead there was the prefab, a structure not much
bigger than a modern mobile home which was only meant to offer
a temporary solution but was still in use well into the 1960s. The

planners were busy planning garden suburbs and new towns; the *Beveridge Report* outlined a magnificent welfare system, including free universal health care; there was to be an end to unemployment; and the Butler Education Act was set to provide a good education for all according to ability, but so far, in 1946, the Labour government, full of fine ideals but struggling to keep up repayments on the $3.75 million loan from America, was finding it difficult to come up with the goods. Democratic socialism was the aim, embracing a mixed economy. Meanwhile, the Ministry of Food announced yet more ration cuts – in poultry, eggs and bacon.

Not surprisingly the British people, well over the euphoria of winning the war and ground down by the hardships of daily life, had little sympathy for the people of Germany, who, they were told, were having an even worse time than the British, literally starving to death, children included. When Mass Observation asked a selected group of people in March, 'How do you feel about giving up some of your food for Europe?' the answers were almost uniformly negative. 'No, I don't think we could do it at present. We're about down to rock bottom,' answered one man. 'I'd be against it myself. It's Germany's turn to go without,' answered another; and a third, answering more fully, replied, 'If it came to it, I suppose I'd do it as willingly as the next. But not to help Germany – only the countries that's been overrun. I wouldn't care what happened to the Germans; they've asked for it.' Women seemed a little more charitable, though not much. 'Yes. Provided we still get something for every meal,' said one. Another said, 'I suppose we'd do it if we had to. I hope it won't come to that.' A third was back to more familiar territory with, 'I think the Germans *ought* to go short, after all they've done.' A fourth agreed: 'I wouldn't go short on half a loaf to benefit Germany.' Oddly, such attitudes didn't much affect the relationships between individual German POWs and the locals they met in the course of their working day; not that they could actually talk to one another due to the ban on fraternisation, but they could smile and nod, or at least not look the other way.

The 27th of April 1946 was a great day for the British nation and for POW Trautmann as well. The FA Cup had started up again that year, and it was the Cup Final, Charlton Athletic v. Derby County, broadcast on the BBC from the Empire Stadium at Wembley straight into the camp canteen at Ashton-in-Makerfield. Bernd, racing back early from his driving duties, settled himself at a table along with other football *Kameraden*, lit up a Woodbine and took a swig from his bottle of beer. For the time being at least, life was good. At the Empire Stadium the 100,000-strong crowd, all in their cloth caps, sang 'Abide With Me'. The hymn rose up like a prayer to God, and it was enough to send shivers up and down your spine, so thrilling was that sound. Bernd thought he'd never heard anything like it, except perhaps '*Sieg Heil! Sieg Heil!*' at Nazi rallies, and yet it wasn't the same, not the same at all, though he couldn't put his finger on how. The King had arrived, said the wireless commentator, wearing a grey overcoat and a bowler hat; apparently that was significant, though for the life of him Bernd couldn't imagine why. Then the match started, and it was no different to any other match he'd ever listened to crouched over the wireless set at Wischusenstrasse 32, and he shouted and swore just the same as then, thumping the table and laughing out loud when Ted Turner scored twice in one minute, once for his own side, Derby County, and once for Charlton Athletic. Football was football, wherever you were. In the end Derby County won 4–1, and everyone was happy. Everyone except Charlton Athletic, that is.

'Post for Trautmann!' Bernd was in the canteen again, seated at a table over a cup of tea, real coffee not being available, reading *Ausblick*, which was nothing but rubbish in his opinion, when he heard the call. It stopped him dead. He hadn't had news from home for almost two years, ever since the chaos of France. He went to the camp office and collected the letter, holding it for a while before opening it, looking at his mother's neat hand. '*Mein lieber Berni*,' she wrote, and it took him straight back home to Bremen, that single phrase, straight into the kitchen with the smell of her cooking and the look of love on her face. He was close to tears as he read it, not because of the hardships she described, which were unbelievable, but because of her voice and that memory of her face. His father was unemployed now, she explained, and so was Karl Heinz, who had somehow made it home from Hungary after the war. Helga was still living back at home with her mother; the Mrozinzskys and Wittenburgs were all back in their flats again because Wischusenstrasse hadn't suffered much damage – a miracle, really, given that they were so close to the docks, which had been 80 per cent bombed. But there was no food and no work, and in winter there'd been no coal, and most people had nowhere to live and nothing to wear. But they were alive, and God be thanked, so was Berni. The International Red Cross had delivered his card to them that morning, after many weeks, apparently, telling them he was a POW in England, at Camp 50. She begged him to write a letter to tell her if he was being treated well, and give them all his news. When was he coming home? That was the main thing. When was he coming home? *Vati* sent his good wishes, so did Karl Heinz; Helga sent a big kiss, and she sent him her love, signing it '*Deine Mutti*'.

He sat alone for a long time after that, not speaking to anyone; so many thoughts, so many feelings. He was interrupted by a group coming into the canteen after one of the re-education classes. They were having a heated argument, evidently carried over from the discussion in the session. '*Wir sind nicht Kreigsgefangene!*' 'We're not prisoners of war!' shouted one POW, known for his Nazi sympathies. 'Of course we are!' shouted another. 'We started a war; we lost it, and now we're POWs, and if you don't change your views you'll be one for a long time yet.' They almost came to blows. 'This is a labour camp, not a POW camp!' shouted the first. 'As prisoners of war we should have been repatriated at the end of the war. This is nothing but a labour camp, no different to those we had in Germany.' 'Blockhead!' the other one shouted as his *Kameraden* pulled him away. 'No one in our labour camps in Germany started a war. They'd done nothing wrong, except try to fight you Nazis.' Bernd got up and left the canteen.

The British people couldn't begin to understand the bitter meaning of an argument like that, having enjoyed the benefits of a democratic system for so long they took it for granted. So when some of them agreed with the ex-Nazi that the Germans should be repatriated they misunderstood the real issues, merely feeling sorry for the underdog. It was the Churches who made the first official moves at reconciliation, pursuing the views they'd held all along, namely that not all Germans were Nazis, which they knew for a fact because throughout the 1930s many Church members were part of the German opposition who had made contact with the British Foreign Office and government begging for help to overthrow Hitler.

By the spring of 1946 German POWs were allowed to attend services on Sundays at local churches, but because of the ban on fraternisation they still weren't allowed to speak to anyone, just march in two by two in their POW uniforms and sit quietly in the front row, where everyone could see them, behaving themselves. Imagine their surprise when the wheezy organ struck up the introductory bars of one of the hymns, Glorious Things of Thee Are Spoken, and it turned out to be '*Deutschland, Deutschland Uber Alles*'. How they sang, how they laughed, and the dear, naive parishioners had no idea why. About 60 per cent of POWs were Protestant, 40 per cent Catholic, and many had returned to their old religion, abandoned during the Nazi years, because of the shock and depression they experienced after the defeat, or just because they wanted a Sunday outing and the chance to belt out '*Deutschland, Deutschland Uber Alles*'.

In April the Committee of Prisoners of War of the British Council of Churches issued a pamphlet to Church ministers to advise and reassure them about their new parishioners. 'At the best of times the POW is in a difficult psychological situation, but the POW who is on the side which has lost a calamitous war is beset with special difficulties,' the pamphlet explained, going on to remind the reader, 'A few have not had news from their families for months. A sense of isolation and uncertainty regarding the future makes the POW apt to see things out of proportion.' The advice was simple: 'A handshake in German is the same as in English.' Keen to see the best in their former enemies, the British Council of Churches misunderstood much of what Nazism had meant for their new parishioners, assuming that anyone who was a churchgoer couldn't also have been a convinced Nazi, especially ministers. 'Among the prisoners are over 150 ordained Protestant ministers, most of whom were serving as combatants,' the pamphlet was pleased to note. In the British army ministers were ministers and combatants were combatants, so this was new territory, but they felt the camps were fortunate indeed to have so many ministers. Great efforts were made to distribute them evenly, the Churches unaware that not all of them were anti-Nazis.

Bernd didn't go to church; he never had and he didn't intend to start now, disliking the hypocrisy of some of his *Kameraden* who professed religion just for the chance of a Sunday outing. Bernd's religion was sport, and his Sundays were taken up with handball and, increasingly, football. This came about through a lucky chance: one of the camp administrators was a Scottish major who was mad about football. The CO was still the swash-buckling one with his easy ways, and when the football-mad major asked whether he could get up POW football teams, the CO was happy to oblige. The camp lay within the grounds of a grand house called Garswood Park and the football pitch was on the far side of the park, right next to Haydock Racecourse. It was sheer joy for Bernd to go out on a bright Sunday afternoon across that parkland with its ancient oak trees and lake and gracious views, with Haydock grandstand in the background, to play a game of football just like the old times in Bremen, tearing up and down the pitch shouting to his *Kameraden* to pass the ball, feeling free, forgetting for a while that they were still living in captivity behind barbed wire.

After a while the Scottish major realised that his best team, the one with POW Trautmann playing centre half, was too good to play only the other camp teams. Would it be all right, sir, he asked the easy-going CO, if he contacted a few of the local teams for his first eleven to play against? Good for morale, good for community relations, that kind of thing. The CO gave it some thought, bearing in mind the ban on fraternisation, but it didn't take long for him to agree. Within two weeks the first local team arrived to play the POWs at Ashton-in-Makerfield, and then it was head to head, the Germans against the Brits, each side determined to win and beat the hell out of the enemy, albeit in a friendly manner. The local team came in a coach, the POWs arrived two by two, already attired in their football shorts and boots, accompanied by their guards, each team eyeing the other with a mixture of curiosity and fear. Bernd was surprised how keyed up he felt as he lined up opposite the visiting team waiting for the outcome of the toss. These were young men of his own age, miners most of them, men who'd fought in France and maybe crossed the Rhine into Germany, men he'd aimed at with his machine gun, killing some, wounding others.

The toss went in the POWs' favour and now winning was all that mattered. The hardened *Fallschirmjäger* who'd spent three years fighting the partisans in Russia wasn't about to be beaten by some local team of puny, bandy-legged, white-skinned Tommies. His national pride resurfaced with a vengeance during the first half and the referee had a job controlling POW Trautmann's aggression. But the British team fought back hard, targeting the centre half, who was by far their best player, and Bernd sustained a small injury. 'You'd better go off and get that seen to,' said the referee, pleased to be rid of him. Trautmann refused. Go off? Now? Against the enemy? Certainly not. He wasn't that badly hurt, he shouted, and anyway, what did it matter? A fight almost broke out, and then the German goalkeeper stepped in. Couldn't POW Trautmann take over in goal? Couldn't they swap places? He indicated the swap with hand gestures, pointing first to Trautmann and then to himself. Bernd shrugged and accepted the compromise, likewise the referee. And so began Bernd Trautmann's career as a goalkeeper.

The game was a walkover for the Germans, and Bernd strode off the pitch feeling that old national pride: We are the masters. Behold! Someone caught up with him and tapped him on the shoulder. It was the English goalkeeper. 'Well done, lad!' he said, clapping Bernd on the back. 'Well played!' Bernd was quite taken aback. All over the pitch the English team were congratulating their German opponents. 'Thank you,' said Bernd, embarrassed, and shook the man by the hand.

After that they played all the local teams, every Sunday, home games and some away too. It was 'magnificent', that's how Bernd put it, using a new word he'd just learnt from the English footballers. Magnificent. They played Haydock and Burscough, Newton-in-the Willows, various teams from Wigan, and even Skelmersdale, which was 100 miles away. The Scottish major contacted them all, and along they came in their coaches, bringing their supporters with them. The POWs had their own supporters too, quite apart from the other POWs – local supporters, the ones they still weren't allowed to talk to. Up from Ashton-in-Makerfield they came, curious to watch this team of Jerries, who weren't half bad, especially that chap in goal. There wasn't much to do in Ashton-in-Makerfield of a Sunday afternoon. Belle-Vue Speedway and the greyhounds were Manchester way, as were the two great football teams, Manchester City and Manchester United, but locally there wasn't much, so they were more than pleased to come and stand on the sidelines, cheering their former enemy. As news of the Jerry team spread, more and more came up to Garsfield Park to watch the game, and as there were no stands the spectators stood about on the grass at the edge of the pitch, eventually up to a thousand of them, all coming to watch the POWs, but especially the star of the team, that tall blond chap in goal called Trautmann. And many fathers were surprised to find their daughters taking a new interest in football; no fraternisation ban on earth could stop a girl smiling at her favourite player and cheering him on.

These unofficial contacts between German POWs and local populations were being replicated all over Britain. And whether it was that or the fact that the economic situation was gradually improving, by the autumn of 1946 the animosity of the British towards the German POWs was virtually gone, increasingly replaced by sympathy for the underdog. Only the Labour government and Attlee held out, and even there opinion was wavering with questions again being asked in the House. In the end it was the newspapers and the newsreels, Movietone and Pathe News, which grasped the nettle, sensing the mood of the public and having a nose for a good story which might run and run.

That autumn the British public, off to the cinema for their weekly treat, the latest American cowboy film or romance, were shown a newsreel with a bold title, accompanied by a dramatic music score: PATHE OPINION POLL: PRISONERS SEND THEM BACK. 'These are German prisoners of war. Controversy ranges around them. Pathe News brings it to the streets,' went the commentary over pictures of POWs in their uniforms marching two by two out of one of the camps, past the barbed-wire gates and the guards, off to work. The film cuts to an interviewer in a smart sports jacket and tie approaching the vicar of St James's, Piccadilly. 'What do you think, sir?' he asks, standing casually by the wall of the church, holding out a large black microphone. 'No one could have been more opposed to Fascism than I was myself,' replies the vicar, nicely framed by the arch of the church porch but sounding stilted, trying to remember his words, mindful of the seriousness of the issue which lies before him. 'But this is a great human question,' he concludes, turning to address the camera. 'These men want to return to their homes.'

'That is a considered opinion. We know there are other opinions, no less honestly held,' opines the Pathe News interviewer over pictures of the same POWs now in the camp office queuing up in a polite and docile manner for their week's pay, saluting smartly, followed by a scene of them seated quietly at desks in a re-education class listening attentively to the teacher. 'These Germans now looking apathetic and harmless were once confirmed Nazis. They carried German arms over Europe and Western Russia.' This to shots of the POWs, mostly blond and young, in the canteen playing cards, and then in the camp bakery taking loaves of bread out of the oven. 'They must take their share of responsibility for German crimes,' says the interviewer sternly, and then, 'You, the people of Britain, must decide the men's fate. From a poll of opinions we bring you men and women from the street.'

The film cuts to a Mrs Tucker and her friend standing on a street corner, wearing hats and coats and carrying handbags. 'What do you think, Mrs Tucker?' asks our interviewer. 'Well, they're human beings the same as us!' she replies in broad cockney, and then, like the vicar, she turns to camera for her finale: 'And they should be sent home to their country the same as our boys 'ere.'

The pressure of public opinion on the government became too strong, and gradually Attlee was forced to make concessions. It was democracy in action, as some of the German POWs, the ones who attended their re-education classes, could clearly see. By October 1946 the POWs were allowed to send the money they earned on the farms and the building sites back home to Germany, to help out their families. And on 18 December the ban on fraternisation was finally lifted, just in time for Christmas.

The very next day people all over Britain came up from the villages and towns to their local POW camps and invited the men into their homes for Christmas Day. Each family was allowed to invite two POWs, and there was hardly a POW in the land who didn't receive an invitation. Bernd was invited by the Benson family, who lived just down the road from Garswood Park, together with Egon Rameil, the dentist in the camp. He couldn't believe it. How could these people, so recently their sworn enemies, be so forgiving, so warm-hearted, so friendly? Years later, thinking back to that moment, tears still come to his eyes. No amount of re-education classes in democracy could have achieved what that simple statement of kindness by the people of Britain achieved that Christmas. Of course, not every family in Britain felt the same, especially those who had lost someone, nor did every POW accept an invitation, some still seeing it as consorting with the enemy, but the general mood of the British public and the German POWs had turned by Christmas 1946, outpacing the government, taking reconciliation into their own hands. The war's over, they seemed to be saying, and we want to forgive and forget.

The camp at Ashton-in-Makerfield became a hive of activity in that week before Christmas. Most POWs managed to lay their hands on some kind of material to make simple presents for their hosts, especially for families who had children. Felt slippers were a favourite, but wood was the easiest material to get hold of and many POWs, being farm boys before the war, knew how to carve and whittle and hammer something together. They made figurines and toys, picture frames and walking sticks; one POW made an entire dolls' house, another an aeroplane, carefully painting the Royal Air Force insignia on the wings; another even managed a rocking horse. Extra tools and materials were brought into the camp by those who worked out on the farms and by drivers like Bernd, who had access to all sorts of forbidden places and a positive talent for 'finding' things.

Two days before Christmas the Accrington Male Voice Choir came from the other side of Manchester up to the POW camp to give a concert of carols and folk songs. The Germans had put up a traditional Christmas tree in the canteen, hung with decorations made by themselves, stars and hearts and painted angels, and the tree was ablaze with candles. Attendance was voluntary but the canteen was crammed. The men from Accrington began with some old English favourites, and then they sang a German folk song, in German, before launching into the Christmas carols, some of which they sang in English with a last verse in German. It touched the POWs very much that these men, workers in the cotton factories for the most part and many who'd been in the war, had learnt enough German to reach out to their former enemies in this way. They had fine voices, these men, and Bernd, sitting in the third row among his football *Kameraden*, could feel a lump rising in his throat. Then the POWs' own choir stood up and sang some German carols, ending with '*Stille Nacht*', and Bernd wasn't the only one in that Nissen hut to wipe his eyes and look away. Peace on earth, they were saying, peace on earth, after which the men filed out row by row, shaking hands with the Accrington men at the door of the canteen, then standing out in the night, waving them off in their coach, back across Manchester and home.

On Christmas morning there were queues in the camp showers: everyone wanted to look as smart as possible for their British hosts in spite of their POW uniforms. Boots were polished, trousers pressed, hair smoothed down with water. Bernd had always been fussy about his appearance. He liked to look neat and clean, and had polished the family's shoes as a boy at home in Bremen. So now he spat and polished and spat again till his boots came up like new. In point of fact POW Trautmann, well over six foot tall, always looked good and always attracted the most attention from the local girls in the football crowd, but he wasn't sure enough of himself to be properly aware of this, so he polished his shoes one more time and returned the shirt he wore under his uniform to the camp laundry to be better ironed, and only then did he feel ready to face his hosts.

At twelve noon the POWs left, two by two, to make their way on foot to the homes of their hosts. Bernd couldn't account for it, but he felt nervous as well as curious as he and Egon walked out of the camp, through the wrought-iron gates of Garswood Park and down the road to the Bensons' home, which was one of a modest row of semi-detached houses, not much bigger than those he'd seen from the train on his journey north. It was years since either Bernd or Egon had been inside a normal family home, and the first time they'd ever been inside an English one. What would it be like? How should they behave? They walked up the short garden path and hardly had time to knock on the door before it was opened by Mr Benson stretching out a hand in welcome. Mrs Benson was waiting in the front parlour, smiling and dressed in her Sunday best, just as Bernd's mother would have been; beside her stood Phyllis, their only daughter, who was nineteen. Years later Phyllis remembered her first impression of the two Germans: no jackboots or clicking of heels like in the films, no arrogance, but a certain formality nevertheless as they bowed, saying, 'Good Day', and, 'A very happy Christmas to you,' with strong German accents. The Bensons spoke no German, Bernd and Egon spoke little English, but with hand gestures and miming and a lot of smiling, they managed.

Bernd and Egon had brought a bottle of camp-made elder-flower wine as their Christmas present, which Bernd had managed to exchange for two packets of cigarettes, and very welcome it was too, in those days of scarcity and rationing.

'Have a seat, Mr Trautmann. And you, Mr Rameil,' said Mr Benson, indicating two armchairs either side of a coal fire so small

it only warmed the immediate area, and adding, 'Am I pronouncing that right, Mr Rameil?'

Mr Rameil nodded and pronounced his name for them and
they all had a go getting it right. Mrs Benson sat down on the
settee with Phyllis shyly beside her, while Mr Benson wrestled
with the bottle of elderflower, which had the cork jammed in
tight. Bernd got up to help him out saying, 'May you allow?'
feeling rather proud that he remembered the word 'allow' from
all those years ago in Mrs Payman's English classes. His parents
had been surprised at the time that Berni was prepared to get up
early just to go to these classes, which were not part of the regular
curriculum and therefore held before school began. What for?
they had wondered. Berni hadn't known why himself, only that
he enjoyed them; but now look. *Schicksal*, fate, is what it was.
When he managed to uncork the bottle everyone clapped and
laughed.

It was strange for the two Germans to sit in a room so different
to anything they had ever known, and try to make conversation
in a foreign language. The whole atmosphere was different,
thought Bernd, sipping his elderflower, looking discreetly around.
Apart from the armchairs and the settee, there was a sideboard
displaying pieces of china and glass and some framed family
photographs, and in the corner of the room was an upright piano
with some sheet music open. Even the Christmas decorations
were different: no tree, just two candles and some holly and ivy on
the mantelpiece, a few balloons and some strange, brightly
coloured paper chains strung across the room from above the
mantelpiece to the curtain pelmet in the bow window. The
window looked out over a small, neat front garden with a clipped
privet hedge. Bernd liked that: the neatness and the cleanliness of
the place made him feel at home.

'Shall we go and eat our Christmas dinner, Mother?' asked Mr Benson.

They sat down to Christmas dinner in the back room, which was neat and clean like the rest of the house but smoky from the coal fire. Mr Benson indicated it with his hand, shrugging his shoulders. There was just room for all of them to sit at the table, what with the kitchen stove and the sink and one old chair by the fire and the budgerigar in its cage in the corner chirping away. The meal came as a shock: tripe in vinegar. *Gott im Himmel*, how was he going to eat that? wondered Bernd. But he noticed Egon making a good show of enjoying it, and, once he got used to it, he found it wasn't too bad. There was a thing called trifle and custard for pudding. 'No Christmas pudding, I'm afraid,' explained Mrs Benson. 'Rationing.' Neither Bernd nor Egon knew what Christmas pudding was, so they just smiled and nodded, and Mrs Benson smiled and nodded back.

After the meal they went back into the front parlour, more relaxed with one another now. Phyllis sat down at the piano and played 'Roll Out the Barrel', a cheerful old song which she insisted on teaching the Germans, laughing at them each time they got it wrong. Egon had rather a good voice, it turned out, and came in for some praise. Then they played Christmas games, starting with charades, which was open to endless misunderstandings and had to be abandoned for a game of cards, ending with a rowdy balloon game where you had to see who could keep a balloon in the air longest; no prizes for guessing who won that. It was amazing, they agreed, how well they understood each other, considering. After three hours the two POWs left with many handshakes and thanks, gratefully accepting another invitation to dinner the following week, on New Year's Day.

13

Staying On

The re-education of the German POWs was turning out better than expected, with a notable exception: those who arrived in Britain in early 1946 from captivity in the USA and Canada proved much more difficult. They'd been told they were being repatriated back to Germany but had found themselves diverted to Tilbury or Liverpool instead. It was a profound shock and caused many to claim they'd been 'sold to Britain like slaves' and to complain bitterly that the Allies were no better than the Nazis, with their lies and their double standards. In April 1946 some of the POWs newly arrived from North America hoisted home-made swastika flags in their camps on Hitler's birthday. 'Under National Socialism I was told to believe all that I was told,' a POW is quoted as saying in one of the POWD reports. 'I was promised lots of things but most of the promises were never kept. But in America I was promised that I was on my way back home to Germany. That promise was also broken. How do you now expect me to believe anything at all?' The two kinds of promises were hardly comparable, what with the Nazis having incarcerated millions in concentration and extermination camps as part of their stated political philosophy, but it gave these POWs a chance to blur the distinctions, venting their resentment.

Worst of all were the 33,400 POWs who arrived from Canada, because the majority of them had been in the Afrika Korps and in captivity since the early years of the war. Many were young Nazis who hadn't experienced the long and disillusioning war in eastern Europe and Russia, where terrible atrocities were committed which every German soldier who fought there had seen or taken part in, even if he wouldn't admit it. The POWs who had fought in Europe were generally susceptible to re-education into another political system, which if not perfect was certainly better than the ruthless dictatorship they had known so far. But the Afrika Korps POWs were intransigent, holding fast to their elite group identity with fanatical pride and resisting all attempts at re-education. As a screener report explained,

> The vast majority are young men in their 20s and 30s who fought with the Afrika Korps and have been prisoners from as early as 1941/2. All these men picture Europe and Germany as they were before the war and cannot appreciate the vast material changes and the alteration[s] in the mental outlook of Europeans which have taken place in that time. The German camp staffs were all senior NCOs and former Party members, fanatically imbued with Nazi philosophy. Even the slightest criticism or expression of doubt as to the eventual German victory was suppressed with all the ruthlessness of Nazi terrorism. The POWs lived in a political vacuum up to the end of the war and the types of men who would have been 'greys' a long time ago in the camps in this country are today still 'blacks'. On arrival in Britain many of them gave the Hitler salute, and discarded very reluctantly the Nazi insignia.

About 10 per cent of German POWs remained suspicious of re-education, whether offered in classes at the camps and hostels or, more informally, through contact with local people. Some wondered whether the British government had ordered the population to be friendly to them, because they still couldn't understand it or believe it was genuine. Sometimes the two extremes of pre-war German politics found themselves in tentative agreement over so-called democracy. A former communist commented, 'The British people had to shut up and do what it was told just as we did. Proof: I spent the First of May of 1946 in Dumfries. There was no workers' celebration and not a single banner that would let you guess that this was the greatest holiday for all workers.' A report compiled in Germany by A. Mitscherlich in 1948 from interviews with thousands of repatriated black POWs explained some of the early problems of language and manners which accompanied fraternisation. 'The British say "How do you do?" No one answers, nor is an answer expected. Instead, the other person says it too. The men say British politeness is purely superficial, "The British are only superficially gentlemen. They keep their real feelings to themselves and behind the surface politeness there is selfish materialism."' Some liked to point out that the Nazis were not the only racists by referring to the British Empire and the way Indians and Africans were treated. Mitscherlich was interviewing those black POWs who were repatriated last; nevertheless he reported that 91 per cent of the men did fraternise, and 70 per cent said they had learnt to esteem the people they knew.

For most, re-education became a regular feature of daily life in the camps, and was greatly helped by the increasingly friendly attitude of the local population. 'In Britain they wanted to re-educate us,' remembered a former POW. 'Who can blame us if we were distrustful? And then came fraternisation. We could talk to the Britishers, visit them in their homes. At first cautious feelers were put out, politenesses were exchanged and they smiled us goodbye and invited us back. And so began our real acquaintance with democrats.' The British too were being re-educated, albeit informally. A British civilian told a POWD field worker,

> I remember one Christmas when I started to feel sad for them for the first time. I saw three of them walking in the snow. They were just boys and I had a sudden impulse to ask them if they had any cigarettes. However, I just did not have the nerve to walk up to them in the street and speak. So I tossed a packet of Players right over their shoulders and watched. The fags were picked up. They turned round, smiled and waved. As I walked away my feelings were utterly confused. I felt an absolute idiot and a bit of a traitor as well. When the Jerrys first came to the area the general feeling from the public was a mixture of indifference and hatred of anything German. Serves the b's right was the attitude. But this didn't last long. Eventually it became: 'Poor b's, it wasn't their fault. They didn't want to fight. They had to do what Hitler ordered.'

The woman went on to describe the classic distinction between feelings about an anonymous group and feelings about a single individual of that group: 'My husband had to go up to the POW camp. I said I did not wish to speak to any Germans. But at the camp I was introduced to William.' Wilhelm was already William when he was invited to their home for Christmas Day 1946. 'By the time we took him back to the camp I had to admit that there were some Germans who were both human and charming . . . I think there were some course lectures, etc. arranged for German POWs. Subject: Democratic Government. William laughed about this and called it "Democrazy". Of course I argued over this. Can you think of anything better? Of course, he didn't have an answer for that.'

'We are all concerned in the process of re-education, and there is no better way of re-educating the Germans than by allowing them to have continued contact with ordinary decent British folk,' opined the Bishop of Sheffield in the House of Lords. A young girl put it differently. 'We grew up with the lads in the village and know them like brothers,' she told a POWD worker. 'That's not interesting any more. And it's too dangerous to go steady. Everyone knows about it and thinks there's going to be a wedding. So you have to watch it. But no one takes the prisoners seriously. That's just being friendly. Besides, you want to know what they are like.' It might have been a bit of fun for most of the girls, but in the end 796 British girls married POWs. And who knows how many children were born out of wedlock?

As far as Bernd was concerned, girls weren't the point. Sport was the thing, and he spent every free minute dedicated to it; it saw him through, just as it had during his boyhood in Bremen and on those few miraculous occasions in Russia when he was given a break from fighting the partisans to play handball against other regimental teams far away from the front line. As to re-education, he didn't need it and he didn't want it. He remembered the time a Nazi Party political officer arrived in a jeep somewhere down in the Crimea back in early 1942 to give Bernd's unit of *Fallschirmjäger* a pep talk. The *Kameraden* were still heady with the speed of their conquest of first Poland and now the Ukraine, and Bernd for one wasn't inclined to give up his precious free time to listen to some official toeing the Nazi Party line, but, having no choice, he went to the village meeting place along with the rest and settled himself down on the mud floor with his back against a wall, preparing to doze through it.

'What do you think you're doing here?' began the political officer. 'Torching and killing and being killed?' That wasn't the usual way these talks began and it came as something of a shock. Everyone including Bernd was listening now, but no one answered. 'Well? What are you doing and why are you here?' His tone was combative. Eventually some poor mutt in the back row put up his hand. 'For the Führer and the glory of the Reich, *Herr Leutnant*,' he offered, as per usual. The officer just laughed at him. 'Glory of the Reich? No one ever went to war for glory, *Kamerad*. Man goes to war to get something, that's the only reason man ever went to war.' This was a new one on them, and now they were waiting to hear his answer. 'We're here for the oil,' he said. 'The oil and *Lebensraum*.' Bernd knew all about *Lebensraum* but he'd never given oil a thought; he wasn't even sure there was any oil in the Crimea. So now, given the choice, Bernd had no wish to attend re-education classes; he'd had enough politics to last him a lifetime.

By April the bitter winter of 1946/7 with its blizzards, snowdrifts twenty feet deep, power cuts, frozen fields and coal shortages was finally giving way to spring. Spells of sunshine were followed by dark clouds, rain and flooding, but the freezing weather was over. At Camp 50 the POWs were out in the gardens which surrounded each hut, digging and hoeing and weeding. The huts were made of wood and concrete with corrugated-iron roofs, and lined up in neat rows. Gardening was popular with the men, offering a link to their lives at home and helping to pass the time. They planted a mixture of flowers and vegetables in the German style and there was great competition between huts as to which garden looked best. Vegetables were especially prized as fresh supplements to the camp canteen food.

Those who didn't garden found something else to occupy their minds. Virtually every POW camp had a chapel in a converted Nissen hut, serving all denominations, and the men decorated them with wall paintings and mosaics, some of them real works of art. Artists were always in demand; apart from the chapels, many huts and most canteens had paintings on the walls: pine forests,

Bavarian farmhouses, stags on alpine peaks, sunsets over the North Sea, anything to remind the POWs of home. Some men did woodwork; some sewed; others read German books supplied by the POWD library service; others again spent their time writing, mostly diaries and letters home. Officers, especially, engaged in many cultural activities, because the arts had always been a part of their lives and because they had so much time on their hands, not having to work. They wrote and performed plays; they acquired musical instruments and formed small orchestras or bands; they held recitations of the classic German poets, even Shakespeare, always trying to involve the men, but with little success. After the war the men had scant respect for their officers; the only thing they shared with them was the camp choir. Virtually every camp had one, and it turned out that singing was the most effective way of dispelling the depression of captivity, as well as providing a natural point of contact between the POWs and the local community.

And Bernd got back to his sport – if not actually playing then sitting at one of the tables in the camp canteen with a Woodbine and a cup of tea, listening to all the sporting fixtures on the wireless relayed via the loudspeakers as usual. They were all back now: the Grand National, cricket at Lord's, the Oxford and Cambridge Boat Race and the FA Cup Final. At times like this Bernd felt a contentment he thought he'd lost for ever; he was even acquiring a liking for tea. During the bitter winter 140 football fixtures had been postponed and there was a backlog which was due to last well into June, which suited POW Trautmann to perfection.

One Saturday in May Bernd was sitting in the camp canteen with his football *Kameraden* listening to a match relayed by the BBC from Hampden Park in Glasgow; apparently there were 34,000 spectators and who knows how many millions of listeners.

It was the Great Britain versus the Rest of Europe match and it was as close to another war as you could get, bar the killing. BRITAIN MUST BEAT EUROPE. OUR PRESTIGE AT STAKE screamed the headlines in the *Daily Express*. Parola, playing for the Rest of Europe, was described as a 'sinister figure', and further as 'the sallow-skinned and dark surly-haired Italian centre half, who is said to be a master stopper', who, with absolutely no sense of decency, was wearing 'the briefest of briefs'. Britain needn't have worried: the famous Stanley Matthews of Stoke City was playing right wing, with Tommy Lawton of Chelsea and Wilf Mannion of Middlesbrough backing him up. They each scored twice and the home team won 6–1. Matthews signed to Blackpool that same night, for a fantastic £11,500.

EUROPE IS NOW CONVINCED THAT THE BRITISH ARE BOSSES OF SOCCER, announced the *Daily Express* the next morning. 'What *Scheisse*! What a load of rubbish!' said POW Trautmann to his *Kameraden* as they left the canteen. 'These British never change: double-dealers, empire builders, hypocrites.' They reminded one another of the British Featherweight Boxing Championship held at the Royal Albert Hall earlier that year. Al Phillips of Aldgate had won against Cliff Anderson of British Guiana, but only on points. 'An extremely unconvincing decision,' *The Times* had called it.

That summer Denis Compton beat hell out of the South Africans at Lord's in the Test. Compton was a real sporting hero, even to some of the German POWs, unique in that he played football as well as cricket; but cricket was his first love and where he attained his heroic status, and on 11 June 1947 he proved it once again by saving the match against the South Africans with his 163 runs. The BBC commentator was a newcomer called John Arlott, who had recently given up being a policeman in Southampton. He spoke with a soft Hampshire burr quite unlike the usual upper-class nasal drawl thought suitable for a sport which still had Gentlemen and Players. Gentlemen played for the pleasure of the game; the rest, who were working men, may have played for pleasure, but also did it for pay. The Head of BBC Outside Broadcasts wasn't in favour of Arlott, who had in his opinion a 'vulgar voice', but the public knew otherwise, and quickly took him to their hearts. The spectators who crammed the stands at Lord's had put on their Sunday best, but they still looked post-war shabby.

> Never have I been so deeply touched on a cricket ground as I was in this heavenly summer, when I went to Lord's to see a pale-faced crowd, existing on rations, the rocket bomb still in the ears of most folks – see this worn, dowdy crowd watching Compton. The strain of long years of anxiety and affliction passed from all hearts and shoulders at the sight of Compton in full sail, sending the ball here, there and everywhere, each stroke a flick of delight, a propulsion of happy sane healthy life. There were no rations in an innings by Compton,

wrote Neville Cardus in the *Daily Express*, still thinking of the war, but in a nicer way.

Bernd wasn't interested in making things, and left it to others to produce slippers, photograph frames, toboggans, model aeroplanes, you name it. Bernd was in supply, not production, and he could supply virtually anything. The two best sources were the American depot at Burtonwood, which was only twenty miles away, and Haydock airbase on the far side of Haydock Park racecourse, which was also still used by the Americans. After curfew, groups of POWs would climb through a hole in the barbed wire and go on foraging expeditions, and Bernd, with access to the camp lorries, would come back from these night forays loaded with planks of wood, silk from old parachutes, odd bits of metal, rubber from the linings of old fuel tanks, disused dynamos and, on one memorable occasion, the plastic cockpits from some full-sized gliders found stored in 40-foot wooden boxes in one of the airbase hangars, which were later made into beads and sewn onto pieces of hand-made lace as gifts for the Germans' new English friends in Ashton-in-Makerfield. Everything was 'liberated' in a good cause, thought POW Trautmann, and it was obvious that no one was bothered; by mid-1947 the security at Camp 50 was much more relaxed and the camp guards often turned a blind eye, even warning the POWs before an inspection was due so they could hide their latest acquisitions. Since March of that year the POWs no longer had to wear diamond patches on their uniforms, and in the autumn they were allowed out of camp, within a radius of three miles.

Repatriation had been in operation since September 1946, starting with the whites, who were considered ready to play their part in the new, democratic Germany. But screenings were still a regular feature of POW life and Bernd always emerged from his session categorised as black. He couldn't help himself. He hated the screeners, who were mostly pompous teacher and university professor types, all German speaking, and as soon as he entered the camp office and sat down at the table opposite one of them, his hackles rose. Was it some left-over inferiority complex? Was it a remnant of the old Hitler Youth training and brainwashing? One way or the other, POW Trautmann, veteran *Fallschirmjäger*, never gave the right answers. It offended his pride to fall for their stupid questions about Hitler and the Nazis and why he'd volunteered for the Luftwaffe aged just seventeen. What else would a seventeen-year-old who'd been in the Hitler Youth since the age of ten want to do? But they didn't understand, and he wasn't the one to enlighten them.

As soon as they were allowed out of camp Bernd and his *Kameraden* were off to football matches on Saturday afternoons, and not always within the three-mile limit. They went with a chap called Cyril Morris, one of the players in the Haydock Park team, who'd become a friend. It was Bernd's first introduction to the English league, and they got as far as Liverpool, Bolton and Preston without any of the camp sergeants raising an eyebrow; in fact they turned a blind eye. It was the same at football grounds. 'They're German POWs, is that OK?' Cyril would say to the men at the gate. 'Oh yes, OK,' they'd say, and they'd all jump over the gate without paying. Once inside the officials more often than not let them sit in the front rows, because that's where the empty seats were. It was magnificent, thought Bernd, magnificent. The atmosphere in the stands with the thousands of spectators all out to have a good time was magnificent too, and the singing before the match began, and the excitement of the game itself, but best of all was being part of it and accepted by everyone, even though it was clear they were German POWs. No one minded, just included them naturally as fellow fans who loved football as much as they did.

The team Bernd loved to watch most in those early days was Everton. It was a great team all round, but it was their goalkeeper Bernd was really interested in: Ted Sagar, one of the most famous goalkeepers at the time, brilliant at his craft and tough with it. Bernd watched Sagar's every move, studied it and stored it away, then tried it out the following week when Camp 50 was playing one of the local teams.

On Saturdays when there was no football they were off to Wigan, to the cinema. The first time Bernd went with Bubi Staudinger, one of the football *Kameraden*. It felt strange that first time, getting on the bus from Ashton-in-Makerfield to Wigan in their POW uniforms, paying the fourpenny fare in real English money, then taking their seats among the locals, feeling awkward and conspicuous, all eyes on them. No one spoke to them, but quite a few smiled even though it was stated in the national press that there had recently been some resentment against German POWs because they seemed to be getting better food and have more money to spend than the ordinary people of Britain, who were still struggling with shortages and rationing. So Bernd and Bubi took their seats in the back of the bus and didn't speak, not even to one another; just looked out of the bus window, studying the landscape. Once they got to Wigan they joined the end of the cinema queue, which was all the way down the street and round the corner: husbands and wives standing arm in arm, girls in summer frocks and hand-knitted cardigans, women with shopping baskets straight from Wigan market, young lads recently demobbed from the army – everyone out to have a good time, laughing and talking and not bothered in the least by the German POWs in their midst.

It was an American film called *The Hucksters*, starring Clark Gable and Deborah Kerr, a good-fun film about a Madison Avenue con man who falls in love with a sweet English girl, the kind of film Bernd's mother loved, and not a war film, thank God, though Gable was a war hero, who'd joined the US Air Force in 1942, not long after Bernd joined the Luftwaffe, and probably played his part in bombing Germany to smithereens. War was full of surprises. Apparently Gable was Hitler's favourite male film star, and the Führer had offered a sizeable bounty to anyone who managed to capture him.

'What are you laughing at?'

'This film star Gable. He was Hitler's favourite, wasn't he?'

'How do you know that?' Bubi was used to it: Bernd was always coming up with some fact he'd read somewhere. Once Bernd had his head in a book there was no moving him.

'Read it in the newspaper.'

'English?'

'*Daily Express.*'

They were near the front of the queue when Bernd spotted him, a crippled war veteran, propped up against the wall of the cinema by the box office, with an old army cap on the pavement in front of him, begging. Written on a piece of cardboard was 'D-Day War Veteran', and most people stopped laughing for a moment, giving him a penny and wishing him good luck. The closer Bernd got to the cripple, the worse he felt; he found he couldn't look at him, with one leg missing and only half an arm and a disfigured face. D-Day. Bernd had been there too, and at Caen and Cherbourg and the Seine – killing and taking prisoners, Tommies like this one, and sometimes shooting them on the spot, because war was war, and both sides did that in the hell of those days and weeks following the Allied invasion of Normandy.

Some in the queue were curious to see what the two German POWs would do once they came face to face with the war veteran. These civilians, thought Bernd, they have no idea, no idea at all. Nor did Bubi, who hadn't been in Normandy; only Bernd and this *verdammter* Tommy war veteran knew. Bernd walked straight past the man and up to the box office. There was a woman with a cheery smile inside. 'How many?' she asked. He had his one and nine pence ready, but then he couldn't do it and he turned away abruptly, digging his hand in his pocket for the rest of his money, and, without looking at the Tommy, he threw the whole lot in his cap and walked off fast up the street.

'What are you doing!' Bubi was having to run to keep up with him; he wanted to see the film and have a bit of fun.

'You go,' said Bernd. 'I'm going back to camp.' And without waiting for Bubi to answer, he headed off back to the bus station.

*

Bubi Staudinger was a great hit with the girls, and the Sunday football matches offered him plenty of opportunities. By the autumn of 1947 up to 2,000 spectators regularly turned up to watch the POW games, including many pretty girls, most of them more interested in the players than the football, and of the players it was the handsome POWs Staudinger and Trautmann, the one dark, the other fair, who interested them most. By the time they were allowed out up to three miles Bubi already had a regular girlfriend. Her name was Vera, a good-looker with a shapely figure, and a great dancer, which was important because, almost more than football, Bubi loved to dance: foxtrots, quicksteps, waltzes, tangos, he could do them all. Every Saturday night he was off to the dance hall with Vera, meeting her at the bus stop, where he changed into a pair of trousers and a jacket and tie loaned by one of her brothers before taking the bus in to Wigan, just like any other local lad, as long as he didn't open his mouth.

'Come with us,' Bubi would say to Bernd every week, and every week Bernd would say no, he preferred to stay in camp. The truth is, Bernd was shy; he'd never been with a girl and he didn't have Bubi's self-confidence, so he hid behind aloofness and said he wasn't bothered. The war had done it. From the age of seventeen he'd been fighting and killing or a prisoner of war. Normal life wasn't in it. The girls he'd known in Bremen before the war had been little more than schoolgirls, and not at all like these English girls, who wore make-up, styled their hair, showed off their curves in pretty home-made frocks, and were quite brazen in their way. He didn't know what to make of them, nor what to say to them. At heart Bernd was still a *Muttersöhnchen*, his mother's boy, and he preferred to stay in camp and listen to sport on the wireless or read a book. He felt safer that way.

Bernd's POW Camp 50 at Ashton-in-Makerfield had its own football team and their brilliant goalkeeper, Trautmann, was soon attracting the attention of Lancashire locals.

Trautmann's talent, size, tough character and early training in athletics and handball made him a great goal-keeper, and his blond good looks were a hit with the local girls.

Bernd felt his real education began when he came to England, aged twenty-two. Grateful for his former enemies' forgiveness and understanding, he was glad to give something back with charity matches.

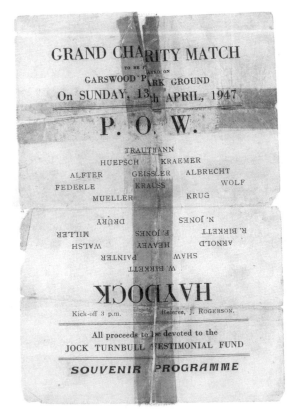

GRAND CHARITY MATCH
TO BE PLAYED ON
GARSWOOD PARK GROUND
On SUNDAY, 13th APRIL, 1947

P. O. W.

TRAUTMANN
HUEPSCH   KRAEMER
ALFTER   GEISSLER   ALBRECHT
FEDERLE   KRAUSS   WOLF
MUELLER   KRUG

W. BARKETT
SHAW   PAINTER
ARNOLD   HEAVEY   WALSH
R. BIRKETT   F. JONES   MILLER
N. JONES   DRURY

HAYDOCK

Kick-off 3 p.m.   Referee, J. ROGERSON.

All proceeds to be devoted to the
JOCK TURNBULL TESTIMONIAL FUND

SOUVENIR PROGRAMME

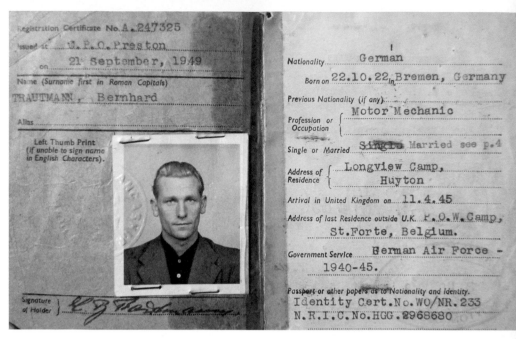

Registration Certificate No. A.247325

Issued at U.P.O. Preston

on 21 September, 1949

Name (Surname first in Roman Capitals)

TRAUTMANN, Bernhard

Alias

Left Thumb Print
(if unable to sign name
in English Characters).

Signature
of Holder

Nationality............ German

Born on 22.10.22 in Bremen, Germany

Previous Nationality (if any)...............

Profession or { Motor Mechanic
Occupation {

Single or Married Single Married see p.4

Address of { Longview Camp,
Residence { Huyton

Arrival in United Kingdom on 11.4.45

Address of last Residence outside U.K. P.O.W.Camp,
St.Forte, Belgium.

Government Service German Air Force -
1940-45.

Passport or other papers as to Nationality and Identity.
Identity Cert.No. WO/NR.233
N.R.I.C.No.HGG.2968680

The British government offered to house and pay POWs who agreed to stay in Britain and help rebuild the country after war. The more Bernd saw of his former enemy, the more he liked them. He loved the football and he got involved with an English girl called Marion. At the end of the year he decided to stay on.

He worked with a bomb disposal unit in the Liverpool docks. Most had done similar work in the war so they were used to the danger.

Bernd, now called Bert, playing for St Helens Town.
Bill Twist (back, 3rd left) was the captain.

Bert's style in goal was tough and aggressive,
charging out of goal to gain possession of
the ball, then kicking it far into the other
half. As his fame grew so did the gate,
from a thousand to over five thousand.

The area round the goal at St Helens Town was often
a sea of mud. But nothing stopped the enthusiasm of
the fans, many of them miners from the Bold Colliery
at the far end of the pitch.

By the 1950 General Election, post-war Britain was changing. Labour held on to the poor, working-class areas, but the suburbs reverted to voting Conservative, and Labour only got in by a slim majority.

By the 1949/50 season Bert was playing for Manchester City where he stayed till he retired in 1964. Here Bert is stopping a goal in typical style in the Manchester City versus Manchester United match in 1952.

By 1955 Manchester City were in the Cup Final. Don Revie (*right*) devised the famous Revie Plan, the key to their success. Captain Roy Paul is on the left.

Bert was integral to the success of the Revie Plan. Instead of kicking the ball to a waiting player, he now kicked it ahead of a player already running down the field.

The *Manchester Evening Chronicle* had paid for Bert's parents to attend the 1955 Cup Final. They pose with Jack Friar, the St Helens Town general secretary and now Bert's father-in-law.

Bert being presented to the Duke of Edinburgh before the 1955 Cup Final. Instinctively he bowed in the German style, amusing his team-mates.

Sixteen minutes before the end of the 1956 Cup Final, Bert charged out of goal to stop Birmingham's Peter Murphy, and Murphy's knee caught Trautmann's neck, knocking him out. When he came round he refused to go off. Manchester City won 3-1.

Bert had broken his neck. He spent weeks in plaster and was told he would never play top-class football again. Luckily the prognosis was wrong. But a month after the Cup Final his son John, aged six, was killed in a car crash. 'It was the worst year of my life,' he says. 'I still find it hard to talk about it.'

Talking to the Collyhurst Lads Club. Bert spent a lot
of time with fans, often signing autographs for over
an hour after a match. 'As a POW I had so much
understanding, so much forgiveness, so much friendship,
I wanted to give something back; show there were
good Germans, not just bad.'

Bert with his
wife Margaret
and their
son John.

Bert watching a Stockport County match when
he was their manager. He brought in Eddie Quigley
from Blackburn Rovers and Jimmy Meadows as
the coach. Within the first year they'd got promotion
from the Fourth into the Third Division and the
average crowd rose from 2,500 to 11,000.

Bert and Marlis, his wife of 24 years, and his sons Stephen and Mark from his marriage to Margaret.

Freda, the baby born to Marion in 1949, never knew her father Bert. But in 2001 she went looking for him. Now they see each other all the time.

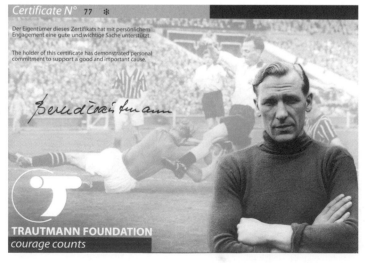

Certificate N° 77 ✳

Der Eigentümer dieses Zertifikats hat mit persönlichem Engagement eine gute und wichtige Sache unterstützt.

The holder of this certificate has demonstrated personal commitment to support a good and important cause.

Berud Trautmann

TRAUTMANN FOUNDATION
courage counts

The Trautmann Foundation fosters Anglo-German friendship through football with young people. 'Courage Counts' is its motto.

Günther Luehr had a girlfriend too. Luehr was the Camp 50 goalkeeper who'd changed positions with Bernd during that match when Bernd was injured, putting him into goal, where he stayed for the rest of his sporting life. Luehr was as popular with the girls as Bubi Staudinger and he had the best girl, called Eileen. You could tell she was from a good home, thought Bernd, by the way she carried herself, the way she dressed and the way she behaved, not brazen like some of the others. This Eileen had a friend called Marion who came to the football matches with her. Marion came from Bryn, halfway between Ashton-in-Makerfield and Wigan, and she was blond and pretty in a quiet sort of way, with a good figure. She was nice too, the kind of girl who wouldn't go out with anyone, just like Eileen. Marion had seen POW Trautmann walking down the road from the camp into Ashton one day, he on one side of the road, she on the other, on her way to see her friend Phyllis Benson, who had been going out with Egon Rameil ever since Christmas 1946, when the fraternisation ban was lifted. Marion thought she'd never seen anyone so lonely in all her life: he was just walking along, head down, shoulders hunched, tall, blond, handsome enough to make your legs go weak, but so alone, even though he was already the star of the Camp 50 football team. She told Eileen she longed to go out with him, so Eileen told Günther, and Günther told Bernd. But Bernd kept saying no. Still, night after night, he lay on his hard straw mattress in his POW hut, thinking of Marion, fantasising, wishing he had the confidence to do it. Finally, after many such nights, he took his courage in his hands and said yes.

After that Bernd and Marion went to the pictures together, and for walks in the park, and on Sundays they often made up a foursome with Egon and Phyllis at the Bensons' house, playing cards, listening to music or just talking round the kitchen table over a cup of tea. On Saturday nights they sometimes went to the dance hall in Wigan with Bubi and Vera, though Bernd never danced, just sat watching from the edge of the dance floor, beer in hand, smiling. It took a while before he got up the courage to kiss Marion, by which time he thought he was in love. In camp, Bubi, Egon and Bernd laughed about the fact that they'd all fallen for English girls – it created a bond between them. Egon was due to be repatriated soon and he meant to take Phyllis with him. Mr and Mrs Benson were devastated. She was their only child, but they could see she was happy, and finally they gave their permission; Egon might be a German, but he was a nice man who loved their daughter, and they knew Phyllis would have a good life over there, better than in England, because Egon was a qualified dentist. So Egon and Phyllis duly got married, and are, by the way, happily married in Germany to this day.

Bubi and Egon's advice to Bernd was to enjoy himself, relax a bit. The following Saturday Bernd and Marion went for a walk across Haydock racecourse instead of the park; it was more private there, on the far side, in the long grass. Marion was crazily in love with Bernd, who was quite different to the local boys: shy but tough and not too full of himself. Bernd was keen on Marion too, and he was feeling almost carefree again with the end of captivity in sight. He thought Marion was just the kind of girl his mother would really like. But Bernd was inexperienced and so was Marion, and one way or another it wasn't long before she had to tell Bernd she was pregnant. It came as an awful shock to him and he didn't know what to do or where to turn. He had many sleepless nights trying to battle it out, on his own, because he felt he couldn't tell anyone else. One thing he knew: he couldn't let her down. Poor Marion was scared stiff – of her parents, the neighbours, the shame and the guilt. But he didn't know what to do.

Came the day when he had to go and meet the parents and face the music. He was so nervous he could hardly speak, but he knew there was no getting out of it. He'd never been to Bryn before, and when he got off at the bus stop his spirits fell even further. It was a desolate place, a mining village with one main street and a row of small, terraced houses, back-to-backs like he'd seen on his train journey from Kempton Park to the Midlands, with scrubbed front steps straight onto the street and outside toilets at the end of sooty backyards. Marion's parents were hostile and unwelcoming, or so Bernd felt, and he was embarrassed, trying, in his broken English, to find excuses for Marion's behaviour, taking the blame on himself. It didn't get him anywhere: all they wanted was for him to marry their daughter and make an honest woman of her, and that's what Marion wanted too of course. But Bernd thought they were narrow-minded and knew they wouldn't ever accept him, being German, and this brought out his own anger and resentment. Nevertheless, he went to Bryn almost every weekend, trudging up the road from the bus stop, eyes to the ground, then into the small dark house, trying to make conversation with the parents, trying to cheer up Marion, trying all the time to do the right thing, but knowing, deep in his heart, that he couldn't.

Bernd was one of the last to be repatriated, in March 1948. The final POWs boarded ships bound for home, carrying the kitbags, battered suitcases and cardboard boxes they'd arrived with, along with the money they'd saved up from their pay to help them start a new life, and laden with presents from their hosts, including clothing, so that every now and again among the crowds boarding the ships there were young men dressed in tweed jackets and ties, English-style. Movietone and Pathe newsreels show them walking up the gangway and turning to wave England goodbye, having promised to keep in touch with their new friends.

But now the moment had finally arrived, Bernd took an unexpected decision: he decided not to go home, at least not for another year. He wasn't the only one: 24,000 German POWs decided to stay on, many because they had nothing left to go home to. Hamburg alone had 36,000 dead in a single night of Allied bombing with hardly a building left standing. Others stayed because their region of Germany was now in communist hands; others again decided to stay because they'd fallen in love, with a girl, with a way of life, with the English.

Bernd's reasons for staying were complicated. Marion was certainly one, but another was his pride. He had no money and no decent clothes, and this wasn't the way he wanted to return home. Home, Bremen. He could hardly imagine life in Wischusenstrasse any more, with his mother and father, his brother Karl Heinz, the Wittenburgs and the Mrozinzskys. News from home was not good, and his mother's letters had a strange feel to them. These days he wrote home regularly, the only time in his life he ever did, and each time a letter came back, almost by return of post. But there was something about the letters – a hidden anxiety, a feeling of depression, of giving up – which made him suspicious and wary. The flats at Wischusenstrasse had suffered some bomb damage, but that wasn't it. Apparently his father couldn't get his job back in the docks and he was still unemployed, so was his brother. What could it mean?

The British government, still struggling to repair the war damage, had made the remaining German POWs an offer: if they stayed to help out for another year they would be housed and paid. That clinched it for Bernd, and he signed up. First he took a job on a farm, later he worked in a bomb disposal unit. He enjoyed working on the farm, but the bomb disposal work was more to his taste. He felt at home there, among men like himself, who were used to blowing things up and familiar with the danger, liking it even. There were nine bomb disposal units operating in England at that time, each run by a team of Royal Engineers who carried out the most technical and dangerous parts of the job, with Germans like Bernd acting as back-up. The Germans had to be under 28 with some suitable training and experience because, even for the back-up teams, it was dangerous work – three were killed and three more were wounded in the course of their work – but morale in these companies was high, and the Germans had great respect for their British superiors, who had, not so long ago, been fighting them in France and Germany.

Bernd's first posting was at Milnthorpe near Kendal in what was then called Westmoreland. He lived, like all the other Germans, in one of the old POW camps, but they were free to come and go like ordinary citizens. Reflecting on this as he lay on his camp bed in his Nissen hut one evening smoking a cigarette, he thought it was the first time in his life he'd known real freedom, meaning freedom of thought as well as freedom of action. Although he'd never admitted it to the screeners, he knew now that his thoughts had never been his own in Nazi Germany, not in the Hitler Youth, not in the Luftwaffe; his head had been filled with nonsense about racial superiority, adulation of the Führer, unquestioning obedience, fighting to the last, sacrificing his life for the Reich, and there had been nothing free about any of it. As to freedom of action, that hadn't existed at all, even as a young boy. Those 'action' days, when the SS and storm troopers, assisted by the Hitler Youth, ordered everyone inside while they arrested communists, Jews, socialists, anyone who opposed them in small ways and large, were enough to terrify anyone into submission. Let the British with their democracy try it some time, thought Bernd. The SS shot people on the spot, and he remembered how, once people were finally let out of their flats and into the street again, the pavements were often covered in blood. It was hard to imagine now, but at the time he thought it was normal; he thought that was what life was like.

One day he was walking back to the bus stop in Bryn after one of his visits to Marion, head down, spirits low, when he bumped into his old friend Cyril Morris.

'Hey up, Bert! What're you doing in these parts?'

Cyril had been the centre forward for Haydock FC, a good one, and the scouts had spotted him, so now he was playing for St Helens Town as a semi-professional. Bernd had heard, and how he envied him, especially because since moving to Milnthorpe Bernd wasn't playing any football at all. Now he mumbled something about visiting friends and prepared to move on, saying he had a bus to catch, but Cyril walked along beside him, talking all the time about what fun it was playing for St Helens Town, what a step up, no comparison to Haydock FC, and you got paid something and all. Like the other English players, Cyril always called Bernd, Bert; those German names were too hard to pronounce for the local lads and they were all anglicised.

'Tell you what, Bert,' said Cyril. 'Why don't you come and try for St Helens Town? We need a good goalie, and there's none better than you.'

Bernd/Bert couldn't believe his luck.

He went down the next weekend for one training session with them, and that was it: they signed him on the spot. From then on he went every Saturday, taking the bus from Kendal to St Helens, a two-hour journey, the whole thing costing him a pound. He only got a pound a week from St Helens, so he made nothing, but that didn't matter. What mattered was the football, the comradeship and the acceptance of the people of St Helens Town. Really, it was football heaven. That's how Bernd saw it, and if it hadn't been for Marion, everything in the garden would have been rosy.

Marion gave birth that July, at home. Bernd wasn't there, but he arrived a few days later, to see the baby and comfort Marion, who hardly needed comforting, she was glowing with happiness. It was a little girl, and Marion decided to call her Freda after Bernd's mother, albeit with an anglicised spelling. Bernd sat by the bed holding Marion's hand in pure panic. They talked about marriage again, but Bernd was just going through the motions. During the past few weeks he'd assessed his life – not so much the things that had happened so far, but the things which would never happen if he married Marion and lived the rest of his life in Bryn among the small dark terraced houses and the miners, and the road which led nowhere. He was 25 and had only ever known war or being a prisoner of war; his life was just beginning. If he married Marion he knew he'd be lost for ever. The question in his mind wasn't whether to stay or go, it was whether to tell her or not.

He didn't tell her. It was the worst thing he ever did in his life, and he knew it, but he couldn't stay and he couldn't tell her he was going, so one weekend he just didn't turn up. He ran away and never looked back. You have to do hard things in war, that's what the Hitler Youth had told him week after week, but no one told him you had to do hard things in peacetime too. Still, he found he could do it, and once he was away he felt, along with the guilt, an instant, heady relief.

News of the Jerry goalkeeper signed by St Helens Town spread fast. This chap Trautmann had everything: he was tall and tough and very fast, with the biggest hands you've ever seen, and he could leap in all directions and stop almost any ball. And he didn't mind danger, he wasn't intimidated by anyone or anything. Of course Bernd knew he was good, he'd known it since he was a boy, and he knew why too. He'd always been an athlete, a fast runner, a high jumper, a great thrower of the javelin and the grenade, and the best player in the handball team, catching the ball and throwing it out again in a split second, just like a goalkeeper. It was a natural talent, God-given, and he had the character to go with it, more so since the gruelling years at the Russian Front. Over and above all this, Bernd knew the most important thing of all: you had to have heart. The goalie's job wasn't just to stop goals; it was to make life easy for his team's defence; to go out there and attack fearlessly; to gain possession of the ball, not hang around in goal waiting for it.

Bernd flourished at St Helens, right from the start. It was the football of course, but it was also the people.

'Want a cup of tea, Bert?' they'd ask as soon as he stepped into one of their homes.

'I don't mind if I do,' he'd reply in his German accent, which was beginning to have some Lancashire in it too.

No wonder St Helens Town was pleased. Football had always played second fiddle to rugby there, but the Jerry's fame spread so fast that the gate takings grew steadily week by week. Where they used to have a regular 1,000 loyal supporters there were now over 5,000. What is a star? Who knows? But you know when you meet one, and Bert Trautmann was a star. Soon St Helens Town had enough money to build its first proper concrete stand, and the takings just went on growing.

As for Trautmann, German POW, he was beginning to feel accepted, beginning to feel at home. He decided, for the second time in his life, to change his name. First he'd been Berni, then, coming back from his Hitler Youth *Landjahr*, he'd become Bernhard. Now he was Bert. Good old Bert.

14

St Helens Town

The summer of 1948 was full of interest for sports fanatics like Bert. On 29 July the first post-war Olympics was held in London, at Wembley, watched by crowds of 85,000 in the middle of a heatwave. It was exactly ten years since Bert had won his medals at the Youth Olympics sponsored by the *Reichsjugendamt* and the Hitler Youth in the Olympic Stadium in Berlin. As to the Berlin Olympics themselves, who could ever forget Siegfried Eifrig running into the stadium and carrying the torch up that endless flight of steps to the brazier high above, the very image of the Aryan athlete. And now it was John Mark, a young doctor from Surbiton in Surrey and a Cambridge Blue, who did it modestly, with no fuss. It was better this way, Bert knew that now, but he'd always remember Siegfried Eifrig.

The British, perhaps still suffering from the exhaustion of war, won few medals. Their great hope was Dorothy Manley, a shorthand-typist from Woodford Green, in the women's 100 metres; but she was beaten by Fanny Blankers-Koen, a mother of two from Holland who became known as the 'Flying Dutchwoman' because she won not just one gold, but four. The Test Match at the Oval in August was no better. 'Two slips, a silly mid-off, and a forward short-leg close to him,' went John Arlott's commentary in his Hampshire burr, as Hollies bowled to Bradman, batting in his last Test. 'And he's bowled! Bradman, bowled Hollies, nought! Bowled Hollies, nought! And – what do you say under those circumstances?' What indeed? Bert, listening on the wireless in the POW camp canteen, hadn't a clue what Arlott was talking about, but apparently England were 52 all out. Luckily there was good news nearer home. At Haydock Park a horse called The Chase won the first race, ridden by a jockey called Lester Piggott who was only twelve years old.

For those not interested in sport by far the most important event of that summer was the start of the National Health Service. From now on everything would be free to everyone: spectacles, dentures, medicines, all free. Doctors' surgeries were inundated with patients, many with ailments they'd been suffering from for years, and the hospitals struggled to cope with the demand. At the same time the National Insurance Scheme, offering 'cradle to grave security', meant the labouring poor were no longer dependent on sporadic charity handouts but entitled to benefits, and no longer needed to fear unemployment in the same way, nor an impoverished old age. Some of the middle classes complained, which was understandable seeing as it was mostly they who had to pay up 4 shillings and 11 pence a week out of an average £7 weekly wage to bankroll Labour's welfare state, but most expressed themselves pleased. It was good and it was fair. After all, how many of these working-class men and women had fought for their country during the war, some of them in the First World War as well? 'We are leading the whole world in Social Security,' wrote the *Daily Mirror*. 'Our State belongs to the people – unlike so many countries where the people are owned by the State. And Social Security converts our democratic ideal into human reality.'

This was all well and good, but in the summer of 1948 – and for a long time yet – the country was still suffering from a serious housing problem, food was still rationed, there were shortages of everything, public transport was so crowded it was a disgrace and the cost of living was going up and up. The only people doing well seemed to be the spivs, flashy types with smarmed-down hair and wide-shouldered coats who hung about street corners offering people anything and everything on the black market. And how many of them were Jews? That's what a shockingly large proportion of the general public, stirred by lurid headlines in the gutter press, were asking themselves in 1948. Oswald Mosley's fascist Union Movement was gaining ground in the poorer districts like the East End of London, and there were anti-Semitic riots in many cities of Britain that year and the next. But the Jews were not the only target; newly arrived West Indians were finding it hard too, first to get lodgings and then encountering prejudice at work, always assuming they got a job at all.

Thank goodness for the royal family. George VI and Queen Elizabeth with their two daughters Elizabeth and Margaret Rose had come through the war with flying colours, moving among their people during the Blitz and even suffering some bomb damage themselves, at the back of Buckingham Palace. In 1948 it was almost impossible to open a newspaper without seeing a picture of the King making a speech or the Queen opening a ward in some hospital. When Queen Elizabeth came to Lancashire to visit the cotton mills and factories that summer the route from Blackburn to Rochdale and Oldham to Manchester was lined all the way with cheering, waving subjects in spite of the pouring rain, and apart from a few killjoys the country went wild when Princess Elizabeth married Prince Philip of Greece, hundreds of thousands camping out all night just to catch a glimpse of the bride sitting next to her proud father the King in the golden coach, on her way to Westminster Abbey, proving that love was alive and well, because anyone could see that this was a love match and not one of those arranged royal marriages. The killjoys disagreed, pointing out that the last thing Britain wanted was for their future queen to be marrying a foreigner and a half-German one at that, and what about the expense during this time of shortages, rationing and make do and mend? But few were bothered; Britain was a monarchy, and proud of it.

That autumn the British government announced it would grant the remaining German POWs who had stayed to help the British back on their feet some home leave. They could go for a month in January, on full pay and with their train and boat fares paid. Unbelievable, thought Bert, but wondered how he'd break it to the management at St Helens Town, including skipper Bill Twist and General Secretary Jack Friar. They'd have to find a replacement goalie, which wasn't easy. Jack Friar was the one Bert minded about most; ever since he had joined St Helens Town Friar had been looking out for him, encouraging him, advising him, taking him under his wing. He was manager of the local Co-op, a self-educated man, a clever man, one who knew his mind and spoke it plainly and fairly. He was very influential locally was Jack, very humorous, very popular, the kind of man who came into a room and everyone knew he was there. Not that he made a lot of it, just told another of his good stories, with everyone gathered round. Bert thought the world of Jack Friar and wished he'd had a father like him.

Bert fitted well into the St Helens Town team, getting on with everyone, including Bill Twist, who'd been signed by Liverpool before the war but was called up and sent off to fight in Egypt. By the time he came back he didn't feel up to the First Division any more, preferring to settle for his local St Helens team, a Liverpool County

Combination Club, playing centre half and making the most of what was on offer. In terms of the pitch, that wasn't much: the constant rain meant it was more like a ploughed field than a well-tended pitch and the area round the goal was usually a sea of mud. The changing rooms consisted of a wooden hut; there was another hut for the supporters' social club; the terracing was cinder; and when Bert arrived there was just one small stand. But the atmosphere and enthusiasm were terrific, the supporters coming mostly from Bold Colliery, which stood at the far end of the field, or from the Pilkington Glass works, the other big employer in the area.

One Saturday that autumn was typical enough. Bert had thought through the game in his mind, as he always did, lying in bed in his hostel on the Friday night. What mistakes had he made the previous Saturday? Who were the dangerous players in the Earlstown team they were playing that weekend? What were their quirks? How should he tackle the new striker? All the usual things he went through every Friday night before the Saturday match. Come the morning, it was pouring with rain. He made his way to the bus stop and got to St Helens with a good hour to spare; Bert always liked to have time in the changing hut to prepare himself, physically and mentally. In those days the goalies wore polo-neck pullovers made of wool. They were an absolute liability in wet weather, absorbing the rain in no time till they hung heavy and shapeless almost down to the knees, with the sleeves flapping over the hands. By the end of the season the colour – blue, green, maroon or whatever it had once been – was all washed out of it, only leaving a few traces round the edges. In the really cold weather some goalies wore gloves, woollen again, with the tips of the fingers cut off. But Bert never did; he'd rather freeze. Once you'd been through a Russian winter you could bear any amount of sleet and ice.

The pitch was waterlogged by the time the game started that Saturday, the goal-mouth the usual sea of mud. The spectators stood watching wrapped up in raincoats, scarves, cloth caps and some with umbrellas; nothing could keep them away. By half-time the score was 1–0 to St Helens Town. Funny, thought Bert. You could have a day of bright sunshine with the pitch in perfect order, and nothing goes right for you. Then there's a day like this one, with the rain pouring down so you can hardly see, and everything goes right.

The two teams retired to the hut for a warm-up and a bit of a dry-out, though nothing made much difference. Bert slid around the goal during the second half, covered in mud, just as he had during the first, till he saw their new striker racing down the field towards him, unchallenged. How often had he gone through this in his mind? The St Helens Town defence was nowhere to be seen, lost in the driving rain. It wasn't Bert's style to hang around in goal and wait for the ball; the old *Fallschirmjäger* nearly always decided to attack, so now he tore out of goal to intercept the Earlstown striker. As he did, he already knew he'd made a mistake and he was too late. Footballs in those days were made of leather, with laces, which made them hard and heavy, and once they were wet, really heavy. The ball hit Bert full in the face, and knocked him out, totally. He was sprawled on the ground in the mud, and there were no doctors like now, waiting in the stands ready with whatever, just a sponge and freezing-cold water to bring him round. It took a good two minutes, but then he was up again, refusing to go off, with the supporters wildly cheering their man, their Jerry goalie, who was frightened of nothing and never gave up.

For the away games the St Helens Town supporters followed their team all round Lancashire, cheering their Jerry, with other spectators turning up from miles around just to watch him. It was curiosity really. Was he really as good as they said he was? They soon found he was, and so his fame spread. Recalling it 60 years later he explained, 'They gave me respect and made me feel like a human being again and I'll always be grateful for it.' By the end of the season St Helens Town had won the George Mahon Cup, beating Runcorn Reserves in a thrilling final at the Prescot Cable grounds, and gaining Bert his first medal in English football.

One Saturday shortly before Christmas Jack Friar invited Bert home to tea with the family after the match. Bert was based at Huyton by then, doing bomb disposal work clearing mines in the Liverpool and Manchester docks and living in a POW hostel with few comforts, so he was only too pleased to accept. The Friars lived in Marshalls Cross Road in the Sutton district of St Helens, a nice part of town full of decent-sized detached and semi-detached houses with well-kept front and back gardens. Bert, always fussy about his appearance and feeling a bit nervous, spruced himself up for the occasion, wearing a newly acquired sports jacket with his shoes well polished. The Friars had two daughters, Margaret, who was eighteen and Barbara, ten. 'I don't like Germans,' announced Margaret before Bert arrived. 'If that German's coming to tea, I'm going out.' And out she went, to the cinema to see *For Whom the Bell Tolls*, with Bill Twist, who was her boyfriend at the time. But Barbara was different: when Bert arrived, bringing a bunch of flowers for Mrs Friar, German style, Barbara instantly fell in love with him. Who says a ten-year-old can't fall in love? When they sat down for tea she sat beside Bert, so close she was almost in his lap, and when he left she stood in the bay window and watched him walking down the road to the bus stop till he was out of sight.

In the event, Bert gave St Helens Town plenty of notice that he'd be going home for a month in January and they took it surprisingly well, only asking him to present himself at the cafe in the High Street the day before he left because they had something they wanted to say to him. 'Will you come at ten o'clock?' they asked. 'Certainly,' said Bert, giving it no more thought. He played his last league match on the Saturday and let in two easy goals, which didn't please the spectators much. The pitch was heavy with rain as usual even though volunteers had worked hard to drain off the surplus water beforehand, but the reason lay elsewhere: Bert's mind wasn't on the game, it was already racing ahead, to Bremen and home to Wischusenstrasse 32. He hadn't seen his family for six years, since his last and only leave from the Russian Front in January 1943. In fact, since he was seventeen he'd hardly seen them at all.

The meeting was on the Monday, and when Bert walked into the cafe he couldn't have been more surprised: the whole supporters' club committee was sitting there at the tables with cups of tea all round, and there was a travelling trunk with iron hinges and leather straps in the middle of the floor, a huge thing which must have weighed fifty pounds or more.

'Hi there, big fella,' they greeted him. 'We know you're going to see your mum and dad, and of course we're sorry you're not going to play for us, but we're pleased for you, and we'd like you to take this with you for your family because we know things are tight over there.'

They indicated the trunk and urged him to open it and have a look. There was everything in there: bacon, butter, sugar, flour, cheese, tins of condensed milk, tins of peaches, even cakes, home-baked, everything; and most things were still rationed, so Lord knows how they had managed it. Then the chairman of the club handed him an envelope. 'And here's a bit for your mum and dad, for whatever they need.' There were fifty pound notes inside. Fifty. Collected from the St Helens Town supporters, though they earned little enough themselves. Bert was speechless, choked, and he was still choked years later, talking about it.

It was easy enough getting the trunk to the station because they took it on a cart, but it wasn't so easy after that, getting it off the train at Manchester then onto the boat train to Harwich, then on and off the boat and onto to the train to Bremen, dragging it all the way, sometimes with help, sometimes not, and with his kitbag slung over his shoulder too.

Bert started feeling apprehensive on the train from the Hook of Holland to Bremen, nearing home. It had been so long, and so much had happened, how would it be? How would he find his mother, knowing she hadn't been well, as Karl Heinz had written? Why didn't his father have a job? What would they talk about? How would he feel? As he looked out of the train window at the flat, white, snow-covered land of northern Germany, he reflected again on the scene in the cafe two days before, and the trunk of food, which was now stuck halfway under his seat so as not to hinder the other travellers, who were mostly British soldiers doing their two years military service in Germany. He remembered coming home to Wischusenstrasse in 1943 with the Führer parcel, and now this trunk, each filled with provisions for his family, the one from Hitler a personal gesture, they were told, to his brave *Kameraden* at the front, the other from the supporters' club of St Helens Town. What was the difference? He knew it now: one was an act of propaganda, the other an act of pure kindness.

He got help with the trunk at Bremen *Hauptbahnhof* and caught a tram which took him to the Heerstrasse. When he got off at the top of Wischusenstrasse he stopped to look around and prepare himself, just as he had in 1943. Then he set off down the road, dragging the trunk through the snow with the help of a dozen small boys in hand-knitted balaclavas like the one he used to wear when he was a boy. Then there he was, in front of number 32, looking up at the kitchen window. He left the trunk in the entrance and ran up the stairs two by two, past the Mrozinzskys' and straight into the flat.

His mother didn't know exactly when he was coming; she just knew from his last letter that he had a month's leave and would be arriving some time in early January, so she'd waited for him day after day, jumping up every time she heard a noise in the street or down the stairs. But this afternoon the wireless was on and she hadn't heard a thing. When he walked in so suddenly, she just threw herself into his arms sobbing; it was too much for both of them after all these long years, and he, the hard man of Russia, was crying too. His father stood up to greet him, looking awkwardly pleased, clapping him on the back: '*So Berni. Bist wieder nach Hause gekommen.*' So, Berni, you've come home again. That made Bert/Berni smile because there'd been a sentimental song during the war which went just like that: '*Junge komm bald wieder, bald wieder nach Haus.*' Son, back home to us soon, very soon.

Karl Heinz was there as well, looking like a grown man now and shaking Bernd rather formally by the hand, but there was no Helga. She hadn't liked living with her mother and her stepfather, a cruel man by all accounts, and she'd left home as soon as possible to marry a man from Danzig, one of the hundreds of thousands of refugees who'd made the great trek from the west after the war, fleeing the Russians. Bernd shook his head; it was hard to imagine little Helga married.

Once everyone had settled down Bernd mentioned the trunk and he and Karl Heinz went to fetch it. '*So, Berni, bist wieder hier!*' Frau Mrozinzsky was standing in the door of her flat, arms folded, smiling, looking a bit older and thinner, but just the same as ever. Berni had to laugh. '*Ja, hier bin ich!*' Yes, here I am.

But was he? It was all so strange, he hardly knew. Was he Berni, or Bernd, or Bert?

When his mother opened the trunk and saw what was inside she just stood there crying her eyes out, and when Bernd gave her the envelope with the 50 pound notes inside, she cried some more. 'This is from England?' Bernd nodded. 'But how?' It was unbelievable – no one could take it in. The money was even better than the food, because by 1949 there was food in the shops again in Germany, perhaps more than in England, but no one except the rich had the money to buy it. Frau Trautmann just shook her head again and again, looking through everything she found in that trunk, trying to understand what it meant, crying.

Bernd tried to explain it to them later. 'They've been very kind to me over there, *Mutti*,' he said. 'Once we could get out of the camp and meet the people we soon found out they were no different to us.'

She nodded, not really understanding, but seeing he meant it. His father was non-committal, Karl Heinz hostile; he'd fought in Hungary during those last desperate months, then made a run for it, all the way home in a stolen farm cart, on his own, through deserted towns and torched villages, along blasted roads with no signs left to guide him, 900 kilometres, with the Russians only hours behind. That's how tough Karl Heinz turned out to be, so now he was in no mood to listen to stories about the kindness of the English.

'Everywhere you go in England, they offer you a cup of tea,' Bernd told them, still trying to explain. 'Friendliness, kindness, forgiveness; that's what I found there, everywhere I went.'

Karl Heinz left the table. '*Bist ein verdammter Engländer geworden!*' he accused. You've become a damned Englishman.

During that first week, as Bernd told his version of England to various members of his family, the aunts, his Uncle Karli, his Uncle Hans, who'd lost his son Hansi in the war, his old school friends, those who'd survived, and to his father's pals at the *Gasthof*, he nearly always met with the same reaction: they didn't believe him or, more likely, they didn't want to believe him. The trouble was that in early 1949 ordinary people in Germany still refused to blame Hitler for the war. They'd suffered too much to admit that the whole thing had been a terrible aberration and all in vain. They were happy to blame the Nazi hierarchy, and happier still to blame the Allies, but not Hitler, their Führer, who had solved un-employment, righted the injustices of the Versailles Treaty and made the Reich great again. At first Bernd was frustrated and kept trying to explain, but he soon gave up and learnt to keep his mouth shut. He realised the problem: they hadn't had the benefit of meeting the enemy at first hand, in peacetime and under a proper democratic system. They were still traumatised by the war, and still brainwashed by Nazi propaganda.

Of course he would have had a different reaction from the old communists and socialists of Bremen, like his Uncle Bencken, who'd been incarcerated till 1943 and only let out then to help the war effort, but Bernd didn't know many others. The people Bernd met had suffered bitterly during the war, followed by the humiliation of defeat. Bremen was in the American zone, and although the young had adapted easily enough, liking the GIs' easy-going ways with their chewing gum for the children and their nylons for the girls, most people resented them, hated the occupation, and couldn't get over the war and the loss of everything promised them by the Nazis during the exhilarating days of the 1930s.

Apart from seeing his family and friends Bernd managed to fit in a couple of games with his old club Tura, playing in goal. It was strange being there, leaping for the ball just as before, like leaping across time, he thought, almost as though the war had never happened. Sitting around in the dressing room afterwards he told his team-mates a bit about England, but not much, because he'd learnt his lesson by now, and because, in truth, there were times when he felt just like they did, forgetting the Englishman he'd become and feeling the same sense of bitterness and anger as they did, a German *Kamerad* once again.

He felt it most strongly when he went down to the Bremen docks with his father, which had been bombed to smithereens, 80 per cent completely gone. It was so shocking, so bitter, he could hardly bear to think of those carefree days when he used to bicycle down there with his father's midday meal, racing across the railway tracks and through the entrance gates to the Kali quay, past the docked ships and on to the canteen, where his father was waiting for him, seated at a long table with all the other loaders and dock workers. Now there was virtually nothing left. He bent to pick up a piece of wood with some lettering on it. 'Look at this, Vati,' He showed him the red letters. '*Achtung!*' was just legible, the remains of a notice written in the Gothic German script, Signs like this had been up everywhere in the docks in the old days, warning of the danger of overhead loads, long before the war, when the word gained another meaning entirely. You might be sad about what happened to the Liverpool docks and Coventry, he accused the English in his mind, but just look at what you did here. Which was worse? At that moment Bernd didn't think that none of this would have happened without Hitler and the Nazis, not Bremen, not Liverpool; he just saw it as tit for tat, proof that all war was bad, for everyone.

He felt the same anger when he looked at his mother at moments when she didn't realise he was watching her and wasn't putting on a good front. It hurt him to see how worn out and ill she looked, she who never hurt a fly, completely done in. He knew she'd been seriously ill during the war but why wasn't she better now, why wasn't she recovering?

He knew the answer, deep down. His father and brother were both still unemployed and there was a reason for that. It wasn't fair, but that's what happened after wars: retribution, revenge, score-settling. The Nuremberg trials had sentenced a few top Nazis to death, and a few more to some years in prison, but most of them had got away scot-free. Later came the local de-nazification trials, at which those who had suffered under the Nazis before the war could finally have their say and get some justice. Bremen had always had a lot of communists and socialists, especially in the docks. In the elections of November 1932 the SPD and the KPD together with the Centre parties had gained 64.5 per cent of the vote, in contrast to the nation as a whole, where they gained 45.9 per cent, while the Nazi Party only gained 20.2 per cent, compared with 33.1 per cent nationwide. Herr Trautmann had voted for one of the Centre parties, but later he became a member of the Nazi Party and benefited from it, keeping his job when others lost theirs. As a result, he was tried by the Bremen de-nazification courts and found guilty. His crime wasn't deemed serious enough for him to be sent to prison, but he lost his job and didn't get it back for over three years.

Frau Trautmann's depression was due to the humiliation and hardship caused by her husband's unemployment, but it went deeper than that: she was suffering from a fundamental loss of hope, because of the war and its aftermath, but mainly because Berni, her most loved son, had gone to England and might never come back. They both knew he'd changed and a link had been broken. Bernd hated to admit it, even to himself, but at the end of the month's leave he was glad to be going back to England, back to his other life – relieved and happy and sad, all mixed in together.

The reason so many top Nazis had escaped punishment was tied up with the Western Allies' extreme fear of communism. It was argued there weren't enough competent men to rule the new Germany unless they made use of many of those who had held high government positions in the 1930s, during the Nazi period. The fact that there had all along existed a secret government in waiting, led by members of the opposition to Hitler, in the government, the Foreign Office, the High Command, in business and industry, all people known to the Allies, was completely ignored. The threat of communism dominated the debate, with the result that many of Chancellor Adenauer's cabinet and party were old Nazis. Not for the first time nor the last it was the little men like Herr Trautmann, caught up in the mayhem created by the real perpetrators, who paid the price.

That, or people who were completely innocent. Worst by far was the case of Ernst von Weizsaecker, the former secretary of state at the Foreign Office. Everyone active in the German opposition, those who were still alive, knew that von Weizsaecker had been one of their truest and most courageous members, his bravery continuing even after Hitler put Ribbentrop into the Wilhelmstrasse to spy on the diplomats, who were known to be secretly anti-Hitler, after which it became even more dangerous to act. At great personal risk to himself and his family he had many secret meetings with Carl Burckhardt, vice president of the International Red Cross, based in Geneva, who acted as one of the opposition's emissaries to the British government. Nevertheless, once the main Nuremberg trials were over the Americans instituted their own further proceedings against other individuals, including members of the army High Command, industrialists and senior civil servants. One case dealt with the central administration of the Third Reich, and it was in this that von Weizsaecker was arraigned, charged with planning and initiating aggressive war and crimes against humanity. There were plenty of affidavits from surviving members of the opposition, and Carl Burckhardt handed over twelve pages of his secret diaries recording his meetings with von Weizsaecker before and during the war, but all to no avail. There was no official written evidence of his opposition, said the prosecution, ignoring the fact that to write anything down in Hitler's Third Reich was tantamount to suicide. Von Weizsaecker was sentenced to seven years in prison, later reduced to five. 'It appears that, after careful weighing of the evidence and pointing out that it was chiefly in favour of von Weizsaecker, the majority of the judges reached the judgement, nevertheless, that he was guilty,' reads a London Foreign Office memo, as ever non-committal.

The Western Allies made no real distinction between Germans and Nazis. In the post-war period it was politic to have no good Germans, and a whole generation of young people in England, France and America grew up with the idea that there was something wrong with the German make-up, an aggressive, warlike Teutonic flaw, existing side by side with a mass mentality which caused them to obey orders without question. And the youth of Germany was landed with the guilt of their father's actions, even those who had never been Nazis and had only lived in fear of them.

There are times when a nation's dilemma finds expression in some aspect of an individual's life. When Bernd got back to England he was always trying to be the good German. It was a resolve which he wasn't even fully aware of himself, but somewhere along the line, during those weeks back home in

Bremen, he'd picked up the idea that he should show the English that there were good Germans as well as bad. It was a strange idea, but he felt it powerfully, and from then on he was determined to be always polite, always fair, always friendly, and always smartly dressed with neatly pressed trousers, freshly laundered shirt and his usual well-polished shoes. The appearance came easily to him, but the rest sometimes needed a bit of effort, because he still had his temper and his bouts of intolerance, especially on the football pitch; but mostly he managed it.

Once back, Bernd now Bert again, returned to his bomb disposal work in the Liverpool and Manchester docks, and to football with St Helens Town every weekend, it already being the mid-season. But not long after his return he fell ill with a chest infection, perhaps a leftover from his years on the Russian Front. Bert was laid up in his POW hostel at Huyton feeling miserable and alone when Jack Friar turned up, got him out of his hard camp bed and into the waiting Hillman Minx, off to Marshalls Cross Road.

It was heaven for Bert to be lying in a proper bed in an airy room with windows onto a garden, being looked after by Dr Chisnall, the family doctor, and Mrs Friar, who fussed around him much as his mother might have done. Even Granny Winstanley, Mrs Friar's mother, who lived with them and who'd refused to talk to the German at first, began to like him now, deciding he couldn't have been a Nazi because he had such nice manners. To Bert, after years of living rough in Russia and France and another four years in POW camps, it felt like a palace. Bert hadn't had a home for years and he yearned for one, and for a family, and to belong, and all this he found at Marshalls Cross Road.

So it came as a shock to hear that he was being transferred to Bristol, to a new bomb disposal unit. He didn't want to go, and nor did Jack Friar want to lose him, he who was almost like a son now, and their star footballer, pulling in crowds like they'd never seen before. Everywhere Bert went in St Helens he was invited in for a cup of tea, and he couldn't walk down the road without schoolboys running up to him asking for his autograph. And then there were the girls. As Bert's fame spread, more and more of them turned up to the matches, waiting for him at the end of the game, literally throwing themselves at the tall, blond Jerry, and quite ignoring the other players, who never got a look-in. It was strange to Bert, this local fame, because under the athletic good looks and a certain arrogance about his sporting superiority he was basically modest and uncertain of himself, aware that he'd left school at fourteen with no proper education, and still confused by what had happened to him during the Nazi years, the war and captivity. But as time went on, and with the careful guidance of Jack Friar – in all matters not only football – he gradually gained in confidence and began to enjoy his popularity, growing more relaxed by the day. But now he was being sent to Bristol, away from it all – the football, the fun, and his new home.

It was May when Bert arrived in Bristol, the start of a perfect English summer with gardens in bloom, boys in shorts and plimsolls, and old ladies on park benches doing their knitting in the sun. When he arrived at the POW camp Bert found Karl Krause there, one of his old Camp 50 football *Kameraden*, who'd also decided to stay on for a year to earn some money before going back home to Germany. Krause was working as an electrician, which is what he'd been before the war, and playing as an amateur for Bristol City Reserves.

'Come and join us at Bristol City,' said Karl to Bert one day as they were kicking a football around up on Clifton Downs. 'Alex Eisentraeger's here too, and doing well. Come and join us when training starts again next week.'

Bert said no, he couldn't do it; his loyalty was to St Helens Town. And just as well, because it turned out he wasn't in Bristol for long – Jack Friar saw to that. With a bit of string-pulling he managed to get hold of the local MP, Hartley Shawcross, who soon fixed things up and got Bert transferred back to the bomb disposal unit at Huyton, just in time to start training for the next season.

Once Bert was back with St Helens Town things moved fast. First Jack Friar applied to have Bert living at home with them so he wouldn't have to travel to and fro from Huyton every weekend for the match and would more easily be on hand for training. He got the permission of course, with a bit more string-pulling, and no one was happier than Bert, who longed for nothing more than to have a roof over his head, a home and a family. By October he was living with the Friars full time, and by December it was clear that Margaret was pregnant. Bert just couldn't believe he'd been so stupid a second time. As for Margaret, beneath all the posturing about not wanting 'that German' in the house and flouncing out with Bill Twist, she'd made her mind up long ago to get Bert, only she didn't tell anyone. It caused quite a falling-out between Bert and Bill Twist, who up till then had been good pals, and it broke many another girl's heart, which was all to the good as far as Margaret was concerned, who was high-spirited and a bit of a flirt. They were married at the local church on 30 March 1950, with Margaret already showing but not so much she couldn't get away with it. Bert's old POW friend Rudi Hering was best man, and the church was crammed with family and friends and well-wishers, including the local press. The only people missing were Herr and Frau Trautmann, who were unable to attend due to ill health and lack of money.

15

Cup Final

The Jerry goalie's fame was spreading fast and football scouts were sniffing about. Bert knew about them even before he was transferred to the Bristol bomb disposal unit, but when the 1949/50 season came round he signed for St Helens Town again, out of loyalty and gratitude, and because he loved the people there. The club was in the Second Division of the Lancashire Combination now and doing well, but the season had hardly started before the scouts were back in force from all over: Bolton Wanderers, Everton, Burnley, Doncaster Rovers and, in late September, Manchester City, who were looking for a replacement for the great Frank Swift. 'Big Swifty', a legendary goalkeeper, though semi-retired was still playing part time for them because City couldn't find a replacement. Jack Friar saw how it was and knew they couldn't keep Bert for much longer – he was too good was the truth of it – but he warned Bert not to act hastily, to take his time and think carefully about his long-term career in the game, and where he might be happiest. Bert didn't fully appreciate the significance of this advice at the time, but he soon found out.

Jack Friar favoured Burnley and had already had informal talks with the club's officials on Bert's behalf; he'd even started negotiations for Bert to get a job with the local National Coal Board, because alien footballers in England couldn't go professional till 1952 and had to find a way of earning a living as well as playing. But then Manchester City joined the race and things became confused, in Bert's mind at least. City officials came to St Helens Town for a secret meeting on 6 October 1949. Jack Friar wasn't at the meeting because he was working in Stockport by then, having taken a new job as manager of the Co-op there. The press, getting wind of a good story, were hanging around outside, but were told nothing. That evening, after the meeting, the Manchester City lot turned up unannounced at Marshalls Cross Road, determined to persuade Bert to join the club. They stayed for four hours, talking on and on, and by the end of it Bert had signed a contract. Perhaps he wouldn't have signed if Jack had been there, but Jack didn't get home till after midnight, tired and furious. He'd gone to Manchester for a meeting with City officials which never materialised because no one turned up.

'I've signed for Manchester City.'

Bert thought it best to come out with it straight away. He didn't know where Jack Friar had been, nor why he was home so late, but he'd waited up for him, feeling bad because Jack had warned him never to sign anything without first discussing it with him, and because he knew that Jack wanted him to join Burnley. Jack Friar realised at once what had gone on. 'Well, you've made your bed, now you'll have to lie in it,' he said, and he left the room without another word.

The next day the papers were full of the news: Manchester City were about to sign Bert Trautmann, the St Helens Town goalkeeper, a German and a one-time Nazi at that. The reaction was ferocious, and took Bert, though not Jack Friar, completely by surprise. Manchester had a large Jewish community dating from before the

First World War, augmented by refugees from Nazi Germany, and now they bombarded the *Manchester Evening News* and the *Manchester Evening Chronicle* with hundreds of abusive letters and phone calls and demonstrated outside City's Maine Road stadium, over 25,000 of them, shouting and waving placards emblazoned with swastikas, 'Nazi!' and 'War Criminal!', threatening to boycott the club unless they got rid of the German. 'When I think of all those millions of Jews who were tortured and murdered, I can only marvel at Man City's crass stupidity,' wrote 'a disgusted season ticket holder'. Another wrote, 'I have been a City supporter for forty-five years but if this German plays, I will ask members of the British Legion and the Jewish ex-Servicemen's Club to boycott the City Club.' Three ex-Servicemen wrote, 'City must be mad to think of signing this man.' A disabled ex-serviceman wrote of 'bitterness in my heart'. Many signed their letters 'Heil!'

Bert was shocked and upset, and didn't know what to do. Jack Friar advised him to keep his head down and wait for the storm to pass; Manchester City took no notice, simply concerned to get the best goalkeeper for the club. Bert stopped reading the newspapers, but it was everywhere and he couldn't get away from it. Then an open letter appeared in the *Manchester Evening Chronicle* from Dr Altmann, the communal rabbi of Manchester, responding to the proposed boycott of the club. 'Each member of the Jewish Community is entitled to his own opinion,' he wrote, 'but there is no concerted action inside the community in favour of this proposal. Despite the terrible cruelties we suffered at the Germans, [*sic*] we would not try to punish an individual German, who is unconnected with these crimes, out of hatred. If this footballer is a decent fellow, I would say there is no harm in it. Each case must be judged on its own merits.' Jack Friar brought Bert the newspaper. 'Read that, Bert,' he said, and left him to it.

Years later, thinking of the moment when he sat reading the letter in the sitting room of Marshalls Cross Road, Bert still felt like crying. He did that day, with his head in his hands and the paper open on his lap. He was so moved, so grateful, that a Jewish refugee from Nazi Germany and a leader of his community could write like that, absolving him, the *Fallschirmjäger* who had seen what he'd seen and done what he'd done in the Ukraine and Russia, and offer him the hand of friendship. It was unbelievable to Bert, who knew very well why the Jews of Manchester had reacted the way they had, and he thanked Dr Altmann silently, vowing to express it to him personally as soon as he could.

He was still feeling bad on 11 October, when he went to meet his new Manchester City team-mates, travelling by train from St Helens to Manchester and then by bus from the station to Maine Road stadium, which was in Moss Side, a tough working-class district with rows of small terraced houses giving straight onto dark cobbled streets. It was raining too, and by the time Bert arrived he was wet through as well as nervous. They were all there waiting for him in the dressing room, including the captain Eric Westwood, who Bert knew had fought in Normandy, probably not far from where Bert had fought himself. But as Bert came in, Eric stepped forward to greet him, hand outstretched. 'There's no war in this dressing room,' he said. 'We welcome you as any other member of staff. Just make yourself at home – and good luck.' It was magnificent, thought Bert, and he felt much better afterwards, but he still had to face the City supporters, and how would he manage that?

He made his debut with the City Reserves on 15 October 1949, in an away game against Barnsley, which they lost 1–0, though it could have been much worse. Normally a reserves game didn't attract the journalists, but they came in force to this one, to watch the new Jerry goalie and assess just how good he was. 'Trautmann is going to be one of the goalkeeper discoveries of recent years,' reported *The Times* the next day, while the local papers agreed Manchester City had found their replacement for Frank Swift.

Bert played only five games with the Reserves before making his debut in the First Division against Bolton Wanderers on 19 November at their Burnden Park stadium. It was nerve-racking waiting to go out there in front of a packed crowd of 35,000, including plenty of the Manchester City protestors, with the press stand full to the brim, and Bert was sitting in the dressing room trying to keep calm and prepare himself when Frank Swift walked in. Big Swifty was a father figure to the team, and now he came to sit on the bench next to Bert. 'You're playing your first league game, son.' Big Swifty called everyone 'son'. 'I'll give you a piece of advice: when you go out, ignore the crowd completely. They're not there, son, you don't even see them.' They both knew what Big Swifty was talking about. The catcalls started as soon as Bert emerged from the tunnel – 'Nazi!' and 'Heil Hitler!' and 'Sieg Heil!' right through the game – but he did what Big Swifty said, and never even looked at the crowd. They lost 3–0 and Bert left the field feeling fed-up, especially about the first goal, a penalty he should never have let in. But Frank Swift was back in the dressing room waiting for him. 'Good lad,' he said. 'You'll do.' Everything was fine after that, and when Bert played his next game, a home fixture at Maine Road against Birmingham City, they won 4–0. By the end of the season there were no more catcalls; as a matter of fact, those same people who had protested so much would have blasted anyone who criticised Trautmann, their very own goalkeeper.

The big test came on 14 January 1950, Manchester City's first game down in London, against Fulham. The morning before, Jack Friar told him, 'You've done nothing yet, Bert. What you have to do now is get the whole of the national press behind you down south, so when you go out on that pitch you'll have to play as you've never played before.' Then it was off to London on the coach, to Bailey's Hotel in Gloucester Road, where the team always stayed for their London matches. Seeing the bomb sites left over from the Blitz, Bert worried about the Londoners' reactions to a German goalie, as well as the reaction of the London Jews, some of whom had been sending hate mail. But he was encouraged by the hundreds of Manchester City supporters who travelled down for the match and did their best to drown out the hostile catcalls with their cheers. City lost 1–0, but it could easily have been 6–0 if it hadn't been for Bert. For some reason almost everything came off for him that day and he could do no wrong, stopping all the shots except that one, which was the one which counted as far as the result was concerned, but not for anything else. As Bert walked off the field at the end of the game the whole stadium stood up, cheering him, and the two teams lined up on either side of the players' entrance, clapping him off.

The next day the papers were full of it, the *Daily Express* including a photograph of one of Bert's amazing saves with four Fulham men crowding around goal and Bert way out, taking possession of the ball, calling it 'one of Bernhard (Bert) Trautmann's spectacular leaps in defence of the goal'. Beaming, Jack Friar brought back a copy from the local newsagent's and showed Bert. It was one of the proudest days of Bert's life, and from then on something changed for him, because now he knew he was accepted by the British public, and he felt he belonged.

Everything was changing in Britain in the early 1950s. The trauma of the war years was abating and the post-war romance with Labour was beginning to fade. The Attlee government called an election for 23 February 1950, not realising how much the mood had altered, and were more than pleased with the big turnout, helped perhaps by the weather, which was not bad for February though it turned to rain towards evening. As the first results came through during the night and into the early hours of the next day they had every reason to feel optimistic that they'd be voted back with a good enough majority to continue their policies of nationalisation, welfare and education reform, which they'd so successfully launched during the previous four years. But the early results came mostly from the cities with large working-class populations, and as the day progressed rural and especially suburban voters showed that change was in the air. Not everyone in England was quite as happy with Labour's sweeping reforms as they had been in the immediate post-war years.

Crowds gathered in all the city centres, where the results were displayed on large boards, constantly updated as each one came in. The atmosphere was friendly and cheerful, almost a holiday mood, with the young wandering around in their duffel coats and scarves, singing and waving their placards, heralding the new age of the teenager. The final result came as something of a shock: 315 for Labour, 298 for the Conservatives, 9 for the two Liberal parties, 2 for the Irish Nationalists, and none for the Communists, leaving Labour with a slim majority of 5, which was no majority at all.

It meant Labour couldn't pursue their policies and would soon have to call another election, which they did the following year. This time the Conservatives, led again by Winston Churchill and buoyed up by the 1950 results, played strongly to the rural and suburban vote, stressing continuing housing problems, massive Labour expenditure and high taxes, which mostly hit the struggling middle classes. The Conservatives won a slim majority, much as Labour had the previous year, not the landslide some had predicted. A young Margaret Roberts, future prime minister, lost at Deptford; Attlee personally gained a large majority of over 11,000 at his West Walthamstow constituency, but the next day he went to Buckingham Palace and tendered his resignation to the King.

Bert watched the democratic process from the sidelines, fascinated by the workings of a system unknown in Nazi Germany, and surprised at the depth of passion it aroused, especially in the working-class districts and mining towns of Lancashire he'd come to know so well over the past five years. By now he'd been fixed up with a job as a motor mechanic at Proctor's Garage in the Greater Manchester district of Hulme, owned by William Proctor, a long-standing Manchester City fan. It was strange being back in a garage, covered in grease, just as he had been all those years ago at Hanomag, before the war and the Holocaust and everything else. But Bert loved the job, not least because the clients were salt-of-the-earth types, full of humour and friendliness, many of them Manchester City supporters who kept coming in for his autograph.

In 1950 the Friar family, including Barbara, Granny Winstanley, Margaret and Bert, moved to the village of Bramhall in Cheshire because of Jack Friar's job at Stockport. John was born there in October, a beautiful baby, blond and blue-eyed like his father. Bert was crazy about him and took him everywhere, showing him off, feeling proud because he was a father now and a proper member of the Friar family, with a wife, a father-in-law, mother-in-law, sister-in-law and all the rest.

Bert spent most of his spare time with his team-mates at Manchester City, either playing or training, and they were steadily growing into a strong team. In those days training was stamina-based, so they ran every day, first up and down the stands forty times a session then twenty miles on the road. It made them tough, which they needed on pitches which were often waterlogged and more mud than grass. But Bert was happy, back to what he did best, and he loved the camaraderie, which was different to what he had had with the *Kameraden*, but just as good. Only his wife presented problems. 'Highly strung' is how some people described Margaret; others called her spoilt. Bert found her hard to please, and every time she was annoyed she brought up the fact that he was German, just to annoy him. Margaret loved the glamour of football and the local fame, but she wasn't happy with how much of Bert's time and energy the game consumed, and the way the women still threw themselves at him. But she was always a good mother, as Bert was the first to admit. 'You should have married me,' said Barbara, still mooning after Bert and seeing how it was between them.

All this time Bert was improving his game, watching other players, studying them, especially goalkeepers, and always learning. Early on there was Ted Sagar, the Everton goalie, with his sound positional sense and his safe pair of hands; later there was Sam Bartram, goalkeeper at Charlton Athletic, who made incredible saves in an unorthodox style, wandering up to the halfway line or clearing the ball with a header, keeping the crowds well entertained at the same time – which was, Bert knew, all part of the job. Bert admired fullbacks like Bill Eckersley of Blackburn Rovers, with his ferocious penalty kicks, and forwards like Stanley Matthews of Blackpool. Tom Finney of Preston North End, Bert reckoned to be one of the greatest players of all, a man you could kick to the ground, and he'd be up again, wiping his shorts, and never say a dicky bird. Nat Lofthouse of Bolton Wanderers always worried Bert as he tore down the pitch making for goal, as did Johnny Hancocks of Wolverhampton Wanderers, the 'Mighty Atom', one of the smallest men in football, who attacked the goal with incredible power and accuracy. There were so many great players, thought Bert; the only thing England lacked was the club system they had in Germany when he was a boy, to bring on gifted young players. Matt Busby at Manchester United seemed to be the only manager with that kind of foresight. Still, there were two things no one could teach a goalkeeper: natural talent and what Bert called 'heart' – fearlessness, which in Bert's case had always been there, honed by years of fighting the partisans in Russia. After that, nothing much would frighten Bert Trautmann ever again.

The next season Les McDowall took over as manager of Manchester City and things quickly began to change. He brought Don Revie, Jimmy Meadows, Dave Ewing and Roy Clarke into the side, with Roy Paul as captain, and the team won promotion into the First Division. Bert was due to report for training in July when a letter arrived from home, from Karl Heinz, in itself unusual, explaining that things were not good at Wischusenstrasse: he and *Vati* still out of work, and *Mutti*'s health was worse, her spirits very low. Bert sat at breakfast with his tea and toast, reading and re-reading the letter, trying to think what to do. He decided to go home for three weeks, and went to ask Les McDowall's permission.

To get to Bremen, Bert had to fly to Düsseldorf. Peter Kularz, his old *Kamerad* from Russia, was coming to meet him at the airport, and they were planning to spend a day or two talking about old times, catching up, before Bert travelled on. The last Bert/Bernd had heard of Peter was that he'd been dumped half dead in the back of an army truck and taken off to a field hospital; he'd never even had time to say goodbye, and for years had no idea where he was, of if he was even alive. But as news of Bert's fame at Manchester City spread, it made the newspapers in Germany, and Kularz got in touch. They'd exchanged a couple of letters since, and now they were going to meet after all that time. Bert knew Peter had been badly disfigured, but nevertheless he was surprised by the man who met him at Düsseldorf: he didn't recognise him at all, not even his voice. It later transpired that the man was an impostor who happened also to be called Kularz, and he'd written the letters hoping to get Bert to come over and sign for Cologne FC. Such are the surprising side-effects of fame. But by some poetic justice the real Peter Kularz, back living in Cologne, saw a photograph of Bert standing next to the impostor at Düsseldorf airport in the local paper. Incensed, he got in touch. And as soon as the real Peter Kularz walked in there was no mistaking him. In spite of the fact that half his face had been blown off, here was his old *Kamerad* with his same wry sense of humour and his same old warmth. Bernd and Peter spent many hours talking and reminiscing, but not once did either of them mention that night deep in the forest in the Ukraine and the horror of what they'd witnessed there.

Before Bernd travelled on to Bremen he and Peter went to visit his old POW football *Kamerad* Karl Krause at Gelsenkirchen, where he was working as the chauffeur of Herr Wildfang, the president of another famous German football club, Schalke. Both Cologne and Schalke made overtures to Trautmann, but Bert never said a word about it when he got back to Manchester City. Later he realised what a mistake he'd made, but for the time being he had other things on his mind: the situation at Wischusenstrasse was as bad as it could be. His father had temporarily left home, whether for another woman or out of sheer frustration over his unemployment was never clear. There was very little money because his brother, now married to Traudel, a refugee from the Sudetenland, was also still out of work. And as for his mother, Bernd could hardly bear to watch her as she struggled to put on a happy face and hold back the tears. When he left he knew he was breaking her heart all over again, and the only way he could console her was by promising to come back to Germany, this time for good.

Still he said nothing when he got back to Manchester City, Bert only dropped a few hints about Schalke to some of his team-mates; he even managed to feign surprise when Herr Wildfang and the trainer Fritz Szepan turned up for talks with City officials in November. It was two days before the news leaked out, but then it was all over the newspapers, causing an instant uproar. City fans were appalled at the thought of losing their Jerry hero, and club officials made it clear they had no intention of releasing Trautmann from his contract. The newspapers received hundreds of letters for and against. It was no more than the law of the jungle if players could be poached regardless of contracts, argued one. How can we talk of the democratic values we hoped to instil in the Germans when, at the first test, we abandon them ourselves, argued another in contrast. Finally Bert put his own case in an open letter to the *Manchester Evening Chronicle* on 3 December, under the headline WHY I MUST LEAVE MANCHESTER CITY. 'I am going back to Germany at the end of the season – no matter what happens,' he stated.

This is one of the hardest decisions I have ever had to make, and believe me I am taking this step only after considerable thought, realising as I do just what it would mean to my family in England, and to my many friends in the football world. My mind is made up and nothing can change my determination to return home. My only hope is when you have read my story you will understand why I am going back, and you will sympathise with me. This is the first time I have spoken freely of my home life in Germany, but I want to go back there because of a promise I made my mother when I saw her earlier this year. She lives with my younger brother, Karl, in Bremen, and for four years now she has been in very bad health. Indeed when I saw her I was shocked at her physical condition, and since my brother, a joiner, finds work very difficult to get, they are living in very poor circumstances. There is little I can do for them while I am in England and for that reason I promised to go back and try and help them . . . I am quite sincere when I tell you this, and I honestly feel that my duty as a son is to help my mother. After all, I have seen her only three times in the last twelve years, and I am afraid her health would break completely if I did not return.

He spoke of his wife and his son John, who would go with him to Germany, and his deep gratitude to his father-in-law Jack Friar, 'who has been my real friend and guide in everything I have undertaken in football', and to all the good friends he'd made through Manchester City, but his mind was made up: he had to go. Even taking into account the help he had with his English in writing it, you can hear Bert and Bernd and Berni in that letter, and feel how he was torn between his new life and the old, the confusion and sadness at everything he'd lost.

Before Bert made his decision he spent days thinking about his life, trying to work things out. In all that time Jack Friar never said a word, never tried to influence him one way or the other, that's what a great man he was. None of Bert's English family wanted him to go, least of all Margaret, who liked the comfort and safety of home, but Jack never said a word, just let him be. And then the drama passed, as suddenly as it had arisen. Another letter arrived from Bremen, again from Karl Heinz, with good news: *Vati* had got his job back and returned home; Karl Heinz himself was getting a job, and *Mutti* was feeling better, so there was no need for Berni to come home, just to make sure he visited often. Bert could feel his mother's hand in the letter, but he took it at face value, knowing how difficult it would be for Margaret to adjust to life in Germany, and how resistant Manchester City was to letting him go.

Up to 1952 Germans were still treated as aliens in Britain, and Bert had to present himself once a year for interrogation at Bellevue, an amusement park with a speedway, fairground and racetrack on the outskirts of Manchester. He was asked about his activities in Russia and in France after D-Day, his capture and his papers, which were all gone along with his dog tag, the same questions he was asked that first time at Kempton Park. The answers were also the same, except about Hitler, who he no longer saw as the great Führer, though privately he still felt that Hitler had done some good as well as bad: just think of those autobahns, and the way he'd restored Germany's pride after the humiliation of Versailles. But mostly the interrogation was cups of tea and friendly chat.

'I see you were between Wesel and Emmerich on 24 March 1945 when we came over, Bert.'

This was a new interrogator, and he'd been there fighting at the same time as Bert, so they got talking, reminiscing like old friends. It was when the Allies were launching their final assault across the Rhine, along a stretch of about 30 miles, and the sky was black with planes. Bert would never forget seeing paratroopers hanging from the trees, hundreds of them, mostly Canadians.

'How many planes do you think we used there?'

Bert thought it might be a thousand.

'I can tell you now,' said his new friend, 'including gliders, we used four thousand six hundred planes.'

The following summer there was a Manchester City tour of Germany with friendlies against Munich, Nuremberg, Stuttgart,

Würzburg and Wuppertal, after which Margaret and John would join him for a three-week stay in Bremen. There was a crowd of 35,000 for the match against 1860 München, and as they were leaving in the coach for the next lap of their tour a man was jumping up and down on the pavement outside, banging on the window by Bert's seat.

'Bernhard!' he was shouting. 'It's me, Kobitska!'

Bernhard stared at him for a minute, disorientated. Kobitska? *Mein Gott!* Kobitska! It was the sergeant who'd thrown him down the coal hole in the blockhouse somewhere in the Ukraine, that Christmas of 1943 when Bernd had got drunk as a lord on a bottle of *kümmel*. Bert asked the driver to wait for a bit, and he and Kobitska stood on the pavement for a few minutes, reminiscing about that time, with no remnants of animosity, only amazed laughter that there they were, alive and well, outside the 1860 München stadium, one a famous footballer, the other, as Bert noted, a funny fellow in a Bavarian jacket, not the fearsome sergeant he remembered at all.

Afterwards Bert sat alone in the coach for a long time, watching the Bavarian countryside slip by but not seeing it, remembering the winter waste of the Ukraine that Christmas, when he drowned out the fear and the longing for home with the *kümmel*. When they arrived at Nuremberg it was the same again, only this time the memory was of the Nazi rallies held there every year and his own triumphs and medals at the 1938 Youth Olympics in Berlin, coming second in the whole of the Reich and feeling so grand he could never even imagine feeling as low as he'd felt that Christmas in the Ukraine. Wuppertal brought him back to himself, where the advance publicity was all about Trautmann, forgetting the rest. 'Grand Football Match! Trautmann Against a Combined Wuppertal XI' read the posters, with 'Manchester City' added in very small lettering under Bert's name. 'Shall we go home and leave you to it, Bert?' asked the team. 'You're the captain now,' said Roy Paul, happily handing over the job. They won the game easily, with Bert doing his leaping and diving, stopping one shot after another. 'Up the Blues!' they heard chanted from somewhere in the stands. There was a British army barracks not far away, and Bert felt at home again.

That autumn, on 25 November 1953, Hungary beat England 3–0 at Wembley; later in the season they did it again in Budapest, only this time it was 7–1. Hungary were unbeatable all through the early 1950s, the 'Magnificent Magyars' taking the football world by storm. How did they do it? all the English teams were asking themselves, admiring their four strikers, Ferenc Puskás, Sándor Kocsis, József Bozsik and Nándor Hidegkuti, studying their tactics and their footwork. Les McDowall and Don Revie set themselves the task of working it out, and devised what came to be known as the Revie Plan, which made use of a deep-lying centre forward and a much more aggressive style of attack.

Trautmann, in goal, was key to the plan, building on his now-established style, described as a fine mixture of power, accuracy, fearlessness and elegance. Bert was never a goal-line keeper, preferring to go out aggressively to claim the ball and clear it, only ever standing on the line for a penalty. If a free kick or a corner was awarded to the other team, he positioned defenders on both posts to cover himself, and, once in possession of the ball, performed one of his legendary goal kicks or throws, which were so long they sent the ball well into the other half. If a forward barged him, which they could as long as both feet were on the ground, he'd go in sideways, meeting him with his shoulder. In the heat of the game Trautmann instinctively fell back on methods he'd learnt fighting the partisans in Russia, countering so hard it took the wind right out of them. 'Next time you barge me, I'll put you in hospital,' he might threaten a player, and likely as not they'd leave him alone for the next few games.

With the Revie Plan, Bert had to learn a new trick to add to his arsenal: instead of kicking or throwing the ball out to a waiting player, he kicked it ahead of him, as he was already running up the field. By the time the other team could react, the ball had already been passed to one of City's strikers, who headed straight for goal. It required length and precision from Bert, but he knew just how to do that from all those early years playing *Völkerball* at home in Bremen, when he had often been the last man standing on his side but still beat the opposition, catching the ball in his large hands and throwing it back with fearsome accuracy at one of the opposing team, till they were all out and he was the winner once again.

At first the Revie Plan didn't work well. The Reserves tried it out in the early part of the season with mixed results, and then the First Division team used it, against Preston North End, and lost disastrously 5–0. The trouble was, a new system needed time; changing tactics, playing more aggressively, it all needed practice, with no guarantee as to the final outcome. The fans were up in arms and the journalists were sceptical, but Les McDowall, the Board and the players were all behind it, knowing that something drastic was needed to stop the team slipping further down the league table. McDowall was the man in the firing line, but he stuck to his guns against all criticism, which Bert thought a fine thing, and the next big game, against Sheffield United at Maine Road, was a different story: they won 5–2, and there was no stopping them after that.

The 'old' Bert came out in the match against Charlton Athletic at Maine Road on 27 November 1954. The referee was a Mr G.W. Pullin of Bristol, and Bert had already had trouble with some of his decisions in the first half, but in the second he couldn't stand it any longer. 'Whoever made you a referee?' he shouted at Pullin, glaring him in the face till Roy Paul calmed him down. Charlton were four goals up when Pullin awarded them a penalty. Bert, beside himself, shouted and jeered at Pullin again, and would have hit him if Jimmy Meadows hadn't stood between them. Trautmann was booked and pandemonium broke out in the stadium. Bert sat on his haunches in the penalty area challenging Pullin to send him off, which he sensibly decided against, but when Eddie Firmani took the penalty for Charlton Athletic, Bert scowled and shrugged his shoulders and didn't even try to stop the goal – he was way, way past that. After the final whistle, as Pullin walked off the field and down into the tunnel to the dressing rooms, he was tripped by some unknown person and stumbled against Bert, who struck him across the face. Pullin was shocked and livid. The subsequent inquiry suspended Trautmann for a week, causing him to miss two important games. Bert felt ashamed of his behaviour and upset at the black mark against the 'good German', but deep down he reckoned it was worth it.

The 1954/5 season was the first of two Cup Final years for Manchester City. Some 75,000 spectators turned up at Maine Road to watch the two great local teams, City and United, battle it out in the fourth round, with the City fans cheering themselves hoarse as Joe Hayes and Don Revie scored the two winning goals. After that it was Luton on 19 February on a treacherous pitch covered in ice and snow in a blinding blizzard, so it was a miracle that Nobby Clarke managed to score their two winning goals. 'Let 'em all come!' was the atmosphere in the coach on the way back to Manchester after that match. Birmingham City, who had beaten them many times, were next up, in the sixth round, at St Andrews. The match was one of those thrillers, with Trautmann making two of his legendary saves, before Nobby Clarke took a free kick and, instead of doing the expected lob, slammed the ball low and hard to Jonny Hart, who flicked it into Birmingham's goal, and there they were in the semi-finals against Sunderland at Villa Park on 26 March, with the rain pouring down and the pitch so sodden it reminded Bert of nothing more than the Pripet Marshes. But Don Revie raced down the pitch like Hungary's Hidegkuti, with his back to Bert, who kicked the ball just ahead of him, and Nobby Clarke scored the winning goal with a great header after a brilliant cross from little Joe Hayes. The Revie Plan had worked and, against all the odds, City were in the 1955 Cup Final against Newcastle United at Wembley.

Wembley, the very thought sent shivers down Bert's spine. He'd been there five months earlier, acting as interpreter in the England v. Germany game, and had walked onto the pitch and into one of the goals, just trying it out, awed by the size of the stadium and all that tradition, never imagining that he might be there himself one day. Now they had two weeks of training at Eastbourne, staying at the Queen's Hotel, their every move reported in the national press: how they trained, what they ate, what they did for recreation, what they said and what they didn't. At the training ground Trautmann was always the star, lining up the players to take penalty kicks at him one after another, entertaining the locals and coincidentally providing the press photographers with plenty of good pictures. One day Bert had a bad fall which set off some fibrositis and rheumatism, which he'd suffered on and off since Russia, and the sports pages were full of it. 'Bert Trautmann, Manchester City's world-class goalkeeper, was ordered to bed with fibrositis today before City's shaken players had recovered from the news that left-winger Roy Clarke was unfit for the Cup Final on Saturday,' reported Bob Pennington for the *Daily Express* from Eastbourne on 4 May, under the heading: TRAUTMANN 'I can't go on' SHOCK.

Don Revie and his forwards were peppering German-born Trautmann with shots on the Wembley-quality turf of their practice ground, Saffrons, when Trautmann grimaced with pain after holding a drive from Paddy Fagan. 'It's no good,' he shouted. 'I can't go on.' City players were silent as Trautmann returned to the team's coach and sat there in pain from his stiffened neck and shoulder muscles. TV cameramen pleaded: 'Let Bert come back for a few more shots with the boys.' But Bert was sent off to a local physiotherapist who put him right.

Pennington went on:

Tonight he rejoined the team saying, "I feel much better." Trautmann, who has complained of rheumatic pains in his shoulders for several weeks, will rest tomorrow and have a work-out on Thursday. Manager Les McDowall took this latest blow calmly. 'We are not worrying unduly. Heat treatment should clear this up in time.' Said Revie: 'The boys felt a bit gloomy this morning. Our luck has been out with Johnny Hart (broken leg) and Roy Clarke (injured knee) missing the Final. But Bert is so tough. I reckon he would play – and play well – even if he were in a plaster cast.

And, sure enough, Bert recovered and soon joined in the training sessions again. In the afternoons the team went for long runs along the cliffs, only the evenings were free, strictly supervised by Les McDowall and player Jimmy Meadows, their self-appointed minder, though even Jimmy couldn't find out who turned on the bathroom taps on the top floor one night, ruining all the ceilings in the rooms below.

'Let's go to the pictures,' someone said, because there wasn't much else to do in Eastbourne of an evening. The choice was between two war films, the *Colditz Story* with John Mills, or *Above Us the Waves*, with John Mills again.

'Oh no,' said Bert. 'I'm fed up with your bloody war films and the way the Germans are always the baddies. If our officers had behaved as stupidly as they do in your films, they'd have been shot.'

'Jerry, we won the war not you,' they'd reply laughing, and set off without him.

The morning of the Cup Final, 7 May 1955, turned out fine and sunny. The team had moved to their 'secret hideout' at the Oaklands Hotel in Weybridge, appearing on a TV show the night before, because Les McDowall knew that entertainment was all part of the game. There were hundreds of good-luck telegrams, and many of the players read their horoscopes over breakfast hoping for good omens. They left the hotel by coach at one o'clock with a police escort, crowds of people standing all along the route waving and shouting, 'Good luck.' As Bert waved back he couldn't help thinking, why me? Why was it me who came through all the horror to this? All through Berdichev and Zhitomir and Dniepropetrovsk. Why me? Where are Bergenthum and Andreas? Where is Schnabel? '*Ich hatte einen Kamerad, ein besseren findest Du nicht . . .*' I once had a *Kamerad*, a better one you'll never find.

At the stadium they had to fight their way through the crowds to the dressing room, where each of them tried to relax in his own way. Bert's routine was always the same: he put his right boot on first and his shirt last; his football socks had to show the same number of rings, and he had to be perfectly turned out. If it was a home game at Maine Road he was always peg 32 – few people knew why, but without that link to home he felt he couldn't go out and play his best. He loosened up for twenty minutes before kick-off, and then he was ready. He didn't mind where he was in the line-up waiting to come onto the pitch. On this occasion he was fourth, next to Jackie Milburn, the Newcastle United forward. 'Aren't you cold?' Bert, shivering in the tunnel, asked Jackie. 'You'll be OK once the game's started,' said Jackie, who'd been there before, 'It's this waiting that gets you.' After that it was out of the tunnel and onto the Wembley pitch to deafening noise and 'Abide With Me' sung by 100,000 voices, rising up to heaven.

'Bert Trautmann, the first German ever to play in a Cup Final at Wembley!' was how skipper Roy Paul, speaking into a microphone, introduced Bert to the stadium as the teams lined up on the pitch. Then the Duke of Edinburgh was introduced to the players, one by one. '*Sehr gut*,' he said when he came to Bert, shaking his hand, and instinctively Bert bowed, in the German way, causing his astonished team-mates amusement for years to come. In the end, City were the 'gallant and sporting losers', 3–1, and those Geordie fans were hoarse with cheering when Newcastle United went up to the Royal Box to receive the Cup and their medals from the Queen.

Bert was disappointed and annoyed with himself for letting in the last goal, which he felt he could have stopped if he'd been more alert, though no one else agreed. *The Times* pointed to the 'devastating opening goal which left a black mark against Manchester's defensive covering. It showed clearly enough the importance of having played at Wembley previously. Before the City players had got used to the lush surface or acclimatised themselves to the atmosphere, or to the distances, White and Milburn swept down the right for Milburn to force a corner from Ewing.' The report ended: 'The final memory was of the great goalkeeping of Trautmann, the German, for Manchester City, a man with wrists of iron, swooping on shots high and low like a predatory eagle. It was an exhibition of grace and power to remember.' As far as Bert was concerned, he'd played at Wembley, that was the thing, and he half believed Roy Paul when he stood up in the coach on the way to the post-match banquet at the Café Royal, promising the lads, in his inspirational way, that they'd be back the following year.

By the time they got to the Café Royal Bert had other things on his mind: the *Manchester Evening Chronicle* had paid for his parents to fly over, and they needed his attention. They'd never been abroad before and they had no notion of what England and the English might be like. His mother had a new coat, hat and gloves, and his father was wearing a new suit, but he could see that they both felt shy and out of place, completely overwhelmed by the whole event, the sheer size of the Wembley stadium and the noise of the crowd, singing and cheering, much of it for their son. 'It's wonderful, and how kind they all are, your English,' said his mother, trying her best. As soon as they could, they went back to their hotel, where Berni joined them later in the evening. The truth was his mother had only agreed to come so she could spend some time with Berni and John, her grandson, but with all the post-match receptions Berni didn't have much time to spare. It was the Friars, once they were all back in Manchester, who took the Trautmanns everywhere, entertaining them. This worked well with Herr Trautmann, who enjoyed everything, especially the English pub, which he thought compared very favourably with the German *Gasthof*. 'I have seen the English people as they really are,' he told Berni afterwards. But Frau Trautmann was only happy when the family was together quietly, in the evenings, except she found it heartbreaking to see her son and grandson living so happily in the bosom of the Friar family, not her own.

It took a while for the team to get back to form after the Cup Final, not so much because of the defeat, more because of the intense build-up and anticipation, which was now all over. Meanwhile Big Swifty gave Bert another piece of advice: 'Never, never ignore the youngsters asking for your autograph.' After Wembley Trautmann was the biggest star of the team for City supporters, and there were times when he stayed on after a match for an hour, even two, signing those autographs. But this wasn't in response to Big Swifty's advice; it was Bert being the good German again, showing the English that Germans could be decent, polite and fair, just like anyone else. To crown it all, he was voted Footballer of the Year; unbelievable, he said to himself: a German voted England's Footballer of the Year. Magnificent.

The other person still offering Bert guidance and advice was his father-in-law Jack Friar. After every match they'd sit down of an evening and talk it through while the women did the clearing-up in the kitchen. For Jack, Bert was the son he'd never had, and they could spend hours talking about football, or life in general for that matter. Bert was semi-professional now, and working for Johnstone's Paint as a salesman to make ends meet, because star that he was, he still only earned £12 a week, and £8 in the close season. But now that he was famous he got endless requests to visit boys' clubs, make appearances at garden fetes and give after-dinner speeches at Rotary clubs. He found the speeches an ordeal and never knew what to say. 'Be yourself, Bert – that's all they want,' advised Jack. 'And always start with a joke to break the ice.' All very well for Jack, who could tell jokes by the yard, but Bert didn't know any, and didn't have the confidence to tell them either. 'Tell them about the time you were waiting for the enemy – us – on the other side of the Rhine in March '45. You know, when you had to get in that bunker which was built by your Home

Guard, and they'd forgotten to put in any windows, so you couldn't see a thing. Tell them that. People always like a war story, and they'll love one about the Germans getting it wrong.' Bert nodded. 'You see, Bert, that way you've taken them head on: about being a German who can laugh at himself.'

Roy Paul's prediction turned out right: by mid-season the team were on form again, making their way through the early rounds of the FA Cup, reaching the semi-final against Tottenham Hotspur at Villa Park by beating Everton 2–1 in the sixth round.

As soon as the Tottenham match was announced Bert started getting hate mail again, this time from the Jewish community in north London. He didn't tell anyone except Jack Friar, who advised him to take no notice, keep his head down and go out and show them what's what on the day, just as he had when he first joined Manchester City. They won the match 3–1, but the day was ruined for Bert partly by catcalls but mostly because, in the heat of the game, he fouled Spurs' left-winger George Robb by holding his leg, stopping a Tottenham goal. The newspapers were full of it that weekend. The photos were damning, and Bert felt he'd let himself down.

Traditionally, there was a long gap between the semi-finals and the Cup Final itself, but meanwhile the league games continued. Bert found he'd completely lost his form, so miserable was he at his fall from grace, the German turned bad again. Eventually Jack Friar persuaded him to tell Eric Todd, the sports writer on the *Evening Chronicle*, about the abusive letters, and Todd wrote a piece about them. Over 500 letters of support for Bert poured in, including some from Tottenham, and that March *Chronicle* readers voted him Player of the Year, with over 3,000 votes. 'You see, Bert,' said Jack Friar. 'I told you so.'

Then it was 5 May, Cup Final day 1956, Manchester City v. Birmingham City. After two weeks training at Eastbourne, City moved on to the Oaklands Hotel at Weybridge for the night before the match again, and a police escort to Wembley the next morning, just as before; and now there they were, for the second year running, waiting in the dressing room, each trying to keep calm in their own way. Bert went through his usual routine – right boot first, shirt last – then into the toilets one more time, before it was 'OK, lads! This is it! Best of luck!' from Laurie, and 'Good luck, boys!' from Les McDowall, and out into the tunnel, where Bert and Gil Merrick, the Birmingham goalie, stood side by side, wishing each other luck. As they waited they could feel the atmosphere and hear the cheering, the Guards band playing, and the singing, conducted by the master of ceremonies dressed all in white standing on a rostrum in the middle of the stadium. Then there was a hush as every cap and hat was removed for 'Abide With Me', followed by an eruption of even wilder cheering as the two teams ran out onto the pitch. It was indescribable, thought Bert, that feeling, running out of the tunnel into the bright light of that vast stadium with 100,000 spectators ranged in stands so high you could hardly see the sky above. Once they were on the pitch, the band played 'God Save the Queen', with everyone standing as the Queen and the Duke of Edinburgh made their way to the Royal Box, followed by the line-up with the Duke of Edinburgh again, and then the whistle for the start of the match, and they were off.

Joe Hayes scored for Manchester City inside three minutes, picking up a fine pass from Don Revie, but Birmingham equalised after fifteen, so they were 1–1 at half-time. The second half needed a lot of work from Trautmann, who made some brilliant saves, tearing out of goal to attack the Birmingham strikers before they had a chance to aim and shoot. Then Jack Dyson and Bobby Johnstone scored for Manchester City one after another, the second of these as a result of Trautmann collecting a ball from Birmingham forward Eddie Brown's feet and throwing it out to launch a counter-attack, which was all part of the Revie Plan. Revie got the ball, passed it to Jack Dyson, who passed it to Bobby Johnstone, who scored the goal.

There were only sixteen minutes to go when disaster struck. Peter Murphy, Birmingham's inside left, had taken possession of the ball and was racing into the penalty area making straight for goal, leaving a tired Dave Ewing well behind. There was nothing and no one between Murphy and the goal except Trautmann. Faced with danger, Bert did his usual thing, charging out and diving for the ball at Murphy's feet. As they fell, Murphy's knee caught Trautmann's neck, knocking him unconscious. Pathe News filmed it all: the collision, the horrified gasps of the spectators, and Trautmann finally staggering to his feet again, holding his neck with his head tilted to one side. The Manchester City supporters cheered him wildly, not knowing that Bert could hardly see and hardly even knew where he was. The medics and the referee were telling him to go off, but he refused. Why would the *Fallschirmjäger* quit now, with victory in sight?

Bert played on to the end of the match in a complete haze, relying on nothing but instinct and an overpowering will to win. His team-mates watched anxiously as he staggered around in front of his goal like a drunk. Birmingham meanwhile redoubled their efforts. Eddie Brown managed to get past Bill Lievers and Dave Ewing, who were desperately trying to protect their injured man, and was heading straight for goal when Trautmann charged out and dived at his feet, grabbing the ball and clearing it all in one move. Ewing managed to clear another ball, but then Murphy was coming at goal again, from the right. It was a high ball and the crowd could only gasp as Bert charged out of goal again, caught the ball and cleared it. Later he confessed he couldn't remember any of it. When the whistle blew it was 3–1 to Manchester City, and the whole stadium erupted, fans from both sides racing onto the pitch to congratulate their heroes, but none more than Trautmann, who was man of the match for supporters of Manchester City and Birmingham alike, a Cup Final legend for ever more.

The Times reported:

From Our Association Football Correspondent

MANCHESTER'S NEW TRIUMPH.
FA CUP ATTACKING PLAN SUCCEEDS

Manchester City have done the city of Manchester proud. Wembley has never looked fairer of a glorious spring afternoon. The grass somehow seemed to hold a richer hue, the massed bands of the Royal Marines, with burnished brass and white helmets, enhanced the day; and even the 100,000 crowd ranged about the steep banks of the stadium took on a new colour and warmth. What one was not prepared for is how Manchester City completely unhinged a Birmingham defence which had conceded only 2 goals in all the previous rounds to the Final. Once more the Revie Plan came into its own. If any one trump was played at the right moment it was played by Manchester at the eleventh hour. It was fascinating to watch. Here was a Birmingham defence now often at sixes and sevens, as Hayes, Dyson and Johnstone picked up the threads of Revie's decoy work. Three times Trautmann was winged painfully leaping to high crosses. But Birmingham's struggle was the struggle of a trout on the line.

It was a straight, cleanly fought tussle between sides in full battle order from start to finish. Never was a Final more worthily won.

DRAMA AND PANIC IN THE DRESSING ROOM was the headline in the *Daily Mirror*. 'You may have been there on the Wembley terraces, surging and swaying and shouting. You may have been sitting tensed on the edge of the front room sofa watching TV. Wherever you were, you didn't SEE IT ALL.' There followed various dressing-room secrets including Roy Little's last-minute 'flaring moment of panic', and ending with

> YOU SAW goalkeeper Bert Trautmann, that great tawny cat of a man, collapse to the flailing approach of the Birmingham inside-left Peter Murphy, YOU SAW trainer Laurie Barnett rush out to tend him. BUT YOU DIDN'T SEE OR HEAR Laurie whisper these four magic words into the ear of the Footballer of the Year: 'Only fourteen minutes left'. TRAUTMANN SAID LATER: 'That was the last thing I remember.' For those last minutes – there were actually sixteen because of extra time for injuries – he remembers only pain.

Bert also remembered very little of the post-match celebrations, but he took part in them nevertheless, not yet realising that his neck was broken. When the team got to Manchester two days later for the grand reception, driving in an open-topped bus, waving and displaying the cup, the whole of the city centre was one mass of fans. No one could move in Albert Square in front of the Town Hall, where the team stood on the steps acknowledging the wild cheering as the dignitaries tried to make their speeches. Through the din one thing could be heard: 'We want Bert! We want Bert!' And finally, as the Pathe cameras turned, we see Bert come to the microphone, head bent to one side but immaculately dressed, looking awkward and embarrassed, saying, 'Quiet, quiet,' to the crowd, then turning away, waiting, because they wouldn't stop cheering their hero, then repeating, 'Quiet, quiet,' again to no avail. 'For he's a jolly good fellow, for he's a jolly good fellow!' sang the crowd, till Bert finally managed a few words of thanks, smiling and waving, completely overwhelmed.

Bert, who was also Bernd the *Fallschirmjäger* and Berni the Hitler Youth, had become an English hero, a football legend, the good German. It was *unglaublich,* thought Bernd, unbelievable. Magnificent.

Epilogue

'Once they knew I'd broken my neck, I was straight into hospital.' Bert Trautmann is sitting in his bungalow in Spain, reminiscing as I record the story of his life for this book, hours and hours of it, and he never seems to tire even though he's 84. His memory is remarkable. When I ask him for small details about Wischusenstrasse, or about his time in prison in Zhitomir, or his first interrogation as a POW at Kempton Park, he never hesitates. And he still looks good – tall and blond, the old footballer, the tough *Fallschirmjäger*. The house is modest because even at the height of his football fame he never earned more than £35 a week, and now he's got no money to speak of. 'Am I bitter?' he asks, talking of players these days who earn hundreds of thousands a week. 'Certainly I am!' he answers in his German Lancashire way, but he's laughing as he says it because, in spite of the lack of money, he feels life has been good to him. Sport has seen him through, he says, and given him so much, he's got nothing to complain about. He's been happily married to Marlis, who is German, for the last 24 years, and although they live in Spain, he makes regular visits back to Manchester, which he still sees as home. When I went to a Manchester City home match with him, to the new Eastlands stadium, although Bert's heyday was 50 years ago, it still took us half an hour to get from the car park to the stadium because people kept coming up to ask him for his autograph.

'They drilled holes in my head and they put calipers in, like U-shaped hooks,' he says. 'I had to lie on a bed of boards, no mattress, no nothing, just a sheet and a blanket. There was a weight over the bed to straighten my spine, and I had glasses like a periscope, so I read my newspaper like this.' He demonstrates, holding his hands out. 'I could read about myself and how I was coming along in the headlines! I couldn't feed myself and I had to stay like that for three weeks. Then they put me in plaster from my head to my waist, only keeping my arms free, and the calipers were still in, so I looked like something from outer space. I was like that till the end of November. I was completely immobilised, and at Maine Road the players would call out "Hey, big fella!" just to watch me turn, like a robot. The doctors warned me I'd never play top football again.

'It was the worst year of my life, being told that, and then trying to recover. But the worst part by far was when our son John got killed. He was just six, and it was a month after the Cup Final. I was out of hospital by then, but still in plaster. The German FA invited me to be their guest of honour at the Germany v. England international in Berlin. They invited Margaret too, but she didn't want to go, and she didn't want me to go either; she wanted us both to spend some time at our caravan in Anglesey instead. But I didn't want to miss the international, and I was fed up with all that time lying in hospital, so I went. Apparently that evening Margaret went off to see some friends and she didn't get back till the next morning. And my father-in-law had a furious row with her about it, though, really, I can see she did it because she was angry I'd gone to Germany. She left the house and took John with her. There was a Tip Top bread and sweets van on the other side of the road, and John asked for some money to buy some sweets. He crossed the road to get them, but didn't have the extra penny for the sweets he wanted, so he ran back across the road, without looking, to ask for some more. He didn't see the car coming.'

Bert shakes his head. He still can't bear to think about it.

'I'd got to Düsseldorf by then and I was in the hotel, in the reception area, when the manager came up to ask if I wanted anything. I said I'd like some strawberries, and just then the reception phone went. As he lifted the receiver I knew – don't ask me how, I just knew. In the plane on the way to London it was cloudy, but every now and again you could see the sun and you sit there and say to yourself, Well he's been in an accident, but at least he's still alive. And you say, If I see the sun come through one more time he'll be OK. But he was dead already of course, killed outright. The hotel manager just hadn't the courage to tell me.

'The driver of the car was a boy of seventeen. He'd only just passed his test, and he was half German actually, just like John. The wife saw it all. She was on the pavement, and as he came running back over, the car hit him, and he was flung in the air just three yards away from her. She never got over it. He was buried at St Helens. There were hundreds of people there, and the press and everything. It was terrible. You'd be sat there talking and you'd be crying your bloody eyes out, and so on. But life has to go on, doesn't it? I'd written a book with Eric Todd when I became Footballer of the Year, and my share of the profits was £3,350, and there was a show house in the Ideal Home Exhibition that year which cost exactly £3,350. Imagine that. So we bought one. Margaret wanted to move out of her parents' house anyway, so we bought it. They come and build it for you, exactly as you want. So we had it built in Bramhall, in Hazel Grove, but she didn't have any interest. There was nothing I could do for her; she had no interest. Desperate.

'So, in a way, I had to fight. I worked pretty hard to forget. Of course I decided to get back into football; sport has always saved me, and that's what I decided to do. So I talked to the doctor, but the doctor said no, I couldn't do it, but my brain said yes, and I insisted. So then he gave me a plan of exercises, and I ran with a leather support for about three weeks and I trained every day and I played my first game on Christmas Day 1956, after just four weeks, without any support. I played for the Reserves, and I was almost OK, but I made a mistake. I went to the cemetery before the match – I don't know why – to visit John's grave. And then I played very badly. I wasn't there really, I wasn't there at all. Everyone thought I wasn't fit enough, but it wasn't that; it was John.

'Why did I carry on? Did I want to prove something? Did I feel lost without the football, without the people, without the applause, without the accolades and so on? I don't know the answer but I carried on, and Les McDowall and Manchester City stood by me, I'll always be grateful and thankful for that. They put me back into the First Eleven, but I realised I had a very long way to go. I had to start all over again like a baby. I'd lost everything – my timing, my sense of anticipation, everything. And I tried to force things because I'd set a certain standard of goalkeeping and I wanted to regain this standard. I wanted to attack the opposition before they had a chance to shoot, like before. But I couldn't do it. I'd say to forwards attacking my goal "Have a shot here, have a shot there" just so I could show that I was still the old man, but it never happened. City kept me there for two seasons while I was a totally indifferent player; they never criticised, never had any complaints, even though I let in some – I have to say it – bloody stupid goals, when I felt ashamed and thought to myself, Christ, how could you? Mind you, three or four people had left us by then: Don Revie, Roy Paul and so on. I didn't have the support any more – the strength and the ability in the side – so I wasn't very happy, the team wasn't very happy and the directors weren't very happy. Anyway, that second season the team went from bad to worse and then one day the directors delivered an ultimatum to us: if we didn't play any better, something would have to happen. But I'd already decided after the team talk on Friday, after training, I would tell McDowall that I was finishing. So after the team talk I said, "Boss, before you carry on, I just want to tell you that I've had enough. I can't carry on, not because of my nerves, but because I know I'm not the same as I was before." And he said, "Well, this is news!" So I said, "Yes, I'm sorry about it but I can't carry on."

'Well, there are moments in your life when you're so down you really feel you can't carry on. But Les McDowall said, "Have you ever thought about the number of points you have saved us throughout the season? Only you have done this, not the team, only you and now you want to quit! No, no." The players also said, "Oh no, big fella, you can't quit." They said carry on, and there was pressure from the directors to carry on, so I decided to stay. And from that moment my confidence came back. It didn't get better all at once but it did get better step by step. Today I say that I was a better goalie later on than I had been before. I think so, yes, as far as my colleagues and myself can judge it. And I was writing a weekly column for the *Manchester Evening News*, so I was getting in a bit more money as well. Then I was selected as honorary captain of the English league team and we had some really great players: Cliff Jones, Denis Law, the Allchurch brothers, George Bartram – a fantastic team, not all English mind, but great players. That was an honour, you know, the acceptance of all these people. Without them Bert Trautmann would be nothing. It was they who encouraged me to improve all the time and become what I became. So I went on playing till 1964, when I retired, and I was 42 by then.

'I played my testimonial match on 15 April 1964. It was a joint Manchester City–Manchester United team against an all-international one and I confess to you I was very nervous that not enough stars would offer to play and not enough people would turn up to watch the game. But Bobby Charlton, Denis Law and Derek Kevan all lined up with me for the Manchester Eleven, with Stanley Matthews, Tom Finney and Jimmy Armfield for the opposition. The attendance was 47,000. Unbelievable. I could already hear the cheering and the noise as we were waiting in the tunnel to go out on the pitch. It was deafening and I was choked, with gratitude really. At the end of the match the score was 5–4 to the Manchester Eleven, but we never managed to finish it properly because the fans just poured onto the pitch. The police had to clear a path for me so I could get up to the main stand for my farewell speech. I could hardly speak really, but I said I'd had some great moments in my life, and the honour of playing with some great players, and living among some of the best people in the world. I managed that much. And I said how grateful I was, not only for myself but on behalf of my family and the German people, and that was it; I was too choked for anything else. The profit from that testimonial match was £6,000 after all the expenses were paid. Magnificent, wasn't it? And would you believe it, the tax people got after me about it. I just wrote and told them I wouldn't pay. Not a penny. It was the only money I had, and I wasn't paying. I never heard a dicky bird after that.'

We had some lunch and a rest. Marlis and I went for a walk along the beach, watching the children running in and out of the sea. Although the house is modest, the situation is lovely, only a stone's throw from the beach and as yet unspoilt by the usual mass of hotels. Later Bert and I sat down at the table, each with a cup of tea, checked the recorder and got going again.

'So you wanted to know about when I finished. I applied for this job as general manager of Stockport County and I got it. It couldn't have been my managerial ability because I'd never done the job before, but I knew how to handle people and how to treat them. One of the first things I did concerned the groundsmen. There were two of them and Stockport County had one of the best pitches in the league, so I got to know them and asked them how much they were earning and they said six pounds a week. God in heaven! So, I surrounded myself with good people. Jimmy Meadows was the coach, and Eddie Quigley from Blackburn Rovers joined the team, and we got promotion in the first year from the Fourth into the Third Division. I told you I'd been working for Johnstone's Paint when I was still playing for Man City? Well, they came and painted the whole ground, for free. Magnificent! At the start of the season the average crowd was 2,500 but by the end of the season it was 11,000. But the chairman, Victor Bernard, was a bad-tempered bugger. He thought he was all-important, always telling me what to do. The *Coronation Street* studio was not far and he kept inviting Pat Phoenix (Elsie Tanner) and the other stars to watch Stockport County, and they spent hours in the bar afterwards, all for free. I told him he couldn't carry on like that – we couldn't afford it – but he just carried on. In the end it was him or me, so one day I'd just had enough, and I walked out. He told the press he had no idea why I left, but he knew very well. In a way, it was a mistake. But it was him or me.'

We talked on for a couple of hours, then I stopped the recorder because I was getting tired, losing my concentration. Indefatigable Bert was quite happy to carry on of course, but we agreed to call it a day. That evening some friends came round for supper. Norbert and Inge are German, but like Bert and Marlis they've lived in Spain for many years, and Norbert is a great paella cook. He arrived with all the ingredients and set to work at a special stove in the garden while we sat drinking Martinis. The garden is beautiful with tall palm trees and an immaculate lawn, mowed by Bert. After the paella we sat late into the night under the palms, with the moon rising and the sound of the waves, drinking *kümmel*. Did it remind Bert of Christmas 1943? I couldn't help wondering. Did he suddenly remember the freezing Russian winter and the fear as we sat relaxed and at peace in the warm Spanish night?

'We moved to Anglesey because Margaret wanted to get away. I would have preferred Germany, where I could find work, but Margaret refused to go. She said she hated everything German.' We were off again the next morning, ten o'clock sharp, Bert needing no prompting from me, leaning over the recorder to make sure I didn't miss a word. 'She'd always liked Angelsey, where we'd had the caravan for years. We had two more boys by then, Mark and Stephen, and I thought it might make things better between Margaret and me, but it didn't. And now I had nothing to do all day but twiddle my thumbs.'

It was a bad time. Margaret's sister Barbara said Margaret blamed Bert for John's death – who knows why – and Margaret was indulgent and overprotective of the boys, who were six and eight by then, giving them all her love and attention, and none to Bert, freezing him out. If there was one thing calculated to offend Bert, his mother's adored Berni, it was this, and given he'd always had a short fuse, he often lost his temper now, storming out of the house to sit for hours by the sea, watching the waves, trying to work things out, completely at a loss as to what to do or where to turn. German football came to his rescue.

'Preussen Münster got in touch and asked me to become trainer of the team. I didn't hesitate and accepted immediately. Margaret refused to go – she said she wanted the boys to be English, not German – so I went alone. I took a coaching course first, organised by the German FA, and then I moved to Münster, which is an industrial town about 100 kilometres north of Düsseldorf. I was happy to be there, believe me, even though it meant only seeing the boys in holiday times. And my mother was happy to finally have me back in Germany, even though it was a long way from Bremen.'

Christmas 1971 spelt the end of the Trautmann marriage. It had been rocky for too long, and Barbara was shocked at how bitter Margaret had become, calling Bert 'that German' and hiding the letters he wrote to the boys before they had a chance to read them. As the family sat down to Christmas dinner that year the atmosphere was tense and the boys were messing about, not settling. Bert told them to sit up straight and behave. He hated the way Margaret let them do just what they wanted, with no manners or discipline. '*Heil Hitler!*' said Margaret, leaping up from the table, giving the Hitler salute and putting a finger over her upper lip to indicate the moustache. At that, Bert grabbed the corner of the tablecloth and pulled it right off, flinging the Christmas dinner – plates, glasses, turkey, sprouts, everything – across the floor. Then he went upstairs, packed his bags and left.

'It was over.' Bert shrugs his shoulders. He doesn't mention the fact that his mother had died a few weeks earlier. Later, when I ask him about her death, he just says, 'She had lost the will to live.' In truth, she never recovered from the traumas of the war and losing Berni to England afterwards. There was nothing much to live for after that: her health was gone, and depression took over. She tried to commit suicide more than once, and by the time Berni came back to Germany it was too late. So it was over for Berni and Bernhard and Bert, all at the same time.

'I flew back to Germany and decided to make my life there, for good. It was a difficult time because I'd left another training job by then and I didn't know what to do. I didn't want to end up like lots of footballers do: like Roy Paul, who was driving a lorry in Wales – imagine it – after all that football fame. But I'd left everything behind for Margaret and the boys and I was penniless. I didn't want to go back home to Bremen and live with my father. I couldn't do it. So I contacted Franz Schein, whom I'd met when he came over to Wembley to watch the England v. Germany game. He said he'd been a long-time admirer of mine, and he'd given me some money then because he'd heard I was hard up. He ran a very successful haulage company and garage in Aachen, and when I contacted him I said I'd be happy to work for him in his garage. He immediately invited me to come and live with them, without hesitation, which gave me a roof over my head and a chance to think about what to do next. Magnificent, wasn't it? I'm a lucky bugger really, because just then the German government and the German Football Association were working together on various Third World aid projects – sports development programmes and so on – and to cut a long story short, I became one of their sports ambassadors.'

Burma, Tanzania, Liberia, Pakistan, North Yemen – sixteen years of coaching and training Third World football teams followed, fascinating years which Bert includes as some of the best of his life. Every posting offered new challenges and interests, and the teams flourished under his expert guidance: no more rows, no more walkouts. He even took the Burmese team to the Olympic Games in Germany in 1972, and then five friendlies against his old Tura team.

Only three things marred those years. The first was his relationship with his boys, Mark and Stephen. Bert had never been a great letter writer, not during his Hitler Youth *Landjahr*, nor from the Russian Front; only when he was a POW in Ashton-in-Makerfield did his mother get regular letters from her son. But now he wrote long chatty letters about life in Burma, Tanzania or Liberia – the people, the landscape, the customs, the football. But he rarely got a reply, and when he did the letters were short and scrappy. Gradually they ceased altogether.

Then there was his second marriage, to Ursula von der Heyde, who came from a well-off family in Rüdesheim near Koblenz, and was working for a firm in Burma when they met. It was a whirlwind affair and Bert felt he was properly in love, perhaps for the first time in his life. They got married as soon as his divorce from Margaret came through, and it was a happy marriage for about eight years, but then they gradually grew apart. Bert was Bernd again now, and when he found out Ursula was having an affair with another man, he went to find him and beat him up.

The last sadness was his father. Things had got better between them over the years, his father becoming more open and affectionate, and Bernd coming to understand the pressures in his father's earlier life: his two years in the trenches, his constant fear of losing his job, the reasons he joined the Nazi Party, the reasons he wasn't always a good husband to Frieda, and all the rest. Herr Trautmann was still living in the same flat in Wischusenstrasse, alone now that Karl Heinz and his wife Traudel had moved out, but managing quite well, doing all his own cleaning and cooking and still going to the same *Stammtisch* in the *Gasthof* up on the corner of the Heerstrasse. On the day he died Bernd was on his way to visit him. When he called up to say what time he was arriving, it was the Mrozinzskys, still living in the same flat, who answered the phone and told him his father had collapsed while doing the vacuum cleaning. That made Bernd smile. Imagine his father doing anything like vacuum cleaning in the old days! But he was surprised how sad he was to lose him. Now all he had left in Bremen was Karl Heinz and his wife Traudel – and Helga of course, the child Herr and Frau Trautmann had adopted, who, after two marriages, was also living back there, contentedly single and always happy to see him.

But Bernd was still the lucky one. In Rüdesheim, Ursula's home town, he met Marlis, and that marriage has lasted, well and happily, to this day. They went to the Yemen together, then they lived back in Rüdesheim for a while, but finally they decided to retire to Spain, where the weather is good and life is cheaper. It suits them both. And for Bert there are regular visits to Manchester.

'Manchester will always be my home – that and the people there.' It's another day of recording, and Bert has come to the subject nearest his heart: the people he came to know and love in 1945, when he came to England as a POW, to the camp at Ashton-in-Makerfield and to a new life. 'So you'll remember Marion Greenhall and the baby she named Freda, after my mother. She spelt it differently, but it's the same name, and that touched me very much. But I couldn't marry her, and I ran away, which was the worst thing I ever did in my life. I always paid, mind, but I ran, and we lost touch completely. And then one day when I was on a visit to Manchester – 1990 it was – one of the newspapermen told me Freda was looking for me, looking for her dad. It was a shock, but the newspaper said they would arrange everything if they could cover the story, and I thought I should do it. The meeting was in Germany to avoid too much other press interest, and I can tell you, I've never been so nervous in my life.'

No more nervous than Freda, who flew to Germany for the meeting, taking her husband David for support. She was 42 by then and never a week had gone by when she didn't think about her father: wonder what he was like, where he was, whether he ever gave her a thought. He was always in the news when she was growing up in the 1950s and 1960s, the glamorous Manchester City football hero, but there was never any mention of her; she might as well not have existed. But her mother never spoke badly of Bert, so she wasn't bitter, just longed to meet him and claim a bit of him for herself. But now the moment had finally come she was so nervous she felt like getting back on that plane and going straight home to Ashton-in-Makerfield again.

The meeting was awkward at first, each shy in the other's company, Bert feeling guilty, Freda desperate that he should like her. But soon enough they relaxed. They were so alike: they looked alike, felt alike. 'You don't look too bad for an old man,' Freda said, teasing him with her Lancashire humour, just like his old football mates used to do. After that he saw Freda every time he came to Manchester, meeting her children, his grandchildren, and a great-grandchild too, and introducing Freda to her other family, Mark and Stephen, who Bert saw more often once their mother had died. These days they often spend time together, one big family.

And then came the day in 2001 when Freda gave the party where Bert and Marion met again. Marion had married and borne four more children, but she'd never stopped loving Bert. For his part, Bert still felt bad about leaving Marion in the lurch with an illegitimate baby, which was an awful stigma in those days. So both were terrified of the meeting, but Freda organised things brilliantly, everyone in her dining room all together at first, and then she pushed the two of them, her father and mother, into the kitchen alone.

'It was difficult at first,' remembers Bert, 'but then we started chatting, like old friends really.' You can sense the relief in him even now. 'And then she said something I'll never forget to the day I die. She said, "I don't blame you, Bert. You did the right thing." Unbelievable, wasn't it?'

There have been two or three times when Bert has been close to tears over these past few days: remembering his mother, recalling the kindness of the English who gave him a second chance, thinking about certain moments in his football life, and now this. He still can't get over Marion's sweetness and generosity – the way she could tell him after all those years that he'd done the 'right thing'. As for Marion: 'In a way, I'll always love him,' she says shyly.

So he's been lucky. There have been many awards in the last few years: in 2000 the Football League voted him one of the hundred Players of the Century; in 2008 the German Academy for Football gave him their Culture Award, one of only three ever to have received it; and in December 2008 he was presented with the German FA insignia before the England v. Germany match. But there was another thing he wanted to achieve. 'In a way, it's the thing that's always mattered to me: to promote Anglo-German friendship through sport, especially with the young. I've done a lot over the years with youth groups in England and some in Germany as well, but never both together. Then one day in July 2003 the telephone rang and it was a man called Mathias Paskowski, a sports journalist from Germany. He wanted to do an interview, so I agreed and he came over. There are always requests for interviews, even after all this time, and guest appearances. Anyway, after the article was published he got in touch again. He knew my interest in Anglo-German friendship and he shared it, and he had some colleagues who felt the same, all Anglophiles who'd studied in England or visited regularly for business and so on. They thought the British still had some funny ideas about the Germans and they thought they could set up a foundation for the young to get to know each other better through exchanges, all based on football. He said the British embassy in Berlin was interested too, and of course I was, so the

Trautmann Foundation was set up, and it's been going very successfully ever since.'

Bert is sitting there, hunched over the recorder as usual, and when he looks up I see a look of real pleasure and satisfaction. It's our last day together, and we're coming to the end of his story. We both know that part of the reason for his pleasure is his own life, Berni and Bert, German and English, finally coming together in this act of friendship and reconciliation. In November 2004 he was awarded the OBE for his work improving Anglo-German relations. There was a reception for him at the British embassy in Berlin, and two days later he was presented to the Queen and Prince Philip at the Berlin Sinfonia. Berlin, where 66 years earlier he'd been presented to Hans von Tschammer und Osten, the *Reichssportsminister*, for coming second in athletics in the whole of the Reich. Two medals, and so much in between.

'People ask, why did I join the Hitler Youth, why did I volunteer to fight when I was seventeen? But they don't understand: we had no mind of our own. Growing up under Hitler, you had no mind of your own. My education, my real education, started at the age of 22, in England. And I shall always be grateful to the people of this country for trying to educate me, or to find my own way. I think this is the way I should express it: to find my own way.' Every time he talks about it, tears come to his eyes. 'The English showed something of forgiveness,' he explains. '"War is war. The war is over. We understand how you feel."

'I was born a German, but in my heart I'm British. I'm still called English, even from my own countrymen in Germany. Many people will be asking why. But I had so much kindness, friendliness, and understanding shown to me. So I stayed. And I'm glad I stayed.'

Notes

1

Page

6 Political demonstrations: M.-L. Ehls, *Protest und Propaganda, Demonstrationen in Berlin zur Zeit Weimarer Republik*, p.191

7 'Too many political parties . . .' E.J. Feuchtwanger, *From Weimar to Hitler*, p.85

11 'How could Germany . . .' Ibid. p.210

20 '"We turn our eyes..."'J. Noakes and G. Pridham (eds) *Nazism: A Documentary Reader*, pp.615, 281

23 '"We train our youth . . ."' A. Rowlands, *Trautmann the Biography*, p.20

2

Page

25 Membership of the Hitler Youth: A. Kloenne, *Jugend Im Dritten Reich*, p.34

26 '"The Hitler Youth asks you today . . ."'Ibid. p.25 (author's translation)

36 '"We who are of German blood..."'Ibid. p.17

37 Structure of the Hitler Youth: A. Kloenne, *Jugend Im Dritten Reich*, p.43

37 Hitler Youths killed: M. H. Kater, *Hitler Youth*, p.18

41 "'This youth, it will learn nothing . . .'" Ibid. p.30 (author's translation)

3

Page

47 "'Twelve months ago the struggle . . .'" Ibid. p.68

48 "'With Jewish blood dripping from . . .'" M. H. Kater, *Hitler Youth*, p.64

49 Unemployed drafted in to work: B. Engelmann, *In Hitler's Germany, Everyday life in the Third Reich*, p.97

52 Hitler Youth Order: A. Kloenne, *Jugend Im Dritten Reich*, p.28

53 Von Fritsch removed: W. Shirer, *The Rise and Fall of the Third Reich*, p.315

55 78,000 Hitler Youth leaders; "'to totally educate . . .'" M. Kater, *Hitler Youth*, p.54

56 Hitler radio broadcast: B. Engelmann, *In Hitler's Germany, Everyday life in the Third Reich*, p.108

58 *Kristallnacht* orders: Ibid. p.113

4

Page

61 Kali Chemicals gold flag: A. Rowlands, *Trautmann the Biography*, p.21

61 Hitler Youth working with SS: A. Kloenne, *Jugend Im Dritten Reich*, p.44

62 Specialist units: M. H. Kater, *Hitler Youth*, p.32

63 Churchill quote: P. Meehan, *The Unnecessary War*, p.2

64 Nazi party statistics: J. Taylor and W. Shaw, *A Dictionary of the Third Reich*, p.231

64 Hamburg and Kiel workers: P. Meehan, *The Unnecessary War*,

p.64; B. Engelmann, *In Hitler's Germany, Everyday life in the Third Reich*, p.78

65 Himmler quote: P. Meehan, *The Unnecessary War*, p.42

65 Hambro's bank employee quote: Ibid. p.52

65 Von Weizsaecker quote: Ibid. p.15

66 Vansittart quote: Ibid. p.18

66 Cadogan quote: Ibid. p.19

70 Ritter von Leeb quote: Max Hastings, review of *Germany and the Second World War, Vol IX/1*, p.11, *German Wartime Society*, ed. Jorg Echternkamp, in *New York Review of Books*, March 2009

73 Roosevelt letter: F. Loewenheim (ed.), *Roosevelt and Churchill. Their Secret Wartime Correspondence*, p.89

5

Page

73 '"Wherever rats appear . . ."' *Der Ewige Jude*, BFI

87 'The train had only three . . .' H. Metelmann, *Through Hell for Hitler*, p.23

89 '"I wish to have a population . . ."' L. Rees, *The Nazis, A Warning from History*, p.146

89 '"We can only talk of these . . ."' Ibid. p.150

6

Page

92 '"Dear Mr Stalin . . ."' R. Murphy, *A Diplomat Among Warriors*, p.257

93 Army Group North: A. Clark, *Barbarossa*, p.12

94 Russian tank strength: J. Keegan, *The Second World War*, p.78

95 *Einsatzgruppen* instructions: L. Rees, *The Nazis, A Warning from History*, p.176

96 "'The commissars are the bearers...'" J. Keegan, *The Second World War*, p.186

97 "'You have only to kick in the door...'" A. Clark, *Barbarossa*, p.43

98 "'Let us pray...'" H. Metelmann, *Through Hell for Hitler*, Epilogue

105 First day of Barbarossa: J.Keegan, *The Second World War*, p.184

109 *V Fliegerkorps* movements: Professor Michael Geyer, University of Chicago, personal communication

7

Page

116 Stalin's radio broadcast:A.Bullock, *Hitler and Stalin, Parallel Lives*, p.687

116 "'He's playing warlord again...'" F. Halder, *The Halder Diaries*, quoted in J. Keegan, *The Second World War*, p.193

118 "'The annihilation of Timoshenko...'"A. Clark, *Barbarossa*, p.157

119 "'The Russian is completely...'" Ibid. p.173

120 German casualty returns: Ibid. p.182

8

Page

129 "'We do not ourselves attach...'" P. Meehan, *The Unnecessary War*, p.309

131 "'For the life of one German...'"A. Clark, *Barbarossa*, p.153

9

Page

147 Führer Conference: A. Clark, *Barbarossa*, p.355

148 Smolensk conspiracy: Ibid. p.306

150 Attitude of German rank and file to opposition: Professor Michael Geyer in L. Rees, *The Nazis, A Warning from History*, p.214

152 Führer Directive 51: J. Keegan, *The Second World War*, p.369

154 "'Now we have them ...'" A. Williams, *From D-Day to Berlin*, p.55

154 "'Mein Führer ...'" Ibid. p.129

154 20 July Plot: L. Rees, *The Nazis, A Warning from History*, p.216

156 "'old and broken man'": A.Williams, *From D-Day to Berlin*, p.267

157 "'The war was won before ...'" Ibid. p.205

165 Sepp Dietrich quote: J. Keegan, *The Second World War*, p.441

166 General Patton quotes: A.Williams, *From D-Day to Berlin*, p.274

167 Rolf Munninger quote: Ibid. p.289

10

Page

174 325,000 had surrendered: J. Keegan, *The Second World War*, p.518

174 "'*Meine Herren*, it's over ...'"A.Williams, *From D-Day to Berlin*, p.316

183 Göring's telegram: W. Shirer, *The Rise and Fall of the Third Reich*, p.1116

184 Hitler's last will and testament: Ibid. p.1124

11

Page

187 Kempton Park: C. Clay, *The Germans We Kept*, BBC documentary

188 POW camp: Ibid.

190 Marbury Hall POW camp reports: H. Faulk, *Group Captives, The Re-education of German Prisoners of War*, p.63

200 2,800 calories: Ibid. p.36

201 *Morgenthau Plan*: R. Robin, *The Barbed Wire College. Reeducating German POWs in the United States during World War II*

202 "'The mass of our youth . . .'" H. Faulk, *Group Captives*, p.73

204 "'The object is neither reproach . . .'" Ibid. p.126

12

Page

213 "'Who still wants to die . . .'" H. Faulk, *Group Captives*, p.138

213 "'If it is treason to refuse . . .'" Ibid. p.138

216 Mass Observation: D. Kynaston, *Austerity Britain*, p.106

220 British Council of Churches: P. H. Taylor, *Enemies Become Friends*, p.5

224 Pathe Opinion Poll: C. Clay, *The Germans We Kept*, BBC documentary

226 Christmas 1946: Ibid.

13

Page

231 POWD report: H. Faulk, *Group Captives*, p.177

232 Screener report: Ibid. p.178

233 Mitscherlich report: Ibid. p.172

235 Bishop of Sheffield: Ibid. p.170

238 *Daily Express* football match report: D. Kynaston, *Austerity Britain*, p.215

239 *Daily Express* Denis Compton: Ibid. p.216

248 POW archive: C. Clay, *The Germans We Kept*, BBC documentary

14

Page

253 Summer 1948 in Britain: D. Kynaston, *Austerity Britain*, p.291

266 1932 election results: Bremen city archives

267 Carl Burckhardt: P. Meehan, *The Unnecessary War*, p.37

268 Von Weizsaecker case: Ibid. p.353

268 British Foreign Office memo: Ibid. p.341

15

Page

274 'Nazi!' placards: B. Trautmann, *Steppes to Wembley*, p.45

274 Rabbi Altmann's open letter: Ibid. p.46

283 '"Why I must leave . . ."' Ibid. p.70

292 Bert's routine: D. Saffer (ed.) *Match of My Life*, p.46

Bibliography

Atkinson, Rick, *The Day of Battle: The War in Sicily and Italy, 1943–1944*, Henry Holt, 2008

Beevor, Anthony, *D-Day*, Viking, 2009

Bullock, Alan, *Hitler and Stalin, Parallel Lives*, Harper Collins, 1991

Burckhardt, Carl J., *Mein Danziger Mission*, Munich, 1960

Clark, Alan, *Barbarossa, the Russia–German Conflict, 1941–1945*, Weidenfeld and Nicolson, 1995

Clay, Catrine and Leapman, Michael, *Master Race*, Hodder and Stoughton, 1995

Echternkamp, Jorg (ed.) *Germany and the Second World War, Vol. IX/1 German Wartime Society*, Research Institute of Military History, Potsdam, Clarendon Press, 2009

Ehls, Marie-Luise, *Protest und Propaganda, Demonstrationen in Berlin zur Zeit Weimarer Republik*, Walter de Gruyter, Berlin & New York, 1997

Engelmann, Bernt, *In Hitler's Germany, Everyday Life in the Third Reich*, Methuen, London, 1988

Faulk, Henry, *Group Captives, The Re-education of German Prisoners of War*, Chatto and Windus, 1977

Fest, Joachim, *Hitler*, Weidenfeld & Nicolson, 1974

Feuchtwanger, E. J., *From Weimar to Hitler*, Macmillan, 1993

Grunberger, Richard, *A Social History of the Third Reich*, Penguin Books, 1974

Halder, Franz, *The Halder Diaries*, Stuttgart, 1960

Hartmann, Christian, *Halder: Generalstabschef Hitlers 1939–1942*, Berlin, 1991

Hastings, Max, *Armageddon, The Battle for Germany 1944–1945*, Macmillan, 2004

Hitchcock, William I., *Liberation, the Bitter Road to Freedom, Europe 1944–1945*, Faber & Faber, 2009

Hrabar, Dr Roman, *The Fate of Polish Children during the Last War*, Interpress, Warsaw, 1981

Irving, David, *Goebbels. Mastermind of the Third Reich*, Focal Point, 1994

Kater, Michael H., *Hitler Youth*, Harvard University Press, 2004

Keegan, John, *The Second World War*, Hutchinson, 1989

Kloenne, Arno, *Jugend Im Dritten Reich*, Eugen Diederichs Verlag, 1982

Kordt, Erich, *Nicht Aus Den Akten*, Stuttgart, 1950

Kynaston, David, *Austerity Britain*, Bloomsbury, 2007

Loewenheim, Francis (ed.), *Roosevelt and Churchill. Their Secret Wartime Correspondence*, Barrie and Jenkins, 1975

Meehan, Patricia, *The Unnecessary War*, Sinclair-Stevenson, 1992

Metelmann, Henry, *Through Hell for Hitler*, Patrick Steven Ltd, 1990

Mitscherlich, A, *Bericht uber eine Befragung heimkehrender deutsche Kreigsgefangener*, 1948

Murphy, Robert, *A Diplomat Among Warriors*, New York, 1964

Murphy, David E., *What Stalin Knew, The Enigma of Barbarossa*, Yale University Press, 2005

Noakes, Jeremy, and Pridham, Geoffrey (eds) *Nazism: A Documentary Reader*, University of Exeter Press, 1988

Rees, Laurence, *The Nazis, A Warning from History*, BBC Books, 1997

Robin, Ron, *The Barbed Wire College. Re-educating German POWs in the United States during World War II*, Princeton University Press, 1995

Rosenheft, E., *Beating the Fascists*, Cambridge, 1983

Rowlands, Alan, *Trautmann the Biography*, Breedon Books, 1990

Saffer, D. (ed), *Match of My Life*, Know the Score Books Ltd, 2007

Shirer, William, *The Rise and Fall of the Third Reich*, London, 1972

Taylor, James and Shaw, Warren, *A Dictionary of the Third Reich*, Grafton Books, 1987

Taylor, Pamela Howe, *Enemies Become Friends, A True Story of German Prisoners of War*, The Book Guide Ltd, 1997

Trautmann, B. and Todd, E., *Steppes to Wembley*, Robert Hale Ltd, 1956

Williams, Andrew, *From D-Day to Berlin*, Hodder and Stoughton, 2004

Acknowledgments

First I'd like to thank Bert Trautmann. I got to know him over ten years ago when he was one of five German POWs in a documentary I made for the BBC. We got on very well and stayed in touch from time to time once the filming was over. Casting around for an idea for my next book, I thought of him. So I rang him up and asked if I could write the story of his life, using it as a way of telling a slice of our 20th century European history. He was a bit surprised, but agreed without even asking for time to think it over. I doubt he realised how strange it would be to read it once it was finished, almost like reading about someone else entirely, a half stranger, or a distant cousin. I sent him the manuscript with some trepidation, anxious that he'd like it, and hoping that he'd feel it represented him and the extraordinary events of his life and his lifetime fairly. I needn't have worried. He took three days to read it then he rang me up. 'That's OK,' he said. 'Have you got a pen?' We went through the pages one by one correcting a date here, a name there, but rarely anything larger. It only took an hour. It was typical of him that, having once decided to trust me, he left me to get on with it, generously and with good humour. He'd been more famous than most, but he wasn't minded to take himself too seriously. For this, and for the hours he spent hunched over that tape recorder recalling every last detail of his life, I thank him.

Bert's family and friends were less surprised than Bert that someone might want to write a book about him, knowing what a dramatic life he's led. I thank them all for their help, especially Marlis, his wife, who became a friend as we chatted during the breaks between taping sessions. I met Freda, the daughter who Bert left in 1948 but found again in 1990, at her home in Ashton-in-Makerfield. It is fascinating to see how like him she is, and I thank her and her husband David for their help and hospitality. Freda's mother Marion is a shy woman, so I thank her especially for agreeing to talk to me about Bert in his POW days, and explaining how she loved him and blamed him for nothing. I'd also like to thank Bert's son Mark who helped with the family story and supplied the single photo we have of Bert/Bernd in Russia; also Barbara, Bert's sister-in-law from Lancashire who fell for him when she was 10; and, in Bremen, Helga his cousin who came to live with the Trautmann family as a small child, and Traudel who married his brother Karl Heinz. As to friends, many died in the war, but Egon and Phyllis Rameil are still alive and happily married after 62 years, living near Cologne. Phyllis, also from Ashton-in-Makerfield, now speaks English with a Lancashire German accent, much like Bert. John Riley, who was one of Bert's many fans as a boy when Bert was Manchester City's greatest star, and later became his good friend, died last year. But I'd like to thank him nevertheless for all the help he gave me on my visits to Manchester.

My thanks to Ingrid von Rosenberg for putting me in touch with Alex Behrens in Bremen who did excellent historical research for me, both general and local. He also took me round Bremen, to Wischusenstrasse, Groplingen, the docks, and the centre of the city, as well as the city archives. Alex is the kind of researcher anyone might want: young, keen, clever, and good company too. In England I was able to rely on my own research, first started when I made the BBC documentary on German POWs. I was lucky then to be able to interview Lt Col Henry Faulk who'd been put in charge of the POWD in 1945 and was 92 by the time of filming, but as acute and humorous as ever. Anthea Combeer was my brilliant BBC production assistant at the time, and not only encouraged me to write the book, but typed out the endless transcripts of the taped interviews, for which many thanks. I also thank John Goodyer, BBC cameraman for over 35 years, turned editor, who helped with the book illustrations and the promotional video.

At Yellow Jersey, Random House, I thank Rowan Yapp for her excellent editing, and Hugh Davis for his equally excellent copy-editing. I'd also like to thank Matthew Phillips, Yellow Jersey's editor, for the work he put into the book, and for promoting it so keenly.

Lastly, I'd like to thank Anthony Sheil, my ever patient agent, for his help and friendship, and John, my husband, for his encouragement and good humour.

Index

Münster, 310
Murphy, Peter, 298, 300

National Health Service, 254
Nazi Party: 'action days', 50, 249–50;
assumption of power, 19; attitude to
religion, 98–9; attitude to sport, 23,
27–8, 36, 48; behaviour in British
POW camps, 190–1, 231–2; British
re-education, 200–5, 213–14, 231–5;
domestic resistance, 63–6, 128–31,
148–50, 156–7, 219; and Jews, 21, 22,
48–9, 50–1, 78–9, 194, 197, 212–13; pep
talks for troops, 235–6; pre-war
government, 19–23, 25–9, 34–41,
49–51, 60; propaganda films, 45,
46–8, 72, 188; racial ideology, 28; rise,
7–8, 19; *see also* Hitler Youth
Nebe, Arthur, 182
Neurath, Konstantin von, 53
Newcastle United FC, 293
Norbert (friend), 308–9
Normandy, Battle of (1944), 154–6
North Yemen football team, 311
Northwich, 189
Nuremberg, 286
Nuremberg Laws, 26–7
Nuremberg rallies, 46–8
Nuremberg trials, 266

Olbricht, General, 148
Olympiad (film), 45, 46
Olympic Games: (1936), 42–6, 48; Youth
Olympics (1938), 59; (1948), 253;
(1972), 311
Orsha, 120, 146
Osendarp, Martinus, 43
Ostend, 181, 186
Oster, Major General Hans, 148, 182
Owens, Jesse, 43–4

Pakistan football team, 311
parachutes, 126, 132–3
paratroopers *see Fallschirmjäger*
Paris, relief of (1944), 157
Parola, Carlo, 238
Paskowski, Mathias, 315
Patton, General George S., 160, 166
Paul, Roy: becomes captain of Manchester
City, 281; on Manchester City tour of
Germany, 287; calms BT down
during match, 289; at 1955 FA Cup

Final, 293, 294; leaves Manchester
City, 305; post-football work, 311
Paulus, *Generalfeldmarschall* Friedrich
von, 137
Payman, Mrs (teacher), 16
Pennington, Bob, 290–1
Philip, Prince, Duke of Edinburgh, 255–6,
293, 297, 316
Phillips, Al, 238
Phipps, Sir Eric, 65–6
Phoenix, Pat, 308
Piggott, Lester, 254
Ploetzensee prison, 182
Poland: German invasion (1939), 63, 70–1,
72; German occupation, 88–90, 197
Poles: German popular attitude, 87; Nazi
propaganda, 30–1
Popitz, Dr Johannes, 182
POWD (Prisoner of War Division), 201–5
POWs: British fraternisation ban lifted,
225–30, 233–5; British re-education of
Nazis 200–5, 213–14, 231–5; British
repatriation of Germans, 223, 240;
British scheme to house and pay
Germans who stay on for extra year,
248, 256; British treatment, 188–214,
217–47; Church attempts at
reconciliation, 219–20; German POW
attitude to British, 233; German
treatment, 121–2; number of German
POWs who decided to stay in
England, 248; Russian treatment,
150–2, 201
Preston North End FC, 288
Preussen Münster, 309–10
Proctor, William, 279
Proctor's Garage, 279
Pullin, G.W., 288–9
Puskás, Ferenc, 287

Quigley, Eddie, 308

racism: in Britain, 255; Nazis, 28; *see also*
Jews
Rainer (school bully), 12–13, 15–17
Rameil, Egon, 226, 228–30, 245, 246
Rath, Ernst von, 58
Reicharbeitsamt (Reich Labour Bureau),
60–2, 66
religion: Nazi attitude, 98–9
Revie, Don: joins Manchester City, 281;
devises Revie Plan, 287; and 1954/5 FA